THE
JAPANESE
MIND

THE JAPANESE MIND

Understanding Contemporary Japanese Culture

Edited by
Roger J. Davies
&
Osamu Ikeno

TUTTLE Publishing
Tokyo | Rutland, Vermont | Singapore

Published by Tuttle Publishing, an imprint of Periplus Editions (HK) Ltd.,

www.tuttlepublishing.com

©2002 Roger Davies and Osamu Ikeno
Cover design by Victor Mingovits

Library of Congress Cataloging-in-Publication Data

Davies, Roger, 1949–
  The Japanese mind : understanding contemporary culture / edited by Roger J. Davies & Osamu Ikeno.
  —1st ed.
  270p. 21cm.
  Includes bibliographical references.
  ISBN 0-8048-3295-1 (pb.)
  1. Characteristics, Japanese. 2. Japan—20th century. I. Title.
  DS830 .D38 2001
  952.03'3—dc21   2001043625

ISBN 978-0-8048-3295-3
ISBN 978-4-8053-1021-2 (for sale in Japan only)

Distributed by

North America, Latin America & Europe
Tuttle Publishing
364 Innovation Drive
North Clarendon, VT 05759-9436 U.S.A.
Tel: 1 (802) 773-8930
Fax: 1 (802) 773-6993
info@tuttlepublishing.com
www.tuttlepublishing.com

Asia Pacific
Berkeley Books Pte. Ltd.
3 Kallang Sector #04-01,
Singapore 349278
Tel: (65) 6741 2178
Fax: (65) 6741 2179
inquiries@periplus.com.sg
www.tuttlepublishing.com

Japan
Tuttle Publishing
Yaekari Building, 3rd Floor
5-4-12 Osaki, Shinagawa-ku
Tokyo 141-0032
Tel: (81) 3 5437-0171
Fax: (81) 3 5437-0755
sales@tuttle.co.jp
www.tuttle.co.jp

ISBN: 978-0-8048-3295-3
24 23 22 21   27 26 25 24

ISBN 978-4-8053-1021-2 (for sale in Japan only)
23 22 21 20   25 24 23 22

Printed in Malaysia   2109VP

TUTTLE PUBLISHING® is a registered trademark of Tuttle Publishing, a division of Periplus Editions (HK) Ltd.

CONTENTS

JAPANESE CHRONOLOGY

Scholars still disagree on the exact dates of the periods listed below.
The following chronology is adapted from Ohnuki, 1987.

ANCIENT (*Kodai*)

Jōmon Period (Neolithic)	8000 BC–300 BC
Yayoi Period (Agriculture)	300 BC–AD 250
Kofun [Tomb] Period (State Formation)	250–646
Nara Period	646–794
Heian Period	794–1185

MEDIEVAL (*Chūsei*)

Kamakura Period	1185–1392
Nanbokuchō Period	1336–1392
Muromachi Period	1392–1603

EARLY MODERN (*Kinsei*)

Edo Period (Tokugawa Shogunate)	1603–1868

MODERN (*Kin-Gendai*)

Meiji Period	1868–1912
Taishō Period	1912–1926
Shōwa Period	1926–1989
Heisei Period	1989–present

Ohnuki, E. (1987). *The Monkey as Mirror: Symbolic Transformations in Japanese History and Ritual*. Princeton: Princeton University Press.

THE
JAPANESE
MIND

Introduction

The Japanese Mind is a collection of essays based on key concepts in Japanese culture. Each essay provides readers with in-depth yet easily accessible information on prevailing cultural values, attitudes, behavior patterns, and communication styles in modern Japan. All of the essays in this book were written over a period of several years by students enrolled in senior seminars in cross-cultural communication at Ehime University in Matsuyama, Japan. A set of discussion questions for classroom use follows each reading. These questions explore the changing nature of Japanese society from the perspective of contemporary issues in intercultural communication.

We have developed this volume as a college-level textbook for two main audiences: university students participating in Japanese studies programs, and Japanese students of English with advanced levels of proficiency who will need to explain and discuss their native culture in English in order to participate effectively in an increasingly globalized world. In addition, the general reader will find a wealth of information on many aspects of life in Japan. The selections cover a wide range of topics, from those that are central to Japanese culture to others that are perhaps less well known. In their totality, they provide an informative overview of Japanese culture from the perspective of the Japanese people themselves.

The Japanese Mind contains twenty-eight chapters, each of which is composed of a short essay and a set of discussion activities. These essays vary in length and are listed alphabetically in the table of contents. It is important to note, however, that they are not designed to be read sequentially, and readers may select from among the chapters in any order they wish. There is also a certain amount of overlap among the selections, and readers will find that many issues are dealt with from slightly different perspectives in more than one chapter. Each of the discussion activities that accompany the readings is composed of two sections, titled "Exploring Japanese Culture" and "Exploring Cross-Cultural Issues," respectively. As these names imply, the former explores issues related to the readings from the perspective of Japan itself, the latter from an external point of view, most often in comparison with the West or other Asian countries. Each section contains a minimum of five questions, but there is much variety in length, format, and content. Some chapters include case studies and references to other works.

The Japanese Mind differs from other publications on Japanese culture in a number of important ways. First of all, the articles in this collection do not require extensive background knowledge, since they have been written with the specific goal of explaining often difficult-to-understand aspects of Japanese culture as clearly as possible. At the same time, the selections are based on thorough research in both Japanese and English, accurately documented in the form of citations, quotations, footnotes, and references. The result is a collection of essays of an academic nature that is easily accessible to the lay reader. Finally, all the readings are accompanied by discussion activities designed to encourage students to explore many diverse aspects of Japanese culture and to enhance their ability to discuss these topics in a clear and coherent fashion.

As mentioned above, the essays in The Japanese Mind were written by university seniors in the Department of English at the Faculty of Education in Ehime University, where the editors themselves are professors specializing in applied linguistics, TEFL, and related fields. All of the student-authors who contributed to this book were enrolled in programs in cross-cultural communication and/or English second language education, and the readings are the result of a multiyear writing program that culminated in a senior seminar in cross-cultural communication, where these essays were written. The articles reflect an intensive collaboration between students and professor in the development of their academic writing skills in English, an effort that began early in their university education with introductory courses in English composition and continued into their senior year, when the emphasis was placed on academic writing skills and research in international communication.

As with all research, these essays began with an investigation of existing materials on topics selected by the students themselves, and a reference section accompanies each article, where sources are documented, often from Japanese works normally unavailable to English-speaking readers. The student-authors then shaped and crafted their own insights around these sources in the development of their topics. This process involved extensive drafting, revising, and reformulating, which took place within individualized writing tutorials guided by their professor. From the outset, the final goal was to produce essays of high academic caliber, written in error-free English, in a way that often complex Japanese concepts could be readily understood by readers from other cultures. It should also be emphasized that many of these concepts remain controversial within Japanese society and are the subject of continuing debate among the Japanese themselves. The goal of our student-authors was not to seek resolution to these issues but to provide a balanced and accurate overview of the selected subjects, emphasizing the need for critical thinking and the importance of understanding Japan's cultural history, so that the issues could then be further explored and debated among the students themselves. In achieving these objectives, the writing process that these students underwent was often difficult and took a good deal of determination and effort. The final products, we believe, speak for themselves.

Finally, all of the essays in this collection have been further modified and revised by the editors in order to provide additional sophistication and to establish a continuity in manuscript style that is necessary for a textbook format. As a consequence, some of the final drafts written by students were extensively edited; others were left relatively untouched. At times, sections of one essay were combined with sections of another in order to provide a more coherent perspective on the selected topic; at other times, the essays of students writing on the same subject, but in different years, were merged for the same reason. The final editions of these readings were then field-tested in courses at Ehime University over a two-year period, and accompanying discussion activities were developed with the assistance and input of participating students. As a result of these circumstances, and because so many individuals contributed to this book over a period of many years, the proceeds from this work will be used to establish a scholarship fund at our university to enable students in financial need to further their studies in English and international communication.

In conclusion, as professors working within the Japanese university system, we believe that this book is of particular significance for contemporary education in Japan. As increasing numbers of Japanese young people take part in study programs and international exchanges throughout the world, it is important for them to communicate what it means to be Japanese to people from other countries. *The Japanese Mind* demonstrates that, given proper instruction, support, and corrective feedback, they are most capable of doing so.

ACKNOWLEDGMENTS

All of the student-authors who contributed to this volume have graduated from Ehime University. Most are now in their mid to late twenties and are pursuing careers of their own or have married and started new families. They are involved in many walks of life, both in Japan and abroad, as housewives and mothers, English teachers, businesspeople, journalists, social workers, and so on. We would like to express our deep appreciation for their efforts and to the many students who participated in field-testing this book project. Our student-contributors are listed below in alphabetical order:

Yoshiho Chiba, Miwako Fukuhara, Kentaro Goto, Yuko Hamada, Yukiko Hino, Naoko Ido, Tokuna Inoue, Chiyoko Isoda, Yukiko Itabashi, Sumi Kadota, Yuki Kagawa, Keiko Kamada, Yoshiko Kiyama, Megumi Manabe, Yoko Mori, Yumi Motōka, Yoko Ohnishi, Tomoko Sakai, Rina Sakamoto, Masato Shuto, Aya Syojima, Yuki Takahashi, Yukari Takeuchi, Chiemi Tanaka, Yuka Utsunomiya, Hiroko Watanabe, Yuko Watanabe, Kosuke Yanai, Miwa Yukimoto

In addition, we would like to thank John Moore, Vice President and General Manager of Tuttle, Japan, for recognizing the potential of this project and for his continued support and encouragement in the completion of our book. Many thanks are also due to the editorial team in Boston, USA, for their advice and suggestions in improving this work. Finally, we would like to state that we are very pleased to be able to support Tuttle's continuing mission of publishing books that "span East and West."

Roger J. Davies
Osamu Ikeno
Ehime University
Matsuyama, Japan

曖昧

Aimai:
AMBIGUITY AND THE JAPANESE

Ambiguity, or *aimai*, is defined as a state in which there is more than one intended meaning, resulting in obscurity, indistinctness, and uncertainty. To be ambiguous in Japanese is generally translated as *aimaina*, but people use this term with a wide range of meanings, including "vague, obscure, equivocal, dubious, doubtful, questionable, shady, noncommittal, indefinite, hazy, double, two-edged," and so on (Oe, 1995 p. 187). The Japanese are generally tolerant of ambiguity, so much so that it is considered by many to be characteristic of Japanese culture. Although the Japanese may not be conscious of *aimai*, its use is regarded as a virtue in Japan, and the Japanese language puts more emphasis on ambiguity than most, for to express oneself ambiguously and indirectly is expected in Japanese society. However, ambiguity can also cause of a good deal of confusion, not only in international communication but also among the Japanese themselves.

THE ORIGINS OF *AIMAI*
The geography of Japan is said to have had a great influence on the development of many of the country's customs and cultural values, a social theory known as geographical determinism. First, Japan is an island country, and because of the dangerous and unpredictable seas separating Japan from the Asian continent, Japanese culture was able

to develop in relative isolation, free from the threat of invasion from other countries. Japan is also a mountainous country and does not have a great deal of inhabitable land; as a result, people had to live close together in communities in which everyone was well acquainted with one another. The concept of harmony, or *wa*, became an important factor in Japanese life, helping to maintain relationships between members of close-knit communities.

In addition, the climate has had an important influence on the development of the Japanese character. It is hot in summer, and the rainy season supports intensive forms of agriculture, such as rice growing, in which the labor of irrigating, planting, and harvesting was traditionally shared communally in order to achieve high production in a limited amount of space. People had to cooperate in this society because they could not grow rice without one another's help, and if they worked together, they were able to grow more food. There developed a kind of "rule of the unanimous," and people tended not to go against group wishes for fear that they would be excluded from the community (*murahachibu*, or ostracism). If people sacrificed themselves and worked for the group, the group supported them, so they made their own opinions conform with their group's objectives and felt a comfortable sense of harmony. Natural communication often occurred without spoken words, and people followed their elders because they had more experience, wisdom, and power. In order to live without creating any serious problems for the group's harmony, people avoided expressing their ideas clearly, even to the point of avoiding giving a simple yes or no answer. If a person really wanted to say no, he or she said nothing at first, then used vague expressions that conveyed the nuance of disagreement. People's words thus came to contain a variety of meanings.

In this way, the social structure of Japan developed a vertical organization that stresses one's place within the group (Nakane; cited in Aoki, 1990, p. 85) and in which one's rank or status is clearly distinguishable, often based on seniority within the group. When people meet, they first try to determine the group to which the other belongs, such as their school or company, and their status within that group, rather than their personal traits. Because such a framework includes people with many different characteristics, a form of unity in which all people aim for the same goal is most important for the group and is strictly enforced. This strong group consciousness brings about a feeling of "in and out" (*uchi-soto*), and people within the group are likely to feel united emotionally. Although this group consciousness has contributed greatly to the economic development of Japan, the need for strong emotional unity has also resulted in an inability to criticize others openly. As a consequence, the development of ambiguity can be viewed as a defining characteristic of the Japanese style of communication:

> Japanese conversation does not take the form of dialectic development. The style of conversation is almost always fixed from beginning to end depending on the human relationship. It is one-way, like a lecture, or an inconclusive argument going along parallel lines or making a circle round and round, and in the end still ending up mostly at the beginning. This style is very much related to the nature of Japanese society. (Ibid., p. 89)

Ambiguity is thus indispensable for maintaining harmony in Japanese life, where it has the quality of compromise. The Japanese carefully weigh the atmosphere that they share with others. People learn to become aware of one another's thinking and feelings instinctively, which is required in order to know who is taking the initiative. Ambiguity protects people in this sense and is regarded as socially positive because it is a kind of lubricant in communication:

> The Japanese think that it is impolite to speak openly on the assumption that their partner knows nothing. They like and value *aimai* because they think that it is unnecessary to speak clearly as long as their partner is knowledgeable. To express oneself distinctly carries the assumption that one's partner knows nothing, so clear expression can be considered impolite. (Morimoto, 1988, p. 22)

EXAMPLES OF AMBIGUITY

In Japan, when people decline offers, they use many roundabout expressions, such as *chotto, demo, kangaete-okune,* and so on. Nobody expects to be told no directly, even if the other person is really in disagreement. People take care to maintain a friendly atmosphere and express themselves indirectly; as a result, ambiguity occurs. One of the most well-known examples of *aimaina kotoba* (ambiguous language) is the expression *maa-maa*, which is frequently used in Japanese conversation. When people are asked, "How are you?" they will often answer, "*Maa-maa*." This is generally translated into English as "not so bad," but the expression is ambiguous and actually has a very subtle range of meanings incorporated within a vague answer, which is regarded as good manners in Japan. When people are asked, "How did you do on the examination?" for example, they will often answer, "*Maa-maa*" even if they did well. If they said, "I did well," they could be thought of as arrogant or overconfident. However, because people cannot define the exact meaning of *maa-maa*, when they hear this term they must take into account the speaker's expression and behavior in order to understand the real meaning.

Ichiō is another example of an ambiguous expression in Japanese. According to most dictionaries, *ichiō* can be defined as "for the present," "at least," "in the first place," and so on. However, the actual meaning in Japanese is more ambiguous. When people are asked questions such as "Will you go home this summer vacation?" "Do you have a car?" or "Have you completed your graduation thesis?" they will often answer, "*Ichiō*," meaning "yes," but indirectly. Peng Hei (1990, p. 167) confirms this as follows:

> At the bottom of the expression *ichiō* is the fact that the Japanese hesitate to assert themselves and like to express themselves ambiguously. This expression is also used to conceal their confusion. This confusion is caused by their fear that to express oneself clearly could be regarded as a display of superiority towards others.

Thus, *maa-maa* and *ichiō* are just two representative examples of ambiguous expressions in Japanese. In fact, however, the number of aimai expressions in the language is so great that they are probably uncountable.

THE CROSS-CULTURAL EFFECTS OF AMBIGUITY

It is often said that the Japanese are shy or inscrutable and that it is impossible to guess what they are thinking. In many cases, however, people may simply be trying to behave politely according to their own customs. Japanese people, too, have their own opinions, but they tend to wait their turn to speak out. If they completely disagree with a speaker, they will usually listen with an air of acceptance at first, then disagree in a rather vague and roundabout way. This is considered the polite way to do things in Japan. On the other hand, because Western people consider directness and the honest expression of one's opinions more important, they tend to express their ideas more clearly. Even though quarrels sometimes arise, they do not usually affect people's relationships, except in extreme cases. In Japan, however, if you go against someone and create a bad atmosphere, your relations may break off completely. People tend to react emotionally, and most are afraid of being excluded from the group.

Silence can also be considered a kind of ambiguity. Between the Japanese and Westerners, there is a different understanding of silence. For the Japanese, silence indicates deep thinking or consideration, but too much silence often makes non-Japanese uncomfortable. Whereas the Japanese consider silence as rather good and people generally feel sympathetic toward it, non-Japanese sometimes feel that it is an indication of indifference or apathy. Too many words, however, are a kind of pressure for many Japanese and make them nervous and ill-at-ease.

Aimai can result in misunderstandings, and people from other countries sometimes become irritated because the Japanese seem unable to answer yes or no directly. For example, if asked "Which will you have, tea or coffee?" a Japanese person will often reply, "Either is OK." This is a reserved and polite answer, but it often causes the host or hostess trouble. In fact, the word that Japanese most often have difficulty in using is no and their use of vague denials also results in criticism: "The Japanese hesitate to deny directly and think of affirmation as a virtue; therefore, troubles between the Japanese and people from other countries often occur. These kinds of vague denials cause others to think that the Japanese are incomprehensible" (Morimoto, 1988, p. 63).

Ambiguity is one of the biggest problems in communication between Japan and other nations today, resulting in a great deal of friction and misunderstanding. To solve this problem, the Japanese need to become aware of their sense of ambiguity because many people simply do not know that it causes problems. With this awareness, they can try to express their opinions more clearly. On the other hand, non-Japanese should try to understand the Japanese mentality and the importance of the role that ambiguity plays in Japanese life.

DISCUSSION ACTIVITIES

Exploring Japanese Culture

1. The Japanese are often very concerned about their reputations and what other people think of them, especially within their groups. How does this contribute to *aimai*?

2. The Japanese are usually uncomfortable expressing disagreement openly, because it is felt that one's opinion cannot be separated from one's personality, and if you reject another's opinion, you are necessarily rejecting the other person as a whole. Discuss this issue and what it means for *aimai*.

3. Ambiguity is important in Japan in maintaining harmony at home, in schools, and in the workplace. However, this way of communicating also has negative effects. What are they?

4. Japanese couples usually do not speak to each other openly but prefer more ambiguous forms of expression. Is it possible to really understand one's partner in this way?

5. Although ambiguous forms of communication have been criticized recently in Japan, it can also be said that changing people's attitudes on this subject will result in changing the basic character of the Japanese people. Discuss this issue.

6. The Japanese language is sometimes said to be very ambiguous

and therefore unsuitable for logical thinking. Do you agree or disagree? Do you think that it is valid to judge languages in this way, or is it simply a form of stereotyping?

7. Ambiguity in Japanese is often associated with aesthetics, or "the beauty of the language." Explain this association.

8. Should Japanese children be taught to express themselves clearly and directly in school in both spoken and written form? What effects will this have on society?

9. It has been claimed that haiku reflects Japanese *aimai* culture because everything does not have to be explained clearly, and readers can share in the author's feelings. Discuss this way of communicating in Japanese.

Exploring Cross-Cultural Issues

1. The Japanese tend to think that people who express themselves openly and clearly are "childish." How does this compare with ways of communicating in other cultures?

2. In Japan, even if you do not express your feelings clearly, others can tell how you feel from your attitude. Besides, the Japanese tend to conceal their real feelings, especially if they are negative and could hurt others. In addition, if you have trouble with others in Japan, it is usually impossible to reestablish the relationship. How does this compare with relationships between people in other cultures?

3. It seems that Japanese people often "beat around the bush," remain silent, or just smile instead of saying no directly and honestly. This can be very irritating for others in cross-cultural communication. What can be done to solve this problem?

4. What kinds of ambiguous expressions are used in other languages of the world?

5. When the Japanese communicate with people from other countries, they often feel uncomfortable expressing themselves directly. Yet ambiguity can cause a great many problems in cross-cultural communication. Offer some solutions.

甘え

Amae:
THE CONCEPT OF JAPANESE DEPENDENCE

Amae, which can be roughly translated as "depending on the benevolence of others," is "a key concept for understanding Japanese personality structure" (Doi, 1973, p. 17). *Amae* is vital for getting along with others in Japan and is the basis for maintaining harmonious relationships in which children depend on their parents, younger people rely on their elders, grandparents depend on their adult children, and so on. Although there are a number of definitions of *amae*, it cannot be directly translated into English, because there are no words in any of the European languages that are its direct equivalent (Doi, 1974, p. 148). According to Doi, *amaeru*, which is the verb form of the noun *amae*, means to "depend and presume upon another's benevolence": "This word has the same root as *amae*, which means sweet. Thus, *amaeru* has a distinct feeling of sweetness and is generally used to describe a child's attitude or behavior toward his or her mother. But it can also be used to describe the relationship between two adults" (ibid., p. 145). Therefore, *amaeru* is related to "self-indulgent behavior by an infant of either sex in presuming on the love of its parents" (ibid.). Definitions of related grammatical constructions provided by Japanese dictionaries include *amayu*, the literary form of the verb *amaeru*, which is described as "dependency on another's affection" (*Daigenkai*; cited in Doi, 1973, p. 167), or "presuming on familiarity in order to 'make up to' the other, or to behave in a self-indulgent manner" (ibid.).

The concept of *amae* greatly affects all aspects of Japanese life because it is related to other characteristics of the Japanese way of thinking, such as *enryo* (restraint), *giri* (social obligation), *tsumi* (sin), *haji* (shame) (Doi, 1973, pp. 33–48). Doi refers to three types of human relationships among the Japanese: relationships in an "inner" circle, those in a kind of middle zone, and those in an "outer" circle:

> One's relatives, with whom no *enryo* is necessary, are in one's "inner" circle but *giri*-type relationships where enryo is present are the "outer" circle. Sometimes, however, *giri* relationships and acquaintanceships are themselves regarded as "inner" in contrast to the world of *tanin* with whom one is quite unconnected, and where there is no need, even, to bring *enryo* into play. (Ibid., p. 40)

In other words, in the inner circle, *amae* is at work and there is no *enryo*, in the middle zone *enryo* is present, and in the outer circle, which is the world of strangers, there is neither *amae* nor *enryo*. In general, the Japanese distinguish strongly between inner and outer, and they have different attitudes toward human relations in each case. For example, they feel *giri* (obligation) when others, toward whom they have *enryo* (restraint), show kindness to them. However, they do not express their appreciation as much to people they are close to and with whom they can *amaeru* (Sahashi, 1980, p. 49). Another example relates to the Japanese sense of guilt, which is "most strongly aroused when the individual betrays the trust of members of his own group" (Doi, 1973, p. 49). With people who are part of the inner circle, however, the Japanese do not usually have as much of a sense of guilt, because they are so close that *amae* gives them confidence in any sin being forgiven (ibid.).

The roots of *amae* can be found in the prototype relationship between mother and child, according to Doi (1973, pp. 7 and 75). Normal infants at the breast have the desire to be close to their mothers, and at the same time "the desire to be passively loved, the unwillingness to be separated from the warm mother-child circle and cast into a world of objective 'reality'" arises in the infant's mind. Doi (ibid., p. 72) suspects that *ama*, the root form of the word *amae*, may be related to the childish word *uma-uma*, indicating the infant's request for the breast or food.

The word *amae* can also be used to describe the relationship between two adults. Dependency among adults is commonly seen in Japanese society, as in relationships such as those between husband and wife, teacher and student, and doctor and patient (ibid., p. 150). However, if the relationship between mother and child is at the root of *amae*, it must be an international concept. Why then does the concept of *amae* seem to be restricted to Japan? Doi (cited in Sahashi, 1980, p. 95) theorizes that in the period of the formation of Japanese society, different people had to migrate and live together on a small island; as a result, the concept of *amae* may have been important in order to maintain the solidarity of the group, because the Japanese have been a people who have stressed group unity since ancient times.

Human relationships in Japan differ from those in the West in many ways and in particular in terms of the concept of *amae*. First, the Japanese have difficulty saying no, in contrast to Westerners, who are able to do so more easily. The reason for this is that Japanese relationships, which are based on *amae*, are unstable (Doi; cited in Sahashi, 1980, p. 79); that is, people hesitate to refuse others for fear of breaking this bond. Doi insists that Westerners can refuse easily because *amae* is not at work in their relationships (ibid., p. 80). Second, when the Japanese want to be close to someone, they offer a present or treat the other to a meal (ibid., p. 87). As a result, the other is in their debt in a sense, and a relationship based on *amae* has been arranged between them. On the other hand, there are no such implications with regard to similar customs among Westerners, and those living in Japan can sometimes be embarrassed by these situations. These examples seem to indicate that *amae* is a specifically Japanese trait; nonetheless, Doi (1973, p. 169) claims that "at the root of *amae* feelings there seems to lie something instinctively common to all mankind." Thus, the concept of *amae* may also exist in Western societies, but on a more hidden level.

DISCUSSION ACTIVITIES

Exploring Japanese Culture

1. Do you think that *amae* is responsible for (or related to) the increasingly serious problems in Japan of *hikikomori* (withdrawal from the world) and *futōkō* (truancy in schools)? If so, explain how *amae* promotes these problems.

2. It has been reported that many students who have emotional and social problems in Japanese schools become better adjusted and successful when they go to the USA or Australia to study. Why do you think this is so? Discuss this issue in terms of *amae*.

3. Japanese companies have traditionally adopted a lifetime employment system, although this approach has recently been collapsing. Discuss Japanese lifetime employment as a reflection of *amae*. As this system is giving way to merit-based employment, what problems are likely to emerge?

4. Japanese students are often less mature than their counterparts in the West. In what ways is this the result of the dominance of *amae* in young people's upbringing in Japan?

5. **Case Study:** Keiko, Haruka, Mayumi, and Ai are best friends and always spend time together. Today, Keiko suggested going to a concert, and Haruka and Mayumi agreed. Ai is not very keen on the idea, because she does not particularly like the band; however, because of a sense of mutual dependence, she feels pressure to agree.
Question: Should Ai agree to go to the concert? Why, or why not? Discuss this issue in relation to *amae*.

Exploring Cross-Cultural Issues

1. Are there any concepts equivalent to *amae* in other countries? If so, describe some situations in which these concepts are reflected.

2. Discuss how the concept of *amae* is related to the prevalence of "parasite singles" in Japan and the Peter Pan syndrome in Western countries.

3. Human relations in Japan are said to be more "wet" (i.e., emotional) than those in the West. How is this related to *amae*?

4. When they travel abroad, many Japanese do not take necessary precautions against robbery and other crimes. It is sometimes said that this is because of *amae* ("*Amaeteiru-kara-da*"). Do you agree with this opinion? How is *amae* responsible for this kind of behavior?

5. Young people in the West generally try to achieve independence from their parents at a relatively young age, whereas in Japan, many young people remain dependent until much later in life. Discuss this issue from the perspective of *amae*.

天下り

Amakudari:
DESCENT FROM HEAVEN

The Japanese people used to believe that Japan, as a nation, would last forever thanks to its strong economy, cooperative spirit, and governmental system. However, since the collapse of the bubble economy and a series of recent financial scandals, this way of thinking has disappeared, and people have begun to realize that structural problems in Japan stem mainly from a kind of bureaucratic dictatorship that was formed in the pre–World War II era (Omae, 1994, p. 36). Government officials in Japan have tremendous authority and often abuse it. Bureaucrats and industrial leaders act in concert to control the reins of government, and a series of well-publicized corruption scandals has brought to light the collusive relations between these worlds.

Amakudari, which literally means "descent from heaven," is a typical example. As a political term, it refers to senior bureaucrats who are allowed to take important positions with private or semiprivate companies after retirement (Gibney, 1996, p. 322). This nepotistic practice gained particular notoriety recently when it became known that many of the upper echelons of failed housing loan companies were former Ministry of Finance dignitaries, and ordinary people have begun to believe that these officials are not able to give direction to modern Japan. In examining the practice of *amakudari*, this chapter will focus on three main topics: the connection between the Japanese government and big business, the repercussions for society, and solutions to the problem.

THE ALLIANCE BETWEEN GOVERNMENT
AND BIG BUSINESS

Government officials regard *amakudari* as necessary because as they move upward through the ranks, opportunities for promotion become fewer and competition and conflict among officials becomes more serious (Ikuta, 1992, pp. 35–37). Friction can be severe, and those officials who fail to win elite ministry posts are expected to resign before they reach the normal retirement age. Bureaucrats who retire early usually take it for granted that they have the right to obtain high-ranking positions in the private sector on the grounds that they passed a first-class civil service exam after graduating from some of the best schools (Tokyo University, for example). Although entering private companies within two years after retiring from a ministry position is a violation of the law according to the Government Officials Act, there is no such regulation for special public corporations. Therefore, most government officials who retire at an early age go straight to these firms as a first step. After two years, they are invited to join private companies, which provide them with high-ranking, lucrative jobs and huge retirement allowances.

The benefits to a firm with *amakudari* executives can be substantial. The Japanese Highway Service Association, for example, is a public corporation in which a large number of *amakudari* officials hold high-ranking positions ("The System to Sustain Monopoly," 1996, p. 34). The association is in complete control of its subsidiary operations and, in fact, has sole responsibility for all highway service facilities in Japan, such as restaurants and gas stations. Companies that have relations with this public corporation run all such facilities in a monopolistic fashion, leading to a complete lack of competition. *Amakudari* officials help to maintain this monopoly.

Hiring influential ex-government officials is also advantageous with respect to running a company smoothly. According to Takahiro Sekimoto, a vice president of the Federation of Economic Organization and the chairman of NEC, *amakudari* officials play a key role in firms. In order to gain useful information from the government, authorization for projects, and preferential treatment concerning regulations, former officials are expected to work as links between government agencies and the firms. As recompense for *amakudari*, not only secret government intelligence but also standard certifications and even financial subsidies are exclusively provided to a particular corporation (Stern, 1996, pp. 260–261).

AMAKUDARI IN TWO MINISTRIES

In Japan, the Ministry of Finance is the most influential ministry because of its great authority in terms of drawing up the nation's budget, managing personnel, and supervising banking, securities, and insurance companies (Ikuta, 1992, pp. 163–138). In addition, the Fair Trade Commission is composed mainly of Ministry of Finance officials, who have great influence. This arrangement shows that the Japanese Ministry of Finance has the special right to intervene not only with financial institutions but also in administrative sectors. For example, in order to maintain stability in financial markets, the government "protects" banks and other financial institutions with rules and regulations, and props them up when crises occur. In 1992, for instance, the Finance Ministry sank public funds into the stock market to maintain stock prices. In the same year, a one trillion seventy billion yen bailout of institutional investors was made, for example, trust banks. The source of these funds was based on public savings, such as postal life insurance, postal savings, and the national pension (Wood, 1996, p. 239). This series of interventions in financial markets ended up increasing their dependence on the government; therefore, the government officials who are concerned with supporting Japanese financial institutions find it easy to gain jobs through *amakudari* practices. As far as public investment is concerned, Ikuta (1992, p. 194) points out that the big-three ministries, the Ministry of Construction, the Ministry of Transportation, and the Ministry of Agriculture, Forestry, and Fisheries, account for 90 percent of all public works spending in Japan. In particular, the Ministry of Construction has a nearly 70 percent share of these projects, based on highways, housing, and sewerage. Receiving public investment is a matter of life and death for construction companies, because public works projects amount to 40 percent of all building investment in Japan. Therefore, most construction companies will try every possible means to obtain government contracts, for example, arranging high-ranking posts for retirees from the Ministry of Construction,

making enormous political contributions, wining and dining Ministry
of Construction bureaucrats at expensive restaurants, and even supporting political candidates who will back their endeavors (Kuji &
Yokota, 1996, pp. 15–22). *Amakudari*, in particular, is widely regarded
as a kind of investment in the future for builders. In fact, a survey
(cited in Omae, 1994, pp. 134–135) investigating the relationship
between construction project orders and *amakudari* among the twen-
ty-four biggest construction companies clearly shows a "back-
scratching" alliance between the government and contractors. For
instance, a major company that has 24.3 percent of its high-ranking
positions filled by *amakudari* executives received exactly the same
percent of orders from the government. This is not a coincidence;
Omae provides details on two other companies with the same results
(1994). In short, the government and the building industry are
engaged in collusive and unlawful activities.

SCANDALS: THE JŪSEN DEBACLE AND ZENEKON

Jūsen (literally, housing loan companies) were established in 1971,
and consist of *botaikō* (literally, mother banks) that are made up of
a complex web of interlocking financial institutions. During Japan's
high-growth period, *jūsen* progressed satisfactorily thanks to the
enormous demands of urban housing developments. In those days,
the value of land was rising dramatically, providing *jūsen* with
opportunities to make loans on speculative ventures. *Jūsen* lent
huge amounts of money to speculators without foreseeing the consequences. Moreover, with their success in the loan business, *jūsen*
enlarged their scale of activities by way of *botaikō*, inviting more
former officials from the Ministry of Finance to join them as
liaisons between the government and individual *jūsen* (Special
Reporters Group, 1996, p. 62). In the bubble economy of the 1980s,
real estate prices soared throughout Japan, and the demand for
loans by businesspeople was too large for most banks to manage
without *botaikō* financial support. However, after the meltdown of
stock prices in 1989, Japan's bubble economy burst, with devastat-
ing effects for the whole financial sector, resulting in irrecoverable
debts in *jūsen* and related businesses. These bad debts have been on
the books of these financial institutions for nearly a decade now,

causing market paralysis in the offering of new loans. As a result, a temporary organization called the Organization for Dissolving *Jūsen* was established. This scheme was instituted by the Ministry of Finance and its purpose was to recall millions of yen in credit within fifteen years. However, this was only the ostensible reason—the actual goal was to give former high-ranking bureaucrats in the ministry who were running *jūsen* after their retirement opportunities to sidestep their responsibilities in the mismanagement that had occurred (ibid., p. 79).

In 1993, several scandals in the construction industry occurred in rapid succession, known as the *zenekon* (general building contractors) scandals. In March of that year, the late Shin Kanemaru, a political boss whom most of the bureaucrats stood in awe of, was accused of tax evasion. His arrest brought to light financial scandals involving the whole building industry, in which illegal contributions, kickbacks, and bribery were prevalent in public investment. In consequence, large-scale investigations were carried out among related companies and the parties concerned. These eventually became known as the *zenekon* scandals, and led to the arrests of the governors of Sendai, Miyagi, and Ibaragi (Kuji & Yokota, 1996, p. 16). This corruption was due to structural defects in the Japanese construction industry. For instance, regardless of criticism, *dangō* bidding (collusive tenders for gaining orders) is still widely practiced between the Ministry of Construction and builders. According to Kunimoto, there are three types of bidding: open public tender, tender by designated companies, and free bidding (1991, p. 93). *Dangō* takes place among companies, resulting in a closed tender. This sort of bidding is very profitable for both the Ministry of Finance and the builders because it is a mutually advantageous relationship. In the process of *dangō*, construction companies and government officials consult with one another and prearrange a bid winner (ibid., pp. 94–95). This system is fundamentally different from that seen in the USA, for instance, where bidding is expected to be transparent and is overseen by independent inspectors. On the other hand, Japan has never had such an independent inspection system, and *dangō* has been widely practiced since the end of World War II. Thus, the recent *zenekon* scandals should be regarded as only the tip of the iceberg.

REPERCUSSIONS FOR JAPANESE SOCIETY

Each year, public and private corporations hire more than 200 bureaucrats in Japan, and nearly 35 percent of them are employed as company executives (Omae, 1994, p. 297). The burden that this imposes on companies is immeasurable. According to Omae, one former bureaucrat is paid at least twenty million yen as a yearly stipend. Moreover, chauffeurs, secretaries, business trip expenses, and other fringe benefits are supplied to each of the *amakudari* bureaucrats by host companies. It is said that private companies pay an average of about thirty million yen for each of these officials. The former bureaucrats often demand the right to speak on behalf of the company, but contrary to their high-ranking status, they are often incompetent to manage private, profit-making firms (Hollerman, 1996, p. 201). Taichi Sakaiya, an economic commentator, has stated that these former officials have been immersed in protected and secure environments for more than thirty years; therefore, they are not accustomed to free competition or to the running of companies. Nevertheless, these former bureaucrats are prone to be self-assertive in all sectors of company operations and often inflict their views on management. As a result, they often cause problems for companies, bringing more trouble and crises.

In recent years, the Japanese financial system has been suffering from a kind of paralysis. This has been due to an increasing mountain of bad debt and to the fact that the entrenched bureaucrats of the Ministry of Finance and the Bank of Japan have assiduously monitored and propped up failing banks, resulting in a weakening of Japan's competitive positions in financial world markets. Many of these debts resulted from the collapse of the bubble economy. According to Omae (1994), although it was not obvious until after the event, in the terminal stage of the bubble economy in the late 1980s, the Finance Ministry froze land prices by regulating the total amount of real estate loans. This practice lasted for more than twelve months, resulting in a disparity in real estate prices between official announcements and the actual figures. In addition, to save Japan's stock market, the Ministry of Finance intervened and supported stocks by using public funds composed of national postal savings and pensions (ibid., p. 43). Ironically, this government intervention resulted in a short-term delay of the bubble's burst but in the end led to the series of bankruptcies we are seeing today.

Government officials, especially Finance Ministry bureaucrats, also tend to expand their influence not only within industries but also inside the government itself through *amakudari*, setting themselves up in charge of certain sectors. The Fair Trade Commission, for example, is a governmental body and is considered a semijudicial office. Yet, according to Yamamoto, the commission usually consists of former officials of the government and retirees from the Ministry of Foreign Affairs, the Ministry of Justice, and the Ministry of Finance (1992, p. 133). Nearly 70 percent of the chairpersons on the commission are from the Ministry of Finance. Hence, although this commission should have great influence in preventing monopolies, its limited force makes it difficult to do so. Consequently, the Fair Trade Practice Commission is virtually *honenuki* (literally, taking the backbone out of system) and tends to grant amnesties to the companies that many former officials work for.

SOLUTIONS TO THE PROBLEM

With the disclosure of massive financial scandals by *amakudari* officials, Japan was discredited, not only in the eyes of the Japanese people but also in the eyes of those in other countries as well. To restore Japan's trust abroad, the government must carry out at the least four measures in general terms: dismantling the alliance between government and industry, making governmental information transparent, raising each bureaucrat's sense of responsibility, and placing legal restrictions on *amakudari*.

First of all, the cozy relationship between officialdom and business circles should be eliminated. The Japanese government has overprotected both financial markets and construction industries, impeding foreign companies' inroads into Japan's markets, which has caused trade friction and even "Japan bashing" throughout the world. Gibney (1996, p. 391) notes that of all the world's trading nations, only Japan has continued the practices of a *sakoku* (closed county), which recall the three-century-old isolationism of the Tokugawa shoguns. As Gibney states, Japan is still a closed country in a variety of fields, most of which are based on a tight relationship between the government and big business. In consequence, Japan's economic situation has deteriorated rapidly because of structural confusion and a lack of measures to solve the problem. The Japanese government is under great pressure to quickly restructure, and this is a must if Japan is to become a true member of the global community. This restructuring will involve great risks for weak companies, perhaps resulting in more layoffs and bankruptcies, but these are matters of course in capitalist economies.

The Japanese government must also disclose essential information not only to the Japanese people but also to representatives of other countries. As foreign critics ceaselessly assert, Japan's government is opaque and exclusive. In particular, in terms of foreign firms, the government has interfered with their entry into Japan's markets by creating excessive red tape in order to prop up Japanese industries (Lake II, 1996, pp. 113–115). Japanese medical institutions, for instance, are protected by many obscure regulations that have not been defined by law. According to a report by the Fair Trade Commission in 1989, standards of authorization are vague and not open to the public; thus, the government is given a free hand concerning the granting of licenses (ibid.). This governmental policy puts foreign institutions at a great disadvantage, resulting in Japan being far from a fair, competitive society. Furthermore, in a democratic society, all people are entitled to know how government officials manage the country. In particular, the people should be well informed as to how their taxes are used for affairs of state such as national welfare, pension schemes, and the incomes of each member of the Diet. Therefore, it is absolutely essential for the government to establish free access to its information for the people.

Japanese officials must also realize that they are accountable. Taking shelter behind governmental authority, many officials still follow in the footsteps of their predecessors of the past fifty years, ignoring ordinary citizens' rights and needs. The Finance Ministry, for instance, should clearly and accurately state the extent of the liabilities contained within the national budget, including hidden loans and bad debts.

Finally, strict legal controls on *amakudari* should be established. Currently, the Government Officials Act prohibits bureaucrats from jumping directly into the private sector after retiring from their government posts. Legally, they must wait two years. However, this policy is only an "official" position. In actuality, many bureaucrats are allowed to enter private companies if the National Personnel Authority permits. These government officials are normally in their late forties or early fifties and have already gained great influence in industrial and governmental sectors (Omae, 1994, p. 297). Hence, to eliminate this back-scratching alliance between government and business, strict legal restrictions for abolishing *amakudari* should be set up. As Karen Van Wolferen states, Japan's government lacks any center of accountability (cited in Neff, 1998, p. 44). The most important priority at the moment is to carry out fundamental changes in governmental policy by way of establishing independent inspectors who will monitor the government at all times and ensure the complete separation of big business and government.

DISCUSSION ACTIVITIES

Exploring Japanese Culture

1. Describe some of the scandals that have occurred recently involving the government and individual companies that are related to *amakudari*. What has been the outcome of these scandals?

2. What measures should the government take to prevent *amakudari* today in Japan?

3. What do you think of the ethics of Japanese bureaucrats?

4. *Amakudari* does not only occur when governmental officials enter the private sector. For example, there is a similar situation at national universities with professors obtaining posts at private universities after they retire and teaching until they are seventy years old or beyond. What do you think of *amakudari* in the Japanese educational system?

5. What do you think bureaucrats should do after they retire, especially if this occurs at an early age?

6. Why do so many Japanese bureaucrats come from Tokyo University? Is this a good practice? If not, how can it be changed?

7. *Amakudari* not only occurs at the national level in Japan but can also be found in local offices at the prefectural and municipal levels. In other words, it seems to be a pervasive practice in Japan. Discuss this issue.

8. In spite of its obvious disadvantages, recent reports in the media suggest that *amakudari* practices are continuing unabated in Japan. Why is it so difficult to stop this practice?

9. How has *amakudari* contributed to the decline of the Japanese economy?

Exploring Cross-Cultural Issues

1. What is the relationship between the government and the business community in other countries? Does *amakudari* exist in other nations? If not, what steps have been taken to prevent it, and what do bureaucrats do after retirement?

2. It has been claimed that the Japanese government is a kind of secret, bureaucratic organization because the independent inspectors who are supposed to oversee governmental institutions are also bureaucrats and cannot monitor the government fairly. In addition, there are few lawyers and judges in Japan, and their superiors are also bureaucrats. How does this system differ from those in other countries?

3. In Western countries, governmental information (e.g., revenues, expenditures) is transparent and open for all to see. This is not the case in Japan, where information is very difficult to access. Compare these two systems.

4. How are companies in other countries organized differently from those in Japan, especially in terms of the power of stockholders? Do companies in other countries employ *amakudari* officials in the same way as Japan?

5. How much power do bureaucrats have in other countries? What is the danger when such people accrue too much power without being accountable to anyone?

美学

Bigaku:
THE JAPANESE SENSE OF BEAUTY

In Japan, it has become popular today for people to wear blue jeans, to listen to rock music, to eat fast food, to sleep in a bed, and to eat with a knife and fork. Since ancient times, the cultures of other countries, especially those of China and Korea, have greatly influenced Japanese life. However, with the opening of Japan in the nineteenth century after many years of seclusion, and especially after World War II, the Japanese have tried to "keep up" with Western people and become like them. As a result, lifestyles from Western cultures have been increasingly accepted and adopted in Japan, and a Westernized way of life is now widespread among the Japanese people. As a result, many people are beginning to ask where one can find original Japanese culture with its deep sense of beauty, which was so apparent in the past but which is now rapidly disappearing. A partial answer to this question can be found in an examination of Japanese aesthetic traditions as they exist today, especially in terms of fashion, music, painting, and language.

The word *wafuku* is taken to mean "original Japanese clothing," such as the kimono. However, women do not wear kimonos very often these days in Japan, and most people wear so-called *yōfuku* (Western clothes), which have taken the place of traditional clothing. In fact, far from rejecting such apparel, the Japanese openly accepted this new way of dressing since they wished to become Westernized, and the wearing of *yōfuku* is now completely natural for all but the very elderly. There seem to be two reasons for the present unpopularity of traditional clothing such as kimonos. One is that they are uncomfortable to move in, forcing women to move very slowly or to remain as motionless as possible. Another reason is that those who wear kimonos are now regarded as relatively high-class, or sometimes as putting on airs, so kimonos have become a kind of formal dress for special occasions such as parties, symposiums, and ceremonies. Consequently, kimonos have not entirely disappeared from the Japanese sense of aesthetics in fashion; however, they are worn not for their beauty but rather to demonstrate people's formality, status, and pride.

Hōgaku, or traditional Japanese music, is also heard much more rarely in Japan these days. Some people try to maintain an interest in these musical traditions, but most Japanese, especially the young, have developed different tastes. Children attending music schools learn to play the piano, the violin, or the electric guitar, but rarely play traditional instruments such as the koto, shamisen, or shakuhachi. "Music" for modern Japanese people seems to have become "Western music," and even the popular enka, which is often sung in karaoke bars and is regarded as an original form of Japanese music, cannot be classified as hōgaku because it is not accompanied by the traditional instruments mentioned above. Modern Japanese music is played with instruments introduced from the West, and many young Japanese study how to play them so that they can create their own songs. In contrast to such music, hōgaku places value on slow movements and long silences, in which the emotions of the player are ambiguously reflected. Because many modern people no longer seem to have the patience to appreciate this kind of music, there are fears that traditional Japanese music is dying out and that aesthetic tastes in music are changing. This may be so, but original forms of Japanese music still remain strong on certain occasions, such as the New Year ceremony, omiai (arranged marriage), or when having dinner at a ryōtei or kappo (Japanese high-class restaurants). On these occasions, people try to be beautifully mannered, so when they hear hōgaku, it reminds them of the feeling of traditional formality.

Japanese art was originally painted in monochrome in such a way that a few simple strokes of the brush in outline could represent entire mountains and forests. It was done with India ink on paper or silk cloth using primitive tools in a contemplative atmosphere. Western art, however, is what most people know as "art" in Japan today, that is, art painted in vivid colors, in a direct, complete, and explicit way. One important difference between these two approaches can be found in "the spirit of the art." Hirayama and Takashina (1994, pp. 22–23) state, for example, that the Japanese sense of beauty is based on a concept known as *mono no aware*, a kind of aesthetic value that comes from feelings, while in Western art, people try to construct something of beauty with a logic of what is beautiful. In contrast, Japanese art focuses not on what is logically considered beautiful, but on what people *feel* is beautiful. The Japanese aesthetic is very subjective, and there are no absolute criteria as to what this should be. In the West, however, what is beautiful is beautiful in and of itself, so there are explicit and well-established criteria for beauty. *Aware* is said to be representative of the Japanese sense of beauty, and it is a term of great subtlety, which is quite difficult to understand because it relates specifically to the Japanese feeling of appreciating something that is regarded as worthless. For example, in the West people tend to think that flowers in full bloom are most beautiful, but when withered they are not. This is not the case with the Japanese sense of *aware*—people are aware of the beauty of full blossoms, of course, but are more touched and deeply moved when these blossoms are falling or beginning to wilt. Similarly, they think that a moon partially covered by clouds is more appealing than one that is full (Keene, 1988). *Aware* is thus connected to feelings of regret for things losing their beauty, and paradoxically finding beauty in their opposite. Moreover, anything can ultimately be appreciated as beautiful in Japan, and what is beautiful depends upon people's subjective point of view. However, such fundamental notions of beauty are sometimes criticized for their vagueness and seem to be less appreciated and are disappearing in modern Japan, and many young people today cannot feel the beauty of *aware*.

The Japanese language is traditionally one that treasures *ma*, or empty spaces. In these blanks, people find unmentioned, hidden meanings and try to determine the meaning of the speaker or writer through feeling the atmosphere created by the words. For many

Japanese, there is great joy in this sense of "reading between the lines." For instance, Japanese haiku (poems with a pattern of 5-7-5 syllables) must be composed in very few words, but the deeper meaning of such verse is to be found in *ma* between the words. According to Ishikawa (1992, pp. 63–68), *ma* is an empty space full of meaning, which is fundamental to the Japanese arts and is present in many fields, including painting, architecture, music, and literature. This concept has also resulted in a good deal of misunderstanding of the Japanese, however, as it is often said that Japanese people never express their real intentions, because of the widespread use of ambiguity arising from the importance of *ma*. Today, the Japanese language is changing as people express themselves more decisively and directly and sometimes become irritated with vagueness for its own sake. However, there is also a danger in losing the ability to appreciate those silences (*ma*) that often seem to be worthless and contain no value (*aware*), except to those who have developed the ability to read between the lines.

In conclusion, the traditional Japanese sense of aesthetics can still be found in Japan, but it is rapidly changing. The greatest changes have been brought about by the Japanese themselves. As Hirayama and Takashina (1994, preface) note, since ancient times the Japanese people have demonstrated the ability to take in foreign ideas and cultural forms and refashion them according to the dictates of the Japanese character, thus creating something new and valuable of their own. Perhaps the modern Japanese are now trying to continue this process of "creating something new and valuable of their own," but the young in particular are often found blindly imitating the Western world. If this trend continues, the ability of people to appreciate traditional Japanese aesthetic qualities is likely to disappear, and this would be a great loss. The Japanese must learn to take pride in their own aesthetic values and find forms of expression for their artistic traditions in the modern world. This means individuals developing a consciousness and awareness of the deeper meaning of *bigaku* in order to appreciate the traditions behind the subtleties of the distinctly Japanese sense of beauty.

DISCUSSION ACTIVITIES

Exploring Japanese Culture

1. Do you think that the sense of beauty in a culture changes with time? For example, would women who were considered beautiful in the Heian era still be thought of as attractive today? What differences have occurred over time in the Japanese sense of beauty?

2. It has often been pointed out that the Japanese are losing their traditional sense of beauty. Is this something that should be lamented, or should it simply be accepted as inevitable, since all cultures are destined to change and evolve?

3. As exemplified in many haiku, scenes with scattered cherry blossoms or a sound fading gradually into silence are considered beautiful in Japan. Why?

4. The Japanese sense of beauty is said to be closely related to the seasons and to nature in general. Describe in what ways this is so.

5. Numerous reports these days detail how nature is being destroyed in modern Japan as the country is being covered in concrete, the rivers polluted, and the air poisoned with dioxins. How can this destruction be reconciled with the professed Japanese love of nature and sense of beauty?

Exploring Cross-Cultural Issues

1. There is said to be a unique sense of beauty in Japan. Compare Japanese aesthetics with the concept of beauty in other countries. Is this notion of uniqueness valid?

2. The Japanese sense of beauty is also said to be expressed in Japanese cuisine. How is this so? How does Japanese cuisine compare with that of other countries?

3. Haiku is a popular form of Japanese poetry, which is thought to express a deeper meaning than in the words themselves. Although haiku is becoming international in scope, many Japanese believe that this deeper meaning is lost when these poems are translated into other languages. For example, the famous poem by Basho, "*Furuike-ya kawazu tobikomu mizuno-oto*," is normally translated as "A frog jumped into an old pond—a sound of water." Do you think that this translation preserves the original sense of beauty? Why, or why not?

4. Compare the following scenes: a vase in which roses are arranged in a precise, geometrical order and a tray on which a variety of flowers are strewn irregularly and interspersed with sprigs of grass. Which would be considered more beautiful in Japan? Why? Which would be considered more beautiful in other countries?

5. Traditional Japanese art forms have had a profound effect on art in the West. Describe these influences and compare them with similar influences in modern times.

武士道

Bushidō:
THE WAY OF THE WARRIOR

In Japanese history, the class that had political power and a position of leadership from the end of the twelfth century to the end of the nineteenth century was the warrior class, called *bushi*, or *samurai*, in Japanese. They appeared as self-defense groups to protect private manors and to maintain public order in the Heian period. Under feudalism, which was a decentralized structure of society in which vassals obtained protection and land as a reward for their loyalty and service to their lord, samurai society became powerful in the Middle Ages (Burns & Ralph, 1955, p. 408). In the Edo era, samurai were ranked the highest of the four classes, which also included farmers, artisans, and tradesmen. In spite of the abolition of this class system during the Meiji Restoration at the end of the nineteenth century, former samurai were actively engaged in the modernization of Japan. As a result, they had a great influence on Japanese society, and the spirit of the samurai, or *bushidō*, was an important factor in molding the Japanese mind.

Bushidō refers to ethics that were formed among the samurai. Although the term was not used until the Edo period, the concept itself was formed in the Kamakura period, evolving through the adoption of neo-Confucian ideals in the Edo period, to become the foundation of national morality after the Meiji Restoration (*Bushidō*, 1988, p. 2111). It is important to note that "*Bushidō* involved not only martial spirit and skill with weapons, but also absolute loyalty to one's lord, a strong sense of personal honor, devotion to duty, and the courage, if required, to sacrifice one's life in battle or in ritual" (Bushidō, 1983, p. 221).

THE ORIGINS OF BUSHIDŌ: ZEN BUDDHISM

Buddhism was introduced into Japan from China in the sixth century and has had a great influence on Japanese culture. At the end of the twelfth century, a Buddhist sect called Zen became established in Japan. While other Buddhist sects affected mainly the religious aspects of Japanese life, Zen contributed enormously to building the Japanese character. Activities that were strongly influenced by Zen included tea ceremony (sadō), flower arrangement (kadō), haiku, and calligraphy (shodō). In addition, Zen had a great impact on bushidō:

> Because [Zen Buddhism] stressed physical discipline, self-control, and the practice of meditation in place of formal scholarship, the sect appealed to the warrior class, who felt that Zen teachings gave supernatural sanction to the attitudes which they had already come to regard as essential to their station. (Burns & Ralph, 1955, p. 503)

The main goal of Zen Buddhism is for practitioners to achieve spiritual enlightenment (satori) through experiencing the Buddha-nature within: "Enlightenment is seen as a liberation from man's intellectual nature, from the burden of fixed ideas and feelings about reality." According to this way of thinking, "the Buddha-nature resides in all things, but . . . this reality could not be taught because it is beyond duality and conceptualization" (Davies, 1998b, p. 1). For this reason, Zen puts emphasis on experiencing one's own body in order to discover truth.

It is said that "to experience satori is to become conscious of the Unconscious (mushin or no-mind)" (Suzuki, 1988, p. 220), and mushin is the secret of the martial arts as well as the aesthetic arts in creating a strong mentality. As the Zen master Takuan, states:

> [No-mind] is a mind that is not at all disturbed by affects of any kind. . . . When mushin or munen is attained, the mind moves from one object to another, flowing like a stream of water, filling every

possible corner. For this reason the mind fulfills every function required of it. But when the flowing is stopped at one point, all the other points will get nothing of it, and the result will be a general stiffness and obduracy. (Ibid., p. 111)

In other words, the state of no-mind unites the body with the spirit. Many samurai trained hard to achieve this state through Zen, and this relieved their fear of death. In Takuan's letter to a great swordsman and one of the teachers of Tokugawa Iemitsu, the Zen master gave him the following advice:

When the opponent tries to strike you, your eyes at once catch the movement of his sword and you may strive to follow it. But as soon as this takes place, you cease to be master of yourself and you are sure to be beaten. . . . Therefore, do not even think of yourself. (Ibid., pp. 95–96)

Thus, the spiritual elements of *bushidō* come from Zen Buddhism, and Zen religious practices were used by samurai to train physically and mentally. They acquired skill in improving their military arts in a way that kept the mind calm, whatever happened, through Zen.

THE ORIGINS OF BUSHIDŌ: CONFUCIANISM

In addition to the primary influences of Zen Buddhism, the modern concept of *bushidō* became established on the basis of Confucian ideology:

Confucianism is first and foremost a rational, utilitarian philosophy of human nature which considers proper human relationships as the basis of society. . . . [It] stresses a social order based on strict ethical rules, centering on the family and state, both of which should be governed by men of education and superior ethical wisdom. [There are four principles]: (1) *jen*—humanism, the warm human feelings between people . . . ; (2) *i*—faithfulness, loyalty, or justice . . . ; (3) *li*—propriety, ritual, respect for social forms, decorum . . . ; and (4) *chih*—wisdom. . . . (Davies, 1998, p. 2)

Neo-Confucianism was developed in China by Zhu Xi (or Chu Hsi) (AD 1130–1200), and it is usually called *shushigaku* in Japanese. This teaching was studied by Zen monks of the *gozan* temples in the Muromachi period and was used when feudal lords enacted laws for their domains. In the Edo period, the Zhu Xi school received strong support from the Tokugawa shogunate (*Shushigaku*, 1993, pp. 1426–1427). The shogunate believed "[Zhu Xi's] philosophy to be enormously useful in justifying or ideologically legitimizing the feudal structure of state and society that had emerged in Japan in the seventeenth century," for the neo-Confucianist school mostly emphasized the principles of *li* (propriety) and *jen* (humanism) in which filial piety toward one's parents and loyalty toward one's lord were valued (Varley, 1986, p. 151). The samurai were ranked as the highest class in the Edo period, and they were not just soldiers, but they also had a political role. Therefore, as Beasley (1999, p. 158) maintains, "Samurai education was developed, in order to provide the ethos and the skills appropriate to an official career. . . . [T]hey were deemed to need 'correct' moral attitudes if they were to play a part in government." Consequently, the Tokugawa shogunate and subservient feudal domains established many schools to enable their retainers to learn Confucian ideas.

In the mid-Edo period, *kogaku* (or "ancient learning schools") were established by Japanese thinkers who rejected Zhu Xi's neo-Confucian orthodoxy because it was difficult to accommodate to Japanese society. Scholars of *kogaku* returned to the works of classical Chinese Confucianism in order to correctly grasp what the ancient sages preached (*Kogaku*, 1993, pp. 808–809). Yamaga Soko was an early major figure who studied the ancient learning and maintained that "a 'sincere' or 'truthful' life . . . was one that adhered to the principles of right conduct, which permitted those who followed them to make contact with what was vital and dynamic in their spirit" (ibid., p. 808). He had samurai origins and was also a scholar of military affairs. In fact, he is said to be one of the main formulators of *bushidō*: "The samurai, he asserted, must cultivate not only his physical skills as a warrior but also his mind and character. . . . [H]e must serve as the exemplar of high mind and character" (Varley, 1986, pp. 183–184).

In summary, Confucianism flourished with the support of the samurai in the Edo period, and Confucian concepts, such as loyalty and humanism, permeated samurai society and gradually spread to the general public, resulting in the continuing existence of strong Confucian beliefs in modern Japan.

LOYALTY

In *Hagakure* (cited in Suzuki, 1988, pp. 72–73), the Edo era samurai Yamamoto stated that "Bushidō means the determined will to die" (*Bushidō towa shinu koto to mitsuketari*). This implies that all samurai had to live admirably and honorably in order not to have regrets when they died, since facing death was a daily occurrence. To act in a praiseworthy manner, there was a strict moral code that the samurai followed, involving justice, politeness, and so on. Moreover, as Nitobe (1935, p. 86) explains, "personal fidelity is a moral adhesion existing among all sorts and conditions of men . . . but it is only in the code of chivalrous honor that loyalty assumes paramount importance."

Loyalty was thus a distinctive feature of feudal society in Japan: the relationship between lord and vassal was called that of "obligations and service" (*go-on to hōkō*) in the Kamakura period. A samurai's life was economically based on fiefs, and the lord guaranteed his servants' territory and gave them additional domains according to their achievements in battle.

There were also antithetical concepts reflected in the samurai's ethical ideology in the Kamakura period. On the one hand, Watsuji (cited in Sagara, 1964, pp. 162–164) states that the relationship among retainers and their master was based on absolute submission and self-sacrifice. They were tied together with feelings; the lord presented lands to his vassals out of appreciation, and the vassals sacrificed themselves freely for their lord. On the other hand, Ienaga argues that samurai served their lord in exchange for remuneration (ibid.). When the exchange was not performed equally, the lord applied sanctions, or the samurai frankly requested more rewards. Accordingly, "honor" involved the relationship of lord and vassal, and the samurai were often torn between autonomy and loyalty to their lord in order to win this honor. In fact, however, the nature of power relationships between lords and their samurai varied greatly, depending on the domain (Ikegami, 2000, pp. 83–84).

HONOR

Samurai valued honor in an extreme and strict way, which was expressed in the adage "Die rather than disgrace yourself" (Ozawa, 1994, p. 13). In battle, samurai who faced death, prized honor and their fame as warriors and desired that this fame should be passed down from generation to generation eternally. They tried to be the first to lead their men into battle and shouted their names to the enemy in order to show their bravery (ibid., p. 65). Honor was very important for samurai as a matter of pride, and achieving an honorable death meant that their descendants were rewarded and treated well by their lord. As an example, in 1582, the troops of Uesugi Kagekatsu were fighting against Oda Nobunaga. When Uesugi's side was in a critical situation and one of his castles was about to fall, his samurai retainers who were defending the castle made the following resolution:

> Just before the fall of their castle, . . . the vassals decided that it would be regrettable if they were captured alive and had their names disgraced by their enemies. They decided to perform *seppuku* and leave their names to posterity. . . . They not only died but each wrote their own name on a wooden tag and fastened it through a hole which they made in their ears. In short, they did this to show who was who. Actually, their names were handed down as a record, and each of their offspring was rewarded by Uesugi. (Nomura, 1995, pp. 8–9)

As this case suggests, *seppuku*, or suicide by self-disembowelment, was the most honorable death for a samurai. The abdomen was regarded as the place where the soul and affections dwelled, so the samurai showed their integrity in this way (Nitobe, 1935, pp. 118–120). Samurai also displayed their courage and mettle and had a feeling of faithful satisfaction in killing themselves with their sword, which was their most precious possession and of utmost importance to them (Okuma, 1995, p. 28).

AFTER THE COLLAPSE OF THE SAMURAI CLASS

The samurai as a class ceased to exist after the breakdown of the feudal system; nevertheless, certain moral characteristics that they espoused, including fidelity, justice, integrity, and honor, still remained strong in the Meiji era (Nomura, 1995, p. 232). However, the Japanese nation abused the concept of loyalty and produced fanatic patriots when it went to war against other countries in the nineteenth and twentieth centuries. They committed atrocities on innocent people in other countries, even though the samurai of olden times observed the proprieties and respected their enemies and one another. However, in modern times, Japanese soldiers fought fanatically for their country and for the emperor, and this caused many tragedies.

As an example, before going to the Russo-Japanese War in 1904–1905, some soldiers killed their children if they had a sick wife and no other guardian, because they did not want to leave their families and let them starve to death. They thought that this was a reflection of loyalty. According to Tomikura et al. (1975, pp. 100–105), these actions were considered laudable since murdering one's children and sick wife expressed devotion to the country and to the Meiji emperor.

Other examples of a perverted sense of loyalty were the suicide (or kamikaze) squads of World War II and the famous suicide of General Nogi. The kamikaze were military pilots who carried bombs and crashed into enemy ships to destroy them; General Nogi and his wife committed seppuku to follow the Meiji emperor into death. Generally, their attitudes were praised as exemplifying the Japanese spirit.

However, while modernization was promoted in Meiji times, society forgot the spiritual center of the Japanese bushidō spirit, and it is argued by some that bushidō vanished as the Meiji period ended (Nomura, 1995, p. 237).

BUSHIDŌ IN MODERN TIMES

As mentioned above, it is claimed that the spirit of bushidō as a Japanese trait hardly exists today; however, some characteristics of bushidō can be still found in the martial and aesthetic arts, which follow certain forms (kata) that are practiced repeatedly until practitioners master the form and enter the state of "no-mind." Manners are also important, and students have to have a strong sense of loyalty and respect toward their teachers.

Unfortunately, bushidō loyalty has also led to the Japanese over-working, which sometimes ends in death (karōshi) as people try to show how they are doing their best for their company and bosses through working hard. Moreover, in modern times, some Japanese are driven to commit suicide when they want to clear an unsavory reputation or when they want to apologize for their sins or mistakes in their company or family. The Japanese people tend to accept and even glorify these kinds of suicides and feel sympathy for the vic-tims, and this has a negative influence on people, especially the young, because they may think that suicide is the easiest way to be released from all pain.

In summary, bushidō has greatly contributed to the formation of the Japanese character. As stated above, bushidō spirit still dominates Japanese society in some ways; nevertheless, in others, it is becom-ing difficult to find this spirit among the young, many of whom have no respect for their teachers and no manners in public. Thus, in mod-ern Japan, some people have a strong awareness of bushidō, whereas others have no interest in it anymore. bushidō, as a Japanese trait, seems to be at a turning point, and its relevance to Japanese life today depends largely on the individual.

DISCUSSION ACTIVITIES

Exploring Japanese Culture

1. During World War II, some Japanese pilots, called kamikaze, delib-erately crashed their planes into enemy battleships. In other cases, Japanese soldiers fought fanatically to the death rather than surren-der. Discuss the relationship between these actions and bushidō.

2. In rebuilding Japan after the war, it was said that Japanese salarī-men embodied the bushidō spirit, and they were even called "corporate

warriors." Do young Japanese work for their companies today in the same way? Why, or why not?

3. Do you think that young Japanese still have the "die-rather-than-disgrace-yourself" spirit? If so, in what present-day phenomena is this spirit reflected?

4. Many Japanese businesspeople work late almost every night. Why? How is this related to the spirit of bushidō?

5. Recently, a number of businessmen in Japan have suffered from mental problems, such as depression, and some have even died because of overwork (karōshi). How are these problems related to the spirit of bushidō?

6. **Case Study**: Ken Goto is a sixth-grader in a Tokyo primary school. He is the pitcher of the baseball team at the school. One day the team had a game against an Osaka primary school and in the bottom of the ninth inning, the second baseman committed a costly error that cost Ken's team the game. Ken was upset and threw his glove to the ground. The team's coach, watching this, approached Ken and slapped him on the face, saying, "Why did you do that to your glove, your most important piece of equipment for playing baseball? You may have excellent pitching skills, but you are not a mature person. Excellent skills and performance are meaningless unless you also have patience and other moral standards."
Question: What do you think of the coach's response? Would you have reacted in the same way? Why, or why not? Discuss this scenario from the perspective of bushidō.

Exploring Cross-Cultural Issues

1. Do you think that bushidō is different from chivalry in the West? If so, what are the differences between the two?

2. It is said that characteristic of bushidō is the spiritual growth of an

apprentice or disciple through the mastery of certain skills under the auspices of a master. Is the relationship between Obi-Wan and Luke Skywalker in *Star Wars* or, later, between Luke and Yoda, the same as the relationship between a master and a disciple in the Japanese martial arts?

3. There are people who point out that American baseball and its Japanese counterpart, *yakyu*, exhibit important differences. In what ways are these differences related to *bushidō*?

4. Many societies in the world have had strong warrior codes. Compare some of these traditions with the Japanese concept of *bushidō*.

5. In Asia, the Japanese are still feared for their military potential. Do you think these fears are justified? Why, or why not?

沈黙

Chinmoku:
SILENCE IN JAPANESE COMMUNICATION

Communication among human beings takes various forms and includes not only verbal but also nonverbal expression such as gestures, facial expressions, posture. Such nonverbal communication is mostly unconscious but nevertheless plays an essential role in human relationships. Silence, or *chinmoku*, in particular, can be viewed as a communicative skill, not just a form of emptiness between spoken words. As Tannen (cited in Lebra, 1987, p. 343) notes, "Silence can be a matter of saying nothing and meaning something." Different societies view silence in different ways, however, depending on cultural values, which determine how silence is interpreted. *Chinmoku* in Japanese communication has certain distinct features, which derive from the underlying values of Japanese culture that determine how silence appears and functions in communication in Japanese society.

THE UNDERLYING CAUSES OF CHINMOKU
In daily conversations, business meetings, and school classrooms in Japan, silence is much more common and is of longer duration than in Western countries. There are a number of reasons for silence being so ubiquitous in Japanese communication, and these causes can be classified into two main categories: historical factors and the dominance of group consciousness in Japanese life.

The Japanese have long treated silence as a kind of virtue similar to "truthfulness." The words *haragei* and *ishin denshin* symbolize Japanese attitudes toward human interactions in this regard. The former means implicit mutual understanding; the latter suggests that people can communicate with each other through telepathy. In short, what is important and what is true in Japan will often exist in silence, not in verbal expression. This attitude is deeply rooted in a Japanese way of thinking known as *uchi-soto*, or inner and outer duality. Lebra (1987, p. 345) provides an explanation:

> [The Japanese] believe that the truth lies only in the inner realm as symbolically located in the heart or belly. Components of the outer self, such as face, mouth, spoken words, are in contrast, associated with cognitive and moral falsity. Truthfulness, sincerity, straightforwardness, or reliability are allied to reticence. Thus a man of few words is trusted more than a man of many words.

Zen Buddhism is thought to have had a great influence on the development of these attitudes toward silence in Japan. The goal of Zen practice is not stated explicitly but is understood only at a deeper intuitive level within learners themselves through constant practice, which puts emphasis on meditation, quietude, and emptying one's mind. Zen training is designed to teach that truth cannot be described verbally, but can exist only in silence. Traditional Japanese arts and the spirit of *dō* (the "way" or "path") reflect this characteristic silence. Japanese music, for example, is said to contain *ma*, meaning "intervals between sounds," which are considered important because "it is the interval which determines the rhythm, while the beat is subsidiary and serves to enhance the interval" (Dan; cited in Lebra, 1987, p. 355). Similarly, in *kabuki* dramas and *Noh* plays, it is the silence between the lines that expresses tension, excitement, and the climax. *Dō* practices such as *shodō* (calligraphy) and *kadō* (flower arrangement) also emphasize quietude and a grave atmosphere in which a controlled attitude contained within silence leads learners to the development of skill and success.

Another reason why the Japanese often become silent among other people is group consciousness, which is symbolized by the saying "The nail that sticks out will be hammered down" (*Deru kui wa utareru*). In Japanese society, where people usually identify themselves primarily as members of certain groups, not just as individuals, silence has played a very important role in creating harmony and in avoiding direct conflict. The person who insists on his or her opinion before the group has reached a consensus is seen as selfish and forward (Naotsuka, 1996, p. 193). In addition, to show off one's ability or knowledge openly makes a bad impression on others in Japan, and such people are considered thoughtless, impolite, and immature. Many people in Japan think that it is better to say nothing than cause misunderstandings or trouble. Silence in Japanese communication is also related to a strong consciousness of social hierarchy within the group and in society at large. In social interactions among the Japanese, it is essential to consider which person is in a higher or a lower position, depending on his or her age, sex, job status, and so on. It is considered rude for a subordinate to speak out openly against a person of higher rank.

THE FUNCTIONS OF CHINMOKU

There are both positive and negative aspects to the functions of silence in Japan. To begin with, it is important to note exactly when Japanese people are silent. Silence occurs when people have nothing to say, of course, but it does not always mean that they have no ideas. Silence is commonly thought to indicate thoughtfulness or hesitation in trying to find a good way to communicate smoothly; therefore, even though people have something to say, they may not express everything that they have in mind and may leave their true intentions unspoken. This kind of silence is known as *enryo-sasshi* (i.e., reserve and restraint). In high-context Japanese culture (Hall, 1970), direct verbal expression, especially negative forms of communication such as anger, hate, refusal, disagreement, and defiance are avoided:

> Ideas and feelings that might hurt the other person or damage the general atmosphere when expressed are carefully sent back for reexamination in an internal self-feedback process. Only those ideas judged safe and vague are allowed to be sent out through the small exit that functions as a screen filter. This message-screening

process . . . is *enryo*; it makes the Japanese appear silent, vague, and awkward in communicating with superiors, strangers, and people from different cultures. (Ishii & Bruneau, 1994, p. 250)

Japanese TV commercials provide a good illustration of *enryo-sasshi* in communication. In ads promoting pharmaceutical drugs, for example, it is common to have famous actors or TV personalities play the role of "warm family members" in promoting a medicine rather than to clearly explain its efficacy because this tends to be felt as "wordy" or "pushy" by Japanese consumers. People prefer being appealed to gradually in a more "feeling" atmosphere in Japanese forms of communication (Akiyama, 1994, p. 48).

Japanese silence occurs not only in public but also in private interactions, particularly in conjugal relationships, because "[the couple] are in love but too embarrassed to express their feelings in speech" (Lebra, 1987, p. 349). Husbands and wives in Japan tend not to use overt verbal communication and try to understand each other by nonverbal means, especially when they attempt to express tender emotions (ibid.). Silence in this case may reflect their feelings of embarrassment caused by closeness or intimacy, or it may have to do with a specific Japanese way of thinking related to *ishin denshin* and *enryo-sasshi*. Silence thus functions as a kind of lubricating oil to create smoother communication because it can help to avoid hurting others and contributes to a peaceful and harmonious atmosphere, allowing people to overcome difficult situations in a calm and unhurried way.

On the other hand, silence can frequently cause misunderstandings, even in Japanese interactions. In fact, it is not unusual for people to feel irritated and impatient when they cannot understand each other because their expressions are too indirect to follow. It is also true that in Japan, actions or judgments tend to be delayed, so it often takes too much time to clarify the facts and solve problematic situations.

The Japanese may also be silent not only to avoid conflict with others but also to hurt someone or to keep them at a distance. When people feel angry or are in disagreement with others, they may not directly express their feelings but often just keep silent and ignore the other person. This behavior characterizes bullying, which has recently become a much more serious problem among Japanese children. If students see someone being bullied, they may not mention anything about the fact and just try to keep a distance from both the assailant and the victim, for fear of being mixed up in the bullying themselves. Similarly, in a train, if people recognize that someone is being molested, they may not say anything to help the victim, because they are afraid of disapproval for their forward behavior, or simply because they are apathetic. In short, silence also means defiance and indifference in Japanese life.

In addition, silence can function as a weapon to protect one's position or to conceal facts when someone has done something wrong or feels guilty. For example, Japanese politicians, business executives, and school principals are known to resort to silence to hide unpalatable facts or evade their responsibilities. These attitudes reflect a Japanese value called *kusai mono niwa futa* ("to sweep the dirt under the carpet"), and not only people with special status but also ordinary Japanese often try to avoid facing up to negative situations.

Silence as a way of avoiding direct or potentially troublesome expression can thus function either positively or negatively. To create a relaxed and harmonious atmosphere, silence may play an important role in Japanese interactions, but it can also arise from less noble attitudes such as shirking responsibility, awkwardness, or apathy.

THE ROLE OF *CHINMOKU* IN CROSS-CULTURAL MISUNDERSTANDINGS

Even in communication among the Japanese themselves, it is sometimes difficult to understand the actual meaning and function of silence. In communication with people from other countries, silence can become a serious obstacle to intercultural understanding.

For one thing, as has been explained, when the Japanese are silent, it may imply a wide range of meanings, such as consideration or sympathy, modesty, agreement, patience, embarrassment, resentment, lack of forgiveness or defiance, and apathy. This can cause confusion for non-Japanese, as they usually do not have similar cultural values that help them to interpret the meaning of silence. In fact, sometimes they will have totally opposite attitudes and values.

Generally speaking, Western cultures have long emphasized verbal expression and communicating opinions and emotions clearly and openly:

> The Western tradition is relatively negative in its attitude toward silence and ambiguity, especially in social and public relations. People seldom recognize that silence does have linking, affecting revelational, judgmental, and activating communicative functions in Western cultures. (Jensen; cited in Ishii & Bruneau, 1994, p. 247)

At the same time, there may be a different concept of time, depending on the communication style. According to Naotsuka (1996, pp. 220–223), many people from other countries consider the Japanese communication style, which is characterized by silence and indirectness, as "wasting time." Japanese society is based on the smooth maintenance of relationships among group members, whereas relationships in the West put more emphasis on individualism, so that time spent in silence or for indirect purposes may be seen as not very productive (ibid., p. 221).

However, Westerners are not always more talkative and frank than the Japanese. In some situations, the Japanese can ask certain kinds of blunt personal questions, such as "How old are you?" or "Are you married?" Although Western people may consider these kinds of questions impolite or "intrusions of privacy" (ibid., p. 113), in Japanese relationships, where people are attuned to depending on one another, personal information of this nature is needed in order to get along with others.

Judging from the above, although there are a number of important cultural differences in communication styles, people may not consciously be aware of them and will judge or criticize others according to their own values or standards of communication. This can be one of the most troublesome obstacles to intercultural understanding.

DISCUSSION ACTIVITIES

Exploring Japanese Culture

1. It is thought that silence plays an important role in maintaining harmony and avoiding conflict in Japan. Do you agree?

2. In the classroom, there are two types of quiet students—those who do not have their own ideas and do not usually think about issues, and those who are thoughtful and very conscious of their own feelings. Most recent problems in Japanese schools have to do with the latter group, who remain silent until their emotions overflow and cannot be controlled. Discuss this problem.

3. Do you think that the concept of *chinmoku* contributes to the rising number of cases of teenage and adult violence in Japan? Discuss this with reference to the case in Niigata of the nine-year-old girl who was held captive in her kidnapper's home for nine years.

4. In what ways do childrearing practices in Japan reinforce the concept of *chinmoku*?

5. In Japan, people often prefer to remain silent rather than hurt someone else's feelings. Discuss the advantages and disadvantages of this approach to interpersonal relations in terms of society as a whole.

6. In Japan, a man of few words is considered a thoughtful person and is trusted more than a man of many words. Moreover, although a Japanese man is looked down upon if he talks too much, most people feel that it is all right for women to talk more openly and freely. How do you feel about these attitudes?

7. Japanese couples often communicate by nonverbal means, and silence is generally an accepted part of the relationship. Can genuine communication develop in this way, and are people really satisfied with this kind of silence in a relationship?

8. In Japanese schools, PTA meetings often go smoothly because nobody interrupts by asking questions or criticizing school policies. People usually do not ask questions officially, but after the meeting they exchange opinions frankly in the corridor, and this is known as a "corridor meeting." What do you think about this way of dealing with issues?

9. Haiku are said to be the shortest poems in the world, and what is not said is considered just as important as what is said. In other words, artistic truth exists in tension created by using limited verbal expression. How does this relate to the concept of *chinmoku* in Japan?

Exploring Cross-Cultural Issues

1. It is quite difficult to show your real abilities and knowledge openly in Japan. For instance, even if you have talent within a company, you are expected to remain silent and do the work you have been assigned diligently. How is this different from other countries?

2. Do you think that *chinmoku* is a barrier to Japan's becoming more internationalized? If so, how can this be overcome?

3. Many Western people are uncomfortable with silence, because it is generally associated with negative feelings or concepts. Indeed, for some, the enforcement of silence is seen as an infringement of "the right to speak." Discuss how this notion of silence causes problems in cross-cultural communication, especially between people of Japan and the West.

4. In English, there is a traditional saying that "children should be seen and not heard." Compare this with attitudes in Japan and other countries of the world.

5. In the West, children are brought up to communicate openly with adults and to express their opinions, ask questions, and even to

criticize. In Japan, however, children are generally shy and do not often know how to speak to adults. What is your view on verbal training in Japan compared with the West?

6. In Japanese schools, students are expected to listen to their teachers without interrupting and without asking questions, and they have few opportunities to express their opinions. Compare this with schools in the West.

7. In homestay situations, Japanese young people staying with Western families sometimes think that being polite means staying silent, but this kind of behavior is often worrying for the homestay family, who may think that the Japanese young person is unhappy. How can this problem be resolved?

8. *Chinmoku* is an important concept in Japan. Does the same attitude toward silence exist in other Asian countries?

男女関係

Danjyo Kankei:
MALE AND FEMALE RELATIONSHIPS IN JAPAN

HISTORICAL PERSPECTIVES

Historically, the relationship between men and women in Japan has changed in accordance with the dominant social system of the period and women's position within it. In the distant past, Japan was a matrilineal society in which women had rights to succeed to the property of a family, and there were many female leaders. Men and women seem to have had equal relations socially, politically, and economically in their daily lives.

Even after men began to assume dominance in the Nara and Heian periods, ordinary people still maintained relatively equal relations, while among the aristocracy, men generally had great power over women. By the end of the Heian period, women's right of succession had weakened considerably, however, and this seems to have accelerated their subordination to men economically.

The most important characteristic of medieval times, known in Japan as the Kamakura and Muromachi periods, was the development of the *ie* system, in which social and political priority was given to men. *Ie* literally means "house" or "home," and the *ie* system involved an extended-membership family system, including not only family members but also servants, household workers, and so on. In this system, the chief male (i.e., the father or grandfather) had great power, and the other members had to obey his decisions. Generally, women marrying such heads of families were expected to have sons, because the first son in the *ie* system had the right of inheritance and an important role in maintaining the family line. This centralization of power in the family was effective in protecting all family members, and it was reflected in similar structures in the government. At this time, Japan developed a multilayered class system, and among the samurai, women played an important role in the ie system, tying families together by marriage for political power. They were expected not only to obey their husbands but also to be strong, as wives of warriors, in supporting their husbands and in running the family during wars.

Male-female relationships began to change completely in the Edo period because Confucianism, which was the official philosophy of the Tokugawa shogunate, had a great effect on people's way of thinking. Because of many of the paternal aspects of Confucianism, the idea of "men outside and women inside" became widespread, and this attitude is still prevalent in Japanese society today.

The next stage in the changing relations between the sexes began in the modern era with the start of formal systems of education for both males and females in the Meiji era, when Japan rapidly tried to absorb ideas from the West. However, education was far from equal for men and women, partly because schooling for females had the goal of intentionally creating *ryōsaikenbo*, literally meaning "good wives and wise mothers." Although women were educated in Meiji times, their training was largely directed toward the household in that they were expected to support their husbands and be responsible for the upbringing and education of their children. It was only after World War II that all people had equal rights guaranteed by the new constitution, regardless of sex. In addition, the Equal Employment Opportunity Law was enacted in 1986 with the goal of abolishing employment discrimination against women. Women's position in society has thus gradually improved, but it is also true that discrimination is widespread in spite of changes in the law.

Relationships between men and women in Japan are changing rapidly nowadays. More women than ever before are working outside the home, and there are widespread changes in sexual mores, as well as a new consciousness toward marriage. These changes can be viewed from a number of different perspectives, which will be discussed below, in terms of Japanese language expressions, changing consciousness toward marriage, and husband and wife relationships in Japan.

JAPANESE EXPRESSIONS

Compared with most Western countries, the position of Japanese women in society is still low, a fact that is often pointed out in this increasingly international world. The reason why women have difficulty in improving their social position seems to be connected with the influence of Confucianism, which exerts an unconscious but still strong influence on Japanese people. An old Confucian adage says, for example, that a woman should in youth obey her father, in maturity her husband, and in old age her son. The Japanese language itself reflects the status of these relationships between males and females. Expressing the term husband in Japanese, most wives use the word *shujin*, which consists of two kanji meaning "main person." On the other hand, *kanai*, which literally means "inside house," is utilized by men as the word for wife. These expressions illustrate certain traditional Japanese ideas about the family, such as the belief that husbands are superior to wives and that wives should always be at home and obey husbands. These traditional concepts are also seen in the literal order of Japanese compound words composed of kanji that describe certain groups consisting of men and women: *danjyo* (men and women), *fūfu* (husbands and wives), and so forth. All of these terms start with kanji designating male groups (i.e., men, husbands).

The Japanese language also has a great many expressions used only for females, which sometimes make fun of women or dictate how they should behave. There are three examples that illustrate this point: *otoko-masari*, *otenba*, and *hako-iri-musume*. *Otoko-masari* means a woman who is superior to men physically, spiritually, and intellectually. However, despite this literal meaning of "a woman who exceeds men," it often sounds negative in Japanese because it carries a connotation of lacking femininity, and such women are usually disliked. *Otenba*, which can be translated into English as "tomboy," generally applies to healthy and active young girls. Parents often use this word to talk about a daughter who is so energetic that they cannot control her. Such a girl, however, will be expected to learn to behave modestly and humbly by the time she becomes an adult. *Hako-iri-musume* is an expression that may be translated as "daughters-in-a-box," which refers to daughters who are brought up very carefully by their parents as if they were some kind of treasure. In the past, most people praised *hako-iri-musume* for their pure image, but recently this has been changing and is now felt to express an overly innocent or delicate female child.

In addition, as far as marriage is concerned, there are two expressions in Japanese that put psychological pressure on single women. *Tekireiki*, the right age to marry, has a disagreeable connotation because it is used to put pressure on women to marry. If they stay single and pass through *tekireiki*, they are often called *urenokori*, which usually indicates a situation where goods or vegetables are left unsold. Because these expressions are so negative, these days people are gradually refraining from using them. However, they still remain in people's consciousness, in spite of the fact that everyone has a right to decide when and whom to marry.

THE CHANGING CONSCIOUSNESS OF MEN AND WOMEN IN RELATIONSHIPS

In modern Japan, the number of people with higher-educational backgrounds is increasing, and their sense of values is also changing in many ways. Conventional ideas with regard to male-female relationships are carrying less weight these days, and sexual mores and perceptions of marriage clearly appear to be changing.

In terms of sexual mores, originally sex between men and women in Japan was freer, more natural, and healthier (Research Group for a Study of Women's History, 1992, p. 106). However, female sexual behavior has been under male control since Confucian principles gave men great power over women in the Edo period. At this time, if women had sexual relations with men other than their husbands, they were punished severely, while men were openly allowed to keep mistresses in order to have sons and maintain the *ie* system. Furthermore, the government officially sanctioned brothels and other places where men visited prostitutes. In the Meiji era, a new idea that unmarried females should be virgins began to spread among the people, and young women were brought up more strictly with regard to sexual matters (ibid., p. 193).

These days, however, it is often said that young people's attitudes toward sexual matters have changed because of the information they receive from the media. Certainly, compared with past generations, people are socially freer to be friends with members of the opposite sex in their teens and twenties, and premarital relations, premarital pregnancy, and even cohabitation are less criticized in society today.

There are two types of marriage in Japan—arranged marriages (*omiai*) and "love marriages"—and this difference is important in understanding Japanese views on the nature of matrimony. Arranged marriages have long been considered as ties between one family and another, rather than just in terms of personal relations between a man and a woman. In the past, men and women who had never met often married in this way. Traditionally, in this case, representatives from both families controlled the couple's choices in terms of partners. Today, the nature of arranged marriages is changing, however, and they remain one of the few chances men and women have to get to know each other in the extremely busy lives of the modern Japanese. If the arranged encounter eventually leads to their building good relations, it can end up in a successful marriage.

According to a survey by the Ministry of Health and Welfare in 1994 (Yuzawa, 1995, p. 83), it is clear that the frequency of "love marriages" is generally increasing. They were more than five times more frequent than arranged marriages in 1990, although the latter were three times more common in 1950. This reflects a changing sense of values toward marriage and what people consider to be important when they finally decide to marry, that is, their parents' wishes or their own personal choices.

Another tendency in recent years has been that more people have been choosing to stay single in Japan, as is generally occurring throughout the developed world, most likely because of the increase in single women with their own careers who feel that they have no need for the financial security that is traditionally associated with marriage. But it would be wrong to generalize from this tendency that fewer people actually want to marry. In fact, a survey by the General Affairs Agency in 1994 (ibid., p. 95) shows that most young people in Japan want to marry at some time in their lives.

Concerning this phenomenon, there are three main reasons why the number of single people is increasing. The first is related to the groupism affecting the Japanese way of life. People consider it important to follow the values of the group in order to maintain harmony. As a result, most Japanese have few opportunities to get to know people of the opposite sex outside of work, much less have enough time to date. In short, contact between the sexes is quite limited in Japan. Second, the existing social system works ineffectively for women in that if they want their own careers, they have little choice but to stay single. In Japan, when women take even short breaks from work, such as maternity leave, it is very difficult for them to return to their former positions. A third reason is the wide gap between the sexes with regard to their views on marriage. In contrast to most women, many single men think of marriage as a social duty, one by which they can gain the trust of others, take social responsibility, or meet their parents' expectations. In regard to this gap, Kumata (1992, p. 118) offers the following viewpoint:

> According to consultants working in dating service industries, women tend to emphasize the quality of "a good partner" in men. However, a lot of Japanese men still have traditional views of women. Frankly speaking, most of them seem to want a kind of a substitute for their mothers, in order to have wives do their housework like their mothers. This does not make sense for women who are taking an active part in society, are independent financially, and aim for a balance between work and family.

HUSBAND AND WIFE RELATIONSHIPS IN JAPAN

Traditional Japanese ways of thinking and living, which date back to Confucian morality in the Edo period, are still easily seen in the family system. In Japan, it is common for husbands to make important decisions in the family, rather than husbands and wives working together as a team. However, this does not mean that married women are always subservient to men in their homes. In fact, they usually have a significant role in managing the family, and wives can often demonstrate their abilities more freely and effectively than men can in the fields of child care, maintaining the household, administrating property, and so on. Indeed, it seems to some Japanese that husbands exist only to support their families financially, because they do nothing to help in any way around the house. Recently, such men are accused of being *sodai-gomi*, meaning "large-size garbage," because when they are off work they just loaf around at home.

After marriage, Japanese wives are often said to have difficulty in socializing freely, unlike their husbands, who must maintain social connections with coworkers or supervisors to maintain harmony in the group. However, women seem willing to play their own roles in maintaining the household as good wives and mothers (Reischauer, 1977, p. 232), and these days, many wives are beginning to take an active interest in networking and volunteer activities, which provide them with more outlets for socializing than before.

From the standpoint of emotional expression between husbands and wives, the Japanese rarely show overt affection to each other, nor do they often speak well of their spouses in public. These husband-wife relationships, as noted by Doi (1975, p. 132), seem to be related to *amae*, or dependency, which is the foundation of personal relationships in Japan. He accounts for the unusual relationships between husbands and wives in Japan, comparing them with those in Western countries, as follows:

> I think a clear difference in husband/wife relationships between Japan and the West is whether couples take each other for granted or not. Although this is permitted for Japanese couples, Westerners generally express their affections for one another in spoken language and other attitudes so as to reveal that they never take the other for granted.

CONCLUSIONS

Male-female relationships in Japan are currently in a state of transition. After World War II, the constitution provided men and women with equal rights, which helped improve women's position in society. In spite of laws advocating equality, however, sexual discrimination in jobs still results in important social problems: sexual harassment, inequality in the workplace, and so on. This occurs partly as a result of a Confucian way of thinking in which men are believed to be superior to women, and such aspects of society are reflected in Japanese language expressions and human relationships.

Recently, many women have obtained a higher level of education and are playing an active role in society, resulting in a number of social phenomena: a higher average age for first marriages, a decrease in the birthrate, and an increase in the number of single people. These changes have probably resulted from a change of consciousness in male-female relationships, resulting in a new sense of values toward marriage. However, conventional ideas such as "men outside and women inside" still exist in society and are supported unconsciously by many people. So whether women continue to work after marriage or not, all housekeeping chores tend to be thought of as women's work, while men are expected to simply work hard and earn money for the family, a remnant of the division of labor prevalent in the old ie system. If these changes are not to have damaging social consequences, the roles that men and women play in society must be more flexible so that the individuality of each is respected, and eventually more cooperative and equal relationships established.

DISCUSSION ACTIVITIES

Exploring Japanese Culture

1. In Japan, women were traditionally expected to get married by their mid to late twenties, and *tekireiki*, or "marriageable age," was very important in Japanese society. Has the concept of *tekireiki* changed in modern Japan? If so, how?

2. It is rare for a Japanese man to praise his wife openly. Why? How do you think that Japanese women feel about this lack of overt affection?

3. Divorce among the older generation is increasing rapidly in Japan. Most often, wives who have obeyed and looked after their husbands

all their lives suddenly want to get a divorce. Explain this situation.

4. Even today in Japan, most men think that their wives should stay home to raise the children and run the household. What do you think about "men outside and women inside"?

5. As more and more Japanese women decide not to marry and opt to have legitimate careers, how will Japanese society be changed?

6. Although the number of well-educated women is increasing in Japan, the position of women in society is still rather low. For example, there are few women politicians, judges, corporate executives, and so on. Even older working women are sometimes called *onna no ko*, or "girls," and are supposed to do low-level or temporary work. Why is this so?

7. After marriage in Japan, the relationship between a couple often seems directed more toward work and parental responsibilities than to male-female relations. A husband and wife sometimes call each other *otōsan* (father) and *okāsan* (mother), and talk to each other with very few words (e.g., *furo* [bath], *kū* [eat], *neru* [sleep], and so forth). Does this mean that they are relaxed at home and understand each other well, or do they lack affection for each other?

8. In modern Japan, it appears that young women are far more progressive in terms of their expectations of marriage and relationships than young men, who are generally more conservative and traditional. Do you agree? If so, why?

9. In job interviews, it is not uncommon for young Japanese women to be asked if they will quit their position if they get married. Is this kind of question appropriate? Discuss this issue.

Exploring Cross-Cultural Issues

1. Compare the status of women in Japan with the status of women in other countries.

2. Compare the husband's role in Japan with the husband's role in other countries.

3. In Japan, there are many women who stay at home and enjoy running the household and doing important tasks such as volunteer work, belonging to the PTA, or providing child care after school. Is it possible to see the role of housewives in this kind of positive light in Western societies?

4. Many Japanese men have to live apart from their families for long periods of time when they are transferred by their company, a policy that is known as *tanshinfunin* (i.e., a job transfer made without one's family). There are too many husbands living alone in Japan, and this situation also has a damaging effect on family life. Is this because the company and the children's schooling are considered more important than male-female relations? Are there other reasons? How does this compare with the situation in other countries?

5. In Japan, women do almost everything in the house, regardless of whether they are working; for example, making meals, washing dishes, cleaning the house, raising the children, and so forth. In other countries, how are these responsibilities shared?

6. Do you think that attitudes within *danjyo kankei* encourage young Japanese women to marry outside their culture? Discuss this issue.

7. Many Japanese people seem to have an image of relationships in the West that is built purely on what they see in the movies. Do they have a realistic view of love and romance in the West?

8. Many young Western people like to have friends of the opposite sex as well as girlfriends and boyfriends. Is this a common practice in relationships in Japan?

道

The Dō Spirit of Japan

Many Japanese expressions contain the kanji *dō*, and these words reflect a wide range of meanings, from the mundane to the profound. The following are examples of the ways in which *dō* can be used in Japanese:

- *dōkyō*: Taoism (Tao = "the Way")
- *shintō*: "the way of the gods"
- *dōro*: street or road
- *dōjō*: practice room
- *dōtoku*: morals
- *dōraku*: entertainment
- *bushidō*: "the way of the warrior"
- *kadō*: flower arrangement (*ikebana*)
- *shodō*: calligraphy
- *sadō*: tea ceremony
- *kendō*: swordsmanship
- *kyōdō*: archery
- judo: "the soft way"
- aikido: meeting/energy/way

Many of these expressions are used for the traditional Japanese arts, both martial and aesthetic; some express religious, philosophical, or spiritual doctrines, others reflect the common usage of everyday life.

The concept of *dō* is thus deeply rooted in the Japanese way of thinking, both traditional and modern, illustrating many of the most significant cultural values of Japan and providing important insights into the Japanese way of learning.

THE ORIGINS OF THE SPIRIT OF DŌ: TAOISM
The origins of the spirit of *dō* in Japan can be found in the Taoist beliefs of ancient China. Taoism affected Japanese culture mostly as a result of its formative influences on Zen Buddhism, although Taoist divination techniques and other magic-religious practices entered Japan starting in the sixth century along with other borrowings from China. Religious Taoism is still found in modern Japan, and Japanese scholarship on the Taoist tradition is considered one of the foremost in the world.

Taoism is thought to have originated with the ideas of Lao-tzu in the fifth century BC, and the Tao (or *dō* in Japanese) is a key notion in all Chinese thought—literally, it means "way," but also *the* Way to be followed, and by extension, a code of behavior and doctrine, as in *bushidō*, the "way of the warrior." The notion of Tao expresses the essential unity of man and nature, and Taoism has long been concerned with techniques aimed at bringing heaven and earth together, blending the sacred powers of the heavens with ritual practice in the mundane world so that human beings can harmonize their life energies with the Tao, or universal spirit.

It is said that the Tao cannot be grasped, but it can be received. Under a master "teaching without words," the adept goes through a cathartic process of emptying the mind of all passions and distinctions until it becomes a "mirror of heaven and earth reflecting the multiplicity of things." The person then becomes inhabited by the Tao and finally reaches enlightenment in the "eternal now" through an experience outside of time and space.

There was never an attempt to implant Taoism officially in Japan, although a random choice of Taoist beliefs and customs has been adopted and modified to the Japanese way of thinking. Taoist mysticism, however, greatly influenced the Chinese Ch'an (Zen) schools of Buddhism, which were transplanted to Japan in the Kamakura period. In fact, the ultimate synthesis of Taoism and Buddhism was realized in the Ch'an tradition, and in Japan, Zen soon became associated with the most important aspects of medieval Japanese culture.

THE ORIGINS OF THE SPIRIT OF DŌ: ZEN BUDDHISM

After its adoption from China in the sixth century, Buddhism gradually permeated the whole intellectual, artistic, and social life of Japan for well over a thousand years. It helped to transform the country from a primitive tribal region into a highly civilized nation-state, and in so doing, had a deep and lasting effect on both the spiritual and aesthetic values of the Japanese people (Reischauer, 1988). Claiborne notes that "so thoroughly integrated into the Japanese psyche have the assumptions and values of Buddhism become that their influence is apparent in every aspect of the lives of the people of modern Japan" (1993, p. 62).

By far the most influential stream of Buddhist thought on Japanese culture was Zen Buddhism. Zen monks engaged not only in religious activities but also in diplomacy and the creative arts, such as literature, painting, architecture, gardening, Noh theater, tea ceremony, and flower arrangement. Zen, and its community of wandering monks, became associated with the most important facets of medieval Japanese art and literature, infusing them with its spirit, emphasizing the immediate, intuitive experience of truth, and the direct transmission of this truth from teacher to disciple. Because it taught such a direct and unhesitating way of life, Zen also had a strong impact on the military class—bushidō, for example, is a combination of Zen training and Confucian loyalty—and as the samurai were also extensively trained in scholarship and the arts, Zen became one of the most important influences on the cultural and aesthetic expression of the Japanese.

Zen, in its original Chinese form of Ch'an Buddhism, was greatly influenced by Taoist thought, which stressed that the Tao (or later, the Buddha-nature) resides in all things, but that this reality could not be taught because it is beyond duality and conceptualization. In Zen, too, essential truth is incommunicable—enlightenment and salvation are sought in immediate experience and spiritual peace, and the Absolute is found in the phenomenal world. Zen emphasizes that all human beings originally possess the Buddha-nature within themselves and need only the actual experience of it to achieve enlightenment (*satori*). This is a state that is seen as a liberation from man's intellectual nature, from the burden of fixed ideas and feelings about reality: "Zen always aims at grasping the central fact of life, which can never be brought to the dissecting table of the intellect" (Suzuki, 1964, p. 51). Those who are enlightened cannot explain this ultimate truth, which is both radically simple and self-evident but beyond the ordinary duality of subject and object. It cannot be conveyed by books, words, concepts, or teachers but must be realized by immediate and direct personal experience.

Zen was introduced into Japan c. AD 1200 by the Buddhist monk Eisai, who founded the Rinzai sect, known for its strict meditational system and use of *kōans*, or enigmatic, paradoxical, nonlogical questions. Another school of Zen, the Sōtō sect, was founded by Dogen, a disciple of Eisai. Sōtō Zen also made meditation its essential practice, but rejected the *kōans*, emphasizing silent sitting and meditating on whatever illumination or insight is received (*zazen*). Although both schools revere the historical Buddha, training and practice is focused on the person of the master, because it is believed that instruction from a master can awaken in a disciple the Buddha-nature that everyone possesses. Based on *mondōs*, or brief dialogues between master and disciple, Zen's particular method of instruction entails simply pointing to the truth, the "eternal now," without interposing ideas and notions about it. For the Zen master, the best way to express one's deepest experiences is by the use of paradoxes that transcend opposites (e.g., "Where there is nothing, there is all" or "To die the great death is to gain the great life"). These sayings illustrate two irreducible Zen dilemmas—the inexpressibility of truth in words, and that "opposites are relational and so fundamentally harmonious" (Watts, 1957, p. 175).

Zen training stresses both stillness and action, and these are expressed through the disciplines of meditation and daily work. Unlike other forms of Buddhism, all Zen schools are self-sufficient, because it is thought that the Buddha-nature dwells hidden in all of the inconspicuous things of daily life and that the harmony of mind and body is "achievable through the simultaneous stilling of one's mind and purposeful activation of the organs of physical perception"

(Claiborne, 1993, p. 76). In all forms of activity, Zen emphasizes the importance of acting naturally, gracefully, and spontaneously in whatever task one is performing, an attitude that has greatly influenced all forms of cultural expression in Japan. The single-mindedness of Japanese martial and aesthetic arts, for example, illustrates the Zen principles of detachment and equanimity, the expanded consciousness beyond the "me-state" in which each moment flows unimpeded by one's awareness of anything except the alert yet relaxed stance of the swordsman or the ritual movements of making tea (ibid., p. 69).

CHARACTERISTICS OF THE TRADITIONAL JAPANESE ARTS

The characteristics most often associated with the traditional Japanese arts are keishikika (formalization), kanzen shugi (the beauty of complete perfection), seishin shūyō (mental discipline), and tōitsu (integration and rapport with the skill). The steps that are followed are as follows:

1. The establishment and formalization of the pattern or form (kata): every action becomes rule-bound (keishikika)
2. The constant repetition of the pattern or form (hampuku)
3. Mastering the pattern or form, as well as the classification of ability en route to mastery, resulting in licensing and grades (kyū and dan)
4. Perfecting the pattern or form (kanzen shugi): the beauty of perfection
5. Going beyond the pattern or form, becoming one with it (tōitsu)

Common expressions in Japanese reflect these steps: kata ni hairu (follow the form), kata ni jukutatsu suru (perfect the form), and kata kara nukeru (go beyond the form). All practice takes place in an atmosphere of quietude, obedience, and respect, mirroring the absolute obedience and respect of the master-student relationship.

Zen originally resisted any kind of formalization of the aesthetic and martial arts that were disseminated in Zen temples, but as the practices became more widespread, ways were needed to pass on instructions to greater numbers of learners and to later generations.

As a result, it became necessary to train many teachers, or masters, and to be able to do this, the formalization of dō practices began in the mid-Edo period (Sakaiya, 1994, p. 277). Thus, in budō (bushidō), sadō, kadō, shōgi (Japanese chess), reading and writing, abacus, and most other types of learning in Japan, there were forms to follow, and teachers needed only to study these forms to train their students. Many terakoya (temple schools) and dōjō (practice halls) that were built in Edo times were based on this approach to learning. The traditional Japanese arts were very different from one another, but all had similar methods of training, many of which are still practiced today. For example, before any practice begins in a dōjō, disciples sit and face the master, who leads them in a moment of meditative silence (mokusō). Then there are patterns or forms to follow, practice is repetitive, and moves must be repeated thousands of times and perfected before new techniques may be learned. The purpose of such discipline is "not only to learn new skills but also to build good character and a sense of harmony in the disciple" (Niki et al., 1993, p. 56). Teaching is kept simple, inflexible, and strictly controlled, and involves imitating the movements of a master rather than detailed and analytical verbal explanations. Forcing students to follow certain patterns causes them to discard extraneous thoughts so that they can move into mushin ("no-mind"). This mushin attitude leads to an acceptance of the world as it is, which is the core of learning in any kind of dō practice. In mushin, thought and action occur simultaneously, and it is in this moment that the essence of the spirit of dō may be found. After long years of repetitive practice in this state of mushin under the direction of a master, the disciple perfects "the way" and is permitted to go beyond the forms and develop new patterns and approaches.

Two other concepts are important in the practice of the traditional Japanese arts: kanzen shugi, or the pursuit of the beauty of complete perfection, in which the aim is to master all patterns completely, and seishin shūyō, or mental discipline, which is developed by a focus on the training of the disciple's mind as well as the craft itself. Sadō, or the Japanese tea ceremony, provides an example. Originally imported from China in the ninth century, the tea ceremony began to be practiced in Zen monasteries, where it gradually became an art form known as the "way of tea." The essence of this ceremony is the aesthetic of perfection and the discipline underlying all movements in the ritual, from the simple act of fetching water from the spring in a tiny garden to the deliberate preparing and serving of the tea in a small and elegantly simple room. Sen no Rikyu transformed the tea ceremony in the sixteenth century with an aesthetic principle known as *wabi*, or the contrast of refinement, simplicity, and rusticity. He advocated the use of plain, everyday Japanese utensils rather than those imported from China in the tea ceremony. Proportions and sizes were carefully chosen to harmonize perfectly with the small tearooms. Not only the utensils but the styles of the buildings and tea gardens, the order and etiquette of the ceremony were designed to be in accord with an atmosphere in which the goal was to perfect one's existence without self-indulgence. Thus, the ideas of simplicity, perfection, discipline, and harmony with nature, which are central to the Zen way of life, are also reflected in *sadō*.

PROBLEMS WITH THE SPIRIT OF DŌ

The spirit of *dō* continues to pervade Japanese culture, and people in many walks of life can be seen seeking after perfection in certain basic patterns as a means of acquiring spiritual satisfaction in their lives. There are also changes taking place in this way of thinking, however, and people are starting to put more stock in the free creation of ideas rather than in conforming to established patterns, although, generally speaking, standards that have become established are still considered more important than originality in Japan. Even today, one will always be accepted in Japanese society as long as one follows the system and its rules. Nevertheless, a great deal of criticism is being leveled at this way of thinking at present, especially in education, because too many people emphasize outer forms, or rules and standards, at the expense of content and original thinking. The Japanese have an expression for such individuals: *kata ni hamatta hito*, or rigid, inflexible people who are stuck in the form and cannot go beyond it. In other words, simply learning patterns by rote, which has never been advocated in Zen thought, does not foster creativity, growth, and development unless you "go beyond the form." Most individuals today, however, tend to follow the forms blindly and stay at surface levels, which, according to some Japanese business leaders, has become Japan's "Achilles' heel." As Tachi Kiuchi, president of Mitsubishi Electric, notes: "Japanese companies have a lot of problems when there is no blueprint or manual to learn from" (Kotkin, 1997, pp. 7–8). Moreover, Japan is being swamped by a tidal wave of "material culture" at present, some of which comes from abroad but much of which is self-generated. As a result, the spiritual and aesthetic values of Japanese culture, which are reflected in the spirit of dō, are rapidly being lost, and nowadays even the *kata* are disappearing, with nothing being created to replace them.

DISCUSSION ACTIVITIES

Exploring Japanese Culture

1. The notions of simplicity, perfection, discipline, and harmony with nature are central to both Zen Buddhism and the aesthetic and martial arts of Japan, as reflected in the spirit of dō. What forms do these qualities take today in the everyday life of contemporary Japanese people?

2. The British scholar of Japanese history George Sansom states that "the quintessence of Japanese thought is to be found in Zen . . . whose doctrines are by definition incommunicable by the written word and can be made clear only by some inner illumination" (1963, p. v). He also describes "the characteristic attitude of the Japanese towards moral and philosophical problems" as "intuitive and emotional," reflecting a "mistrust of logic and analysis." Reischauer (1988, p. 200) concurs:

> The Japanese have always seemed to lean more toward intuition than reason, to subtlety and sensitivity in expression rather than to clarity of analysis, to pragmatism rather than to theory, and to organizational skills rather than to great intellectual concepts. They have never set much store by clarity of verbal analysis and originality of thought. They put great trust in nonverbal understanding

and look on oral or written skills and on sharp and clever reasoning as essentially shallow and possibly misleading. They value in their literature not clear analysis, but artistic suggestiveness and emotional feeling. The French ideal of simplicity and absolute clarity in writing leaves them unsatisfied. They prefer complexity and indirection as coming closer to the truth.

Do you agree or disagree with these statements? Do you believe, as is taught in Zen, that "essential truth is incommunicable"? Do you also believe that people in Japan prefer intuition and emotion to logic and analysis? Discuss these issues in detail.

3. The Japanese of the premodern period have been described as "a people among whom once flourished a great refinement and virtuosity, coupled with superb accomplishment in the arts and crafts" (Reischauer, 1988, p. 166). Do you think these characteristics still hold true today?

4. It has been claimed that the tea ceremony in modern Japan is full of contradictions:

Advocates argue that in addition to its inherent aesthetic and spiritual satisfactions, the practice of tea can be an antidote to the mindless materialism and alienation from nature rampant in modern life. However, some critics see it as yet another example of how aspects of Japanese tradition have been . . . packaged and sold as up-market pastimes—a cult of poverty and simplicity that only the very rich and sophisticated can afford to indulge in properly. (LaPenta, 1998, p. 13)

Do you think that this is an accurate assessment? What forms does the tea ceremony take in Japan today? What are its advantages and disadvantages in alleviating some of the problems of the modern world?

5. It is said that Japanese education has become too rigid and inflexible, that the country is being swamped by materialism, and that young Japanese are forgetting their traditions and losing the forms

(kata) that have long been the key to learning in Japanese culture. Do you think this means that the original spiritual essence of *dō* has become corrupted or perverted in Japanese life today? Are young people in Japan still being influenced by the spirit of *dō*, or are they rebelling against it? Discuss these issues, identify the causes of these changes, and suggest ways in which these problems can be solved.

Exploring Cross-Cultural Issues

1. The formality exhibited in the tea ceremony is a common part of everyday life in Japan, and the daily behavior of all kinds of people is carried out according to fixed patterns. This is illustrated in the following description by a newcomer to Japan regarding the sevice provided by a waiter in a coffee shop in a smart Tokyo hotel:

> When the waiter brought the coffee I was very impressed by the grace and formality with which he gave it to us. First he rolled up a large trolley with two enormous silver coffee jugs on it. Then he stepped back and bowed low to me. After that he put the cup and saucer very carefully on the table, took the two jugs, stepped back, and with a very delicate and precise movement poured the coffee into the cup from a great height. He bowed low again and then put the cup in front of me, with the handle at a certain angle. Then he bowed again. Every single movement was carried out with perfect precision. Next he did the same thing for my friend, repeating the same movements exactly. When he had finished he bowed low again, and took the trolley away [and] did exactly the same thing at every other table. I felt it was more like watching a ballet dancer or a magician than an ordinary waiter at work. It was then that I thought to myself that not only do they have a tea ceremony in Japan but they have a coffee ceremony too! (Pinnington, 1986, p. 14)

Describe other types of work in Japan in which this kind of ritual behavior can be observed. How do you think people in Japan feel about doing a job in this way? Compare this way of working with that observed in other countries.

2. One of the most difficult features of living in Japan for people from other countries is that life can be very formal. In serving customers at supermarkets, department stores, and fast-food restaurants, Japanese clerks, elevator girls, and waiters and waitresses often seem to behave like robots, repeating exactly the same fixed phrases with wooden expressions or insincere, frozen smiles. This criticism has also been raised increasingly by the Japanese themselves, as recent debates in the mass media attest. How do you feel about this kind of robotized service, and how is it different from the description of the waiter in the previous question?

3. Teachers from abroad often comment that classrooms in Japan are extremely formal and that students seem very passive compared with those in other countries: "[R]ather than questioning and challenging their teacher, they listen silently and politely, taking notes . . . [which] they do their best to memorize . . . and to repeat . . . in their exams" (Pinnington, 1986, p. 24). In the West, few students would tolerate not being "allowed to question, challenge, and criticise the teacher," an approach to education that is designed to encourage originality and a questioning mind (ibid.). In Japanese schools, however, most things are done "according to a fixed pattern or plan; then it becomes much easier to learn how to do things—all one needs to do is to learn the patterns from someone who knows them" (ibid., p. 16). Because there is a tendency to formalize learning, "to make everything into a fixed pattern," students tend to "assume that there is a right way and a wrong way to do everything" (ibid., p. 17), that there can only ever be one right answer to a given question. Discuss the process of learning in Japanese schools from the point of view of this critique and in light of the most important qualities inherent in the spirit of dō. Compare this way of learning with that in other countries.

4. In recent times, the Japanese Ministry of Education has begun to stress the need to foster a sense of individuality, originality, and creativity in young people to meet the demands of an increasingly internationalized world and its global economy. Are Japanese ways of learning, as exemplified by the spirit of dō, compatible with these

goals? How can traditional educational practices be adapted to modern goals in order to provide students with the skills they need to achieve success in a rapidly changing world?

5. In the Japanese martial arts, teaching is kept simple, inflexible, and strictly controlled and involves imitating a master rather than providing detailed and analytical verbal explanations:

> The traditional skills in particular are learned not so much by analysis and verbal explanation as by personal transmission from master to disciple through example and imitation. The teacher-disciple bond is a very important one . . . , but of equal importance is the fact that learning is more an intuitive than a rational process. The individual is supposed to learn to merge with the skill until his mastery of it has become effortless. He does not establish intellectual control over it so much as spiritual oneness with it. (Reischauer, 1988, p. 166)

What are the advantages and disadvantages of this way of learning? As the martial arts, as well as some of the aesthetic arts, are being practiced throughout the world today, how well do students from other countries adapt to this approach to learning? Should this approach be maintained in the future?

頑張り

Gambari:
JAPANESE PATIENCE AND DETERMINATION

After the Meiji Restoration in 1868, Japan rapidly modernized itself, and after World War II, the Japanese reconstructed their ruined country to become a powerful economic nation. Even today, the Japanese are often said to be diligent, sometimes to the point of being workaholic, characteristics that are best exemplified in the expression *gambari*, the noun form of the verb *gambaru*.

Gambari reflects an essential component of the modern Japanese character as it has developed since historical times. In daily life, the Japanese use the term *gambari* very often, and this overuse seems to point to certain Japanese characteristics, some of which have negative effects. In addition, the concept of *gambari* is now changing, and the term is losing much of its traditional strength, especially among the young. This chapter will examine the Japanese way of thinking and national characteristics that are based on *gambari*, the reasons why the Japanese are so diligent, and recent changing attitudes regarding this expression.

THE BACKGROUND OF GAMBARI
Gambaru is a frequently used word in Japan, with the meaning of doing one's best and hanging on. For example, students *gambaru* (study hard) in order to pass entrance examinations. Athletes also *gambaru* (practice hard) to win games or medals. Moreover, company workers *gambaru* (work hard) to raise their company's sales. Also,

when the Japanese make up their minds to begin something, they tend to think "*gambaru*" in the initial stages of the project. When a young woman from a small town, on leaving for a new job in the city, promises her friends, parents, and teachers that she will *gambaru*, the implication is that she will not disappoint them. The word is also used by friends as a kind of greeting, often in the imperative form *gambare* or *gambatte*. In this situation the meaning is rather ambiguous. The Japanese use these expressions at least once a day with good-bye and also write them at the end of letters. With this usage, they encourage one another with the implication "Please keep up your hard work until your goals are achieved." The term connotes high achievement, motivation, and orientation to group harmony (Wagatsuma, 1983, p. 5). The word is also used among group members to encourage one another in cooperative activities. For example, during track and field days at school, children can be heard shouting "*gambare*" or "*gambatte*" to encourage their friends running in races. In 1998, the Japanese team participated in World Cup soccer matches, which were held in France, and the Japanese spectators cheered on their team under the slogan of "*Gambare, Nippon!*" During the championship, this slogan was used on TV programs and commercials every day. In addition, several years ago, after the big earthquake in Kobe, the slogan "*Gambarō Kobe*" (*gambarō* is the volitional form of *gambaru*) encouraged the people of Kobe to reconstruct their city and rebuild their lives. Most Japanese use this word frequently, and it is found in newspapers everywhere. *Gambari* has a lot of different grammatical forms depending on the situation, and it is used with a wide range of meanings, from the superficial to the profound.

THE MEANING OF GAMBARI

The meaning of *gambari* has changed greatly over time. Historically, it meant to assert or insist on oneself. According to the *Sanshodo Japanese Dictionary* (Kenbō, 1989, p. 218), *gambaru* is defined in the following ways: (1) to work hard and patiently, (2) to insist on having one's way, and (3) to occupy one place and never leave. In recent times, the first definition has generally been taken to be the principal meaning of *gambaru*. Although the origin of *gambari* is still being debated, two theories have developed. One argues that *gambari* comes from *gam-baru*, "to strain one's eyes, open one's eyes wide, keep an eye on something"; the other contends that *gambaru* is derived from *ga-o-haru*, "to be self-willed," an expression that originally had the negative connotation of asserting oneself against group decisions and norms (Wagatsuma, op. cit.). Since the 1930s, however, *gambaru* has become a positive expression, commonly used to exhort enthusiasm and hard work from others, usually toward group objectives.

According to Amanuma (1987, pp. 51–53), *gambaru* does not have any exact equivalent in non-Japanese languages. In other words, there are no words to express the many nuances of *gambaru* exactly. Amanuma (ibid., p. 51) further states that in a discussion on the subject, scholars, journalists, and graduate students from other countries who know the Japanese and Japanese culture well provided expressions that are close to *gambaru* in their mother tongues, such as a*ushalten*, *beharren*, and *beharrung* in German; *tiens bon* in French; a*guante* in Spanish; and *chā yo* in Chinese. The Americans said that *persist in* or *insist on* were close to a part of the meaning of *gambaru*, but did not completely cover its meanings and did not express its many complex nuances. Amanuma (ibid., pp. 49–50) further states that even the Chinese and Koreans have no equivalent word for *gambaru*, although the word is indicated by a Chinese character that was introduced to Japan from China through Korea. Both Chinese and Korean have the characters that make up *gambaru*, but they do not have expressions that possess the same nuances. This suggests that *gambaru* is an expression that is unique to Japan and expresses certain qualities of the Japanese character.

DIFFERENT WAYS OF THINKING

Different ways of thinking about work, which are related to the concept of *gambaru*, can be seen in the following two proverbs that are famous in America and Japan: "The monk who does not work should not eat" (Japan); "All work and no play makes Jack a dull boy" (America). According to Amanuma (ibid., pp. 131–133), on the whole, to have free time, to do nothing, or not to work gives the Japanese an unpleasant feeling. They tend to think that having free time is wasteful, even shameful, and feel uneasy. As Matsumoto (1994, p. 142) also notes, in Japan working hard and straining when serious are considered to be good; it is neglectful not to try hard, and the ideal is to make an effort seriously, regardless of the results. Consequently, the Japanese try to *gambaru*, and the following two examples illustrate this characteristic. The five-day school week occurred only once a month in Japan until recently, when it was changed to twice a month, putting teachers and parents in a quandary because they did not know what children should do on these additional holidays, and conferences had to be held throughout Japan to develop useful activities for the children. Moreover, as Tsuzino (1993, pp. 159–160) points out, many Japanese men do not know what to do with themselves after they retire, since their purpose in living had always been to work. As a result, the number of elderly people who commit suicide has been increasing, and the problem is now under consideration at the National Diet.

On the other hand, Matsumoto (1994, p. 147) contends that it is crucial for Americans to have free time. In America, people consider ability more important than effort, and the person who can relax and even make a joke in a serious situation is well considered. Many Americans also look forward to retirement (Tsuzino, 1993, p. 158), so stationery stores offer a variety of cards containing expressions such as "happy retirement." Not only in America, but also in France, retirement is well received. François Mitterand, the former president of France, lowered the retirement age from sixty-five to sixty, and this reform was considered one of the most important during his ten years of political power. Matsuoka (1989, p. 135) explains these contrasting attitudes as follows:

> There are some expressions that are often used in America but seldom in Japan, such as "take it easy." Americans say to a person who is busy working, "take it easy" or "don't work too hard"; in contrast, the Japanese say "*gambatte*" (or work hard) as a sign of encouragement. Americans, of course, also think that it necessary to be diligent, but as the proverb says, "all work and no play makes Jack a dull boy," suggesting that working too hard is not good for you.

Even in Korea, which has a culture closer to that of Japan, people have almost the same expression as in America, meaning "take it easy." Lee (1982, pp. 175–176) explains that Korean people often use expressions, the equivalent of "relax" or "soften your body," to someone who is beginning a new project, but hardly ever say "*gambare*" or "work hard." Fluidity and relaxation enable the Korean people to display their potential power (ibid.); in contrast, the Japanese tend to show their ability through strain and effort.

THE DEEPER CAUSES OF GAMBARI

Three reasons can be suggested as to the origins of the *gambari* spirit: rice growing, the geographical conditions imposed on Japan, and equal opportunities in raising one's social class. According to Amanuma (1987, p. 140), rice growing left a permanent imprint on the Japanese character. It has always been the most traditional and intensive form of agriculture in Japan, ever since it was introduced from China in the Jōmon period. This farming style typically needs periods of particularly intensive labor in certain seasons, especially during rice planting and harvest time. Thus, such ancient agricultural customs as working for short periods with all one's strength are said to have helped build the Japanese *gambari* spirit (ibid., p. 143).

In addition, according to Miyazaki (1969, pp. 269–272), the difficult climate and geography of Japan cause characteristic Japanese diligence:

> The climate of Japan has high temperatures and humidity. In addition, geographical conditions are really difficult, for there are a lot of disasters such as floods, typhoons, and earthquakes. Steep mountain ranges penetrate the center of the narrow mainland. The land on both sides is sandwiched between the Japan Sea and the Pacific Ocean, and the seasides have a lot of steep slopes and few plains. Thus, most of the rivers flow rapidly and often overflow because of abundant rainfall. These challenging geographical conditions never give to Japanese a sense of calm and leisure; on the contrary, they make people restless and diligent.

Finally, equal opportunities for raising one's social status provide the Japanese with incentives to *gambaru*. After the Meiji Restoration, a lot of reforms in the class structure and educational system took place. The class system of the Edo period, known as *shi-nō-kō-shō* (samurai, farmers, artisans, merchants), was abolished early in the Meiji, and with the Gakusei Proclamation ("encouragement of studying"), which was promulgated in 1872, about 80 percent of children had the opportunity to go to school. Moreover, in 1947, compulsory education edicts were issued, and virtually all the children received education, giving everybody a chance to go on to a higher level of schooling and attain a better position in society. Amanuma (1987, p. 154) maintains that this chain of reforms enabled individual Japanese to raise their positions in society through their own efforts; that is, through *gambari*:

> Many Japanese who achieved great works came from normal, even poor families. For example, Prime Ministers like Hirofumi Ito and the heads of Honda and Mitsubishi came from the lower classes. So, many students in the Meiji were engaged in *gambaru*, dreaming of becoming a Prime Minister or a doctor in the future. (Kato, 1978, pp. 183–188)

Even today, schoolchildren study very hard in order to pass the entrance exams of higher-level universities because after entering such schools, they will be respected and sure to get a job at a good company. This achievement-based society and the equal opportunities provided by the educational system created a competitive world and reinforced the *gambari* spirit of the Japanese people.

PROBLEMS WITH GAMBARI

For the Japanese, doing one's best and enduring difficult situations patiently in order to achieve one's goals—to *gambaru*—is considered to be one of the highest virtues. However, sometimes this kind of *gambari* causes negative results. A typical example is *karōshi*, or death from overwork, which has been increasing year by year. Businessmen are often forced to work late at night without breaks or holidays, and as a result, some of them die of heart attacks or strokes. The number of claims filed by families for compensation as a result of death from overwork is about 500 a year on average in Japan, but the real figure is considered to be several thousand, because companies often try to cover up to avoid admitting responsibility (Kawato, 1991, p. 8). According to Kawato (ibid., p. 10) . . . ,

> . . . the reasons for overwork are thought to be the worker's diligent character and the nature of the enterprise. First, the worker's assiduity—*gambari*—does not let him take a rest. Second, the atmosphere in the company forces workers to *gambaru*. The worker who takes rests and does not put in extra hours will be estimated poorly. This low estimation will keep him from promotion. In addition, some employees who reject overtime work are laid off.

The fanaticism of the Japanese can also be seen in *gambari*. According to Miyazaki (1969, p. 274), people in Japan are easily influenced by others because of the importance of groupism, adding that some of these people are apt to become fanatical and lose control in certain situations. This fanaticism is reflected in *gambari*, which is often displayed blindly and instantaneously, such as was typically exhibited during World War II:

> During the war, military authorities took full advantage of this Japanese characteristic. The Japanese were forced to *gambaru* and many went into the war blindly. Some people, however, opposed this policy, and they were eliminated. Such blind and fanatical *gambari* made the war terrible. (Amanuma, 1987, pp. 67–68)

CHANGING ATTITUDES TOWARD GAMBARI
The concept of *gambari* is now changing, and the expression is losing much of its traditional strength, especially among the young. According to many recent criticisms, Japanese children today are lacking in patience because they have often been spoiled and given all that they want by their parents and grandparents. According to the *Asahi Daily*, the recent problem of *gakkyū hōkai* (collapse of the classroom) is becoming increasingly serious:

> Teachers cannot control students anymore. The children, especial-
> ly in elementary school, often disobey, use violent language to their
> teachers, chatter loudly, and walk around during class. Decent
> classes cannot be carried out in such situations. In a certain city in
> Tokyo, two-thirds of elementary schools are said to be suffering
> from this problem. ("Collapse of the classroom," 1998, p. 17)

To make matters worse, this impatience among children causes
another problem, absenteeism (tōkō kyohi). According to surveys done
by the Ministry of Education, the number of permanent absentees in
Japanese primary and junior high schools is reaching 150,000 at present and is continuing to increase yearly. Some people say that such
students do not have the ability to *gambaru*, and if people around
them encourage them by saying "*gambare*," they tend to withdraw
and go into their shells (Amanuma, 1987, p. 84). However, Velisarios
argues that changing social conditions are more relevant to understanding these phenomena:

> In classrooms across Japan, the future is something most kids
> would rather ignore. Thanks to a rigorous system of advancement
> based on tests, about 80 percent of all Japanese students are losers
> by the age of 15. They are the ones who do not pass exams to enter
> top-tier high schools. By extension, this kills their dreams of
> attending a good university and building a distinguished, white-
> collar career. In the past, working-class kids could look forward to
> decent jobs on graduation. Today, with Japan's economy shrinking
> and unemployment among young adults approaching 10 percent,
> many average students see little point to staying in class.
> (Velisarios, 1998, p. 16)

In Japan today, people are beginning to think that it is important
to have more leisure time. Recently, a five-day workweek has
become more common, and a standard five-day school week will
also be instituted from 2002, with the Ministry of Education deciding to reduce the content of study in elementary and junior high
schools ("Education in relaxation," 1998, p. 1). Thus, people continue to work hard, but they also think that it is good to have free time,

resulting in significant changes taking place in the Japanese attitude toward *gambari*.

DISCUSSION ACTIVITIES

Exploring Japanese Culture

1. There is no doubt that *gambari* is one of the main factors that has contributed to the rapid economic development of Japan, especially in rebuilding the country after World War II. But do young Japanese people work hard for the country today with a feeling of *gambari*?

2. *Gambari* still seems to be important in Japanese companies, but what is its place in the educational sector, especially among university students and professors? Are they really practicing *gambari* these days to raise educational standards and institute much-needed reforms? Discuss this issue.

3. Recently, a court decision was handed down making a company, which had pressured an employee to work so hard that he committed suicide due to overwork and fatigue, responsible for these actions, and it had to pay a large amount of money in compensation to the bereaved family. Do you think that Japanese companies will change their working environments in the future to discourage employees from working too hard, a policy that sometimes results in death in Japan?

4. Recently, students who *gambaru* have not been treated with respect, and if they study hard, they are called *gari-ben*, which has a negative meaning in Japanese. Does this indicate that the spirit of *gambari* is changing in Japan?

5. In Japan, is the present dilution of the *gambare* spirit viewed as a good thing, as it may reduce death from overwork (*karōshi*), or as a bad thing, as seen in the phenomenon of classroom collapse (*gakkyū hōkai*) in Japanese schools?

6. As the structure of Japanese society continues to change, with more women in the workplace, will *gambari* weaken because it is difficult for family life if everyone works excessive hours, or will it strengthen in response to increased competition for top jobs?

7. Is *gambari* essentially the product of Japan's homogenous, group-oriented society? In other words, because of the homogeneity of Japanese society, people can only be differentiated on the basis of effort, rather than ability. Discuss this issue.

8. In Japan, there are many men who die from overwork or who are transferred to locations where they must live apart from their families for long periods of time. Why do they accept these kinds of situations?

9. What are the roots of the Japanese sense of *gambari*?

10. Do you think that the concept of *gambari* places unrealistic pressures on Japanese people to constantly do their best? Discuss this with reference to the increasing numbers of suicides in Japan resulting from a sense of failure or inadequacy.

11. **Case Study**: Katsunori Nakamura worked very hard for his company all his life. He left his home early every morning and did not return home until late most nights. He also worked on weekends or was so tired that he slept all day. He did not see much of his children as they were growing up, because he led a life that was dedicated to his company and quite separate from that of his wife. When he retired, however, he did not know what to do with his free time and constantly irritated his wife, who was not used to him staying home all day. Instead of his retirement being a reward for a lifetime of hard work, it became a nightmare and eventually led to divorce and the breakup of his family.

Question: How common is this kind of situation in Japan? How is it related to *gambari*? What can be done to remedy the problems caused by *gambari*?

Exploring Cross-Cultural Issues

1. In the last Olympic Games, Japanese athletes did reasonably well in spite of the tremendous pressure the nation put on them, which has often caused them to underperform in the past. Do you think that today's young people are becoming indifferent to such *gambare* pressure? What are the incentives for the athletes of other countries to do well in the Olympic Games? How are these incentives different from those in Japan?

2. Is *gambari* seen as an asset by international companies that hire Japanese workers (e.g., dedication), or as a liability (e.g., exhaustion)?

3. In Japan, because of the social pressures associated with *gambari*, once someone becomes employed by a company full-time, it is very difficult for that person to take a long holiday with pay. What is the situation in other countries?

4. Compare the use of free time in Japan with that in other countries.

5. Do you think the concept of *gambari* is admired and respected by people in other nations?

6. *Gambari* (studying and working hard) is sometimes said to be one of the most important virtues of the Japanese. What are similar virtues in other countries of the world?

Giri:
JAPANESE SOCIAL OBLIGATIONS

A key concept in understanding Japanese culture and certain characteristic patterns of behavior among the Japanese arising from traditional attitudes toward moral duty and social obligation is known as *giri*. The origins of giri are obscure, and precise definitions are difficult to formulate:

> Giri . . . does not have an equivalent concept in English [although in Japan it is considered] the most valued standard in human relationships: master-subordinate, parent-child, husband-wife, brothers and sisters, friends, and sometimes even enemies and business connections. If pressed to define it, *giri* involves caring for others from whom one has received a debt of gratitude and a determination to realize their happiness, sometimes even by self-sacrificing. (Gillespie & Sugiura, 1996, p. 150)

Giri can perhaps best be understood as a constellation of related meanings, the most important of which are as follows: (1) moral principles or duty, (2) rules one has to obey in social relationships, and (3) behavior one is obliged to follow or that must be done against one's will (Matsumura, 1988, p. 653).

The notion of *giri* is thought to have come into being in feudal times, but its exact origins remain in dispute. There are a number of conflicting theories as to how the concept initially arose (Ohshima et al., 1971, p. 932), but it is generally considered a kind of "social norm formed in feudal society by the samurai class" (ibid.). The notion itself has existed since ancient times, however, especially if *giri* is regarded as "a custom of returning something for goodwill" (Minamoto, 1969, p. 41). In the prefeudal age, the term *giri* was not used, but the foundations of the concept were laid in the agricultural communities of the Yayoi period as a result of the historical importance of rice growing in Japanese life. Minamoto (ibid., p. 42) provides the following explanation:

> The basis for life among the ancient Japanese was the rice crop. Working conditions were not severe but it was not as easy as just seeding and awaiting a rich harvest. Rice growing required intense cooperative work for short periods, such as during planting and harvesting. This kind of labor encouraged the formation of hamlets where people had to cooperate with one another. People who received goodwill from others in the rice field in the form of help in transplanting and reaping rice wanted to return that goodwill, and those who provided the assistance must have expected something in return. In addition, people who lived in the same hamlet must have carefully noted whether they actually received something back. This custom of returning something for goodwill is called *giri* today.

Although the notion of *giri* goes back to the origins of Japanese life, the word itself did not come into existence until medieval times. According to Minamoto (ibid., p. 48), "the term *giri* used by Nichiren at the beginning of the Kamakura period is the oldest attested case on record," but at that time, it meant the equivalent of "meaning" or "reason," not the habit of returning something for goodwill. Later, this custom was called *go-on to hōkō* in samurai society and referred to a rule between masters and subordinates in which "a social and psychological obligation [is] taken on with favors received from others" (Gillespie & Sugiura, 1996, p. 149). In reality, *go-on* meant that "lords granted land to followers," and *hōkō* that "the subordinates, feeling *on* toward their superiors, were inclined to pay them respect and render them loyalty" (ibid.). In the Muromachi period, a book of manners was written that formalized this way of thinking, advising that "if you receive a present from someone, you should return something which is of equal value" (Minamoto, 1969, p. 43). In the Edo period, the term *giri* came into common usage, meaning "a rule one has to obey in human relations and social relationships" (ibid.). At this time, the dominant form of learning under Tokugawa rule was called shushigaku, the teachings or doctrines of Chu Hsi (Shuki, in Japanese), or neo-Confucianism. With the neo-Confucian values of the age, *shushigaku giri* came to mean a rule one has to obey in human relations, and this concept eventually developed into the present-day belief in *giri* as a social obligation or moral duty or debt.

Giri initially arose as an unarticulated custom of returning something for goodwill in the tightly knit agricultural communities of prefeudal Japan and evolved through successive periods of Japanese history into its forms of *go-on to hōkō* in the feudal age and *shushigaku giri* during Tokugawa times. Today, the concept continues to play an important role in contemporary Japanese society in the custom of giving presents in the summer and at year's end, called *chūgen* and *seibo*, respectively. In addition, presents on Valentine's Day are often named *giri choko* (*giri*-chocolates), and New Year's cards, called *nengajō*, are likely to be written with *giri* (*giri de kaku*).

Chūgen and *seibo* are the most common examples of the custom of gift giving in Japan. Yamane (1997, p. 1216) explains the history of *chūgen* as follows:

> Chūgen originated with Taoist rituals in China in the form of *jōgen*, *chūgen*, and *kagen*, which were celebrated on January 15, July 15, and October 15, respectively. In Japan, the Tokugawa shogunate adopted the celebration of *chūgen* during the Edo period, and in the Meiji era, people entertained their relatives at dinner and exchanged gifts at the Buddhist Bon festival of July 15th, the same date as *chūgen*. By the end of the Meiji period, people were giving presents in July in order to celebrate *chūgen* and Bon together as a result of an advertising campaign by Mitsukoshi department store, suggesting that presenting gifts signified gratitude for kindness. After this campaign, it became common practice to exchange gifts in July, and people began to call the gifts *ochūgen*, adding the prefix o- to express politeness.

Chinese religious ritual was thus transformed into a custom of gift exchange in Japan, and this habit "remains strongly entrenched to pre-serve the harmony of human relationships" (Gillespie & Sugiura, 1996, p. 156). Compared with the mid-year *ochūgen* gift, *oseibo*, the other major gift exchange of the year, is sent in the middle of December, since the term *seibo* itself originally meant "the end of the year." Both these gifts require giving a present in return, called *okaeshi*: In Japan, "a person receiving gifts without doing *okaeshi* and sending gifts [in return] is regarded as being ignorant of social obligation" (ibid.).

Compared with *ochūgen* and *oseibo*, giving Valentine's gifts is a much newer custom in Japan, but it is also strongly connected with feelings of *giri*, or social duty. In many Western countries, people generally give cards or presents to their spouses, boyfriends or girl-friends, and family members on Valentine's Day; however, in Japan only females give chocolates to their boyfriends or husbands. This custom started with a confectionery company that ran an advertis-ing campaign after World War II promoting Valentine's Day as the only day of the year in which women could say "I love you" to their sweethearts through the gift of chocolates. People sent two kinds of chocolate gifts, called *giri choko* and *honmei choko*. On Valentine's Day, women give *giri choko* to men they may not have any particular liking for as a means of preserving the harmony of human relationships; on the other hand, they give *honmei choko* to men they really care for. In addition, on White Day (March 14), an occasion that is found only in Japan, men have the opportunity to do *okaeshi* by returning these chocolate gifts.

Nengajō and *shochūmimai* are the most popular kinds of greeting card in Japan, and they also reflect the continuing importance of *giri* in Japanese life. The former are New Year's cards, which are often designed with "a picture of an animal appropriately corresponding with that year's sexagenary cycle and sent . . . to arrive on New Year's Day" (ibid., p. 158). The latter means "a postcard asking after one's health in the summer" and is generally sent to greet someone between July 15 and August 8. If it is sent after that, it is called "a postcard asking after one's health in the lingering summer [*zan-shomimai*]" (ibid.). These cards are of two types, business *nengajō* and *shochūmimai*, and those sent privately by individuals. The former are written and sent with *giri* (*giri de kaku*) and most of them are printed and do not contain any handwriting; the latter are written by hand and are sent from the heart.

In conclusion, the concept of *giri* emerged in rice-farming communities in ancient times and was transformed as it absorbed samurai and neo-Confucian influences in the Kamakura and Edo periods. Many *giri* customs that came into being in the past continue to be important in Japanese life, though it may be difficult for those from other cultures to understand why the Japanese expend so much energy giving gifts and sending greeting cards, even when they may not really want to. According to a recent TV program, however, the cost of *ochūgen* and *oseibo* gifts is almost equivalent to the cost of justice in the USA, meaning that the cost of keeping harmony in human relations and that of mediating legal disputes is almost the same. Whether keeping harmony, even though it entails people giving gifts "against their will" is a better idea depends on one's point of view, but it is certainly true that because harmony is so important in Japan, *giri* customs will likely continue to play an important role in Japanese society for some time to come.

DISCUSSION ACTIVITIES

Exploring Japanese Culture

1. In some families, the expense of sending *giri*-related gifts can become a real financial burden, accounting for a substantial portion of the household budget. In your opinion, should such families continue this tradition in spite of the hardships involved? Why would it be difficult to stop?

2. What other occasions and events in Japan are important in terms of social obligations and moral duty?

3. In Japan, if you receive a present from a colleague but do not send one in return, you will be regarded as being ignorant of social obligations. Why do you think this is? How do you feel about this custom?

4. Do you think it is better for a person to act and behave from a sense of social obligation, or on the basis of individual motivation? Give examples of each. Discuss the positive and negative sides of both points of view.

5. Do you think that there is a difference between the generations in how *giri* is viewed today among the Japanese?

6. **Case Study**: Yumi and Mariko are now attending a university in Tokyo. During the summer holidays when they went back to Osaka, they visited the high school they had attended. On this visit, Yumi took cookies as a gift to her former teachers, but Mariko did not bring anything. One of the teachers jokingly said, "Yumi, you have grown up. I did not expect this."
Question: Do you think that Mariko should also have brought some gifts as an expression of Japanese social etiquette? Why, or why not?

Exploring Cross-Cultural Issues

1. People customarily send presents to one another in Japan in mid-August and at the end of each year. When are gifts normally exchanged in other nations? What are the reasons for doing so? What are equivalent concepts of *giri* in other countries?

2. It is not uncommon for people from other countries living in Japan to neglect their *giri*-related obligations. What do you think about this kind of omission?

3. In Japan, even if you do not like alcohol, you may often feel obliged to go out drinking with your friends or colleagues. Why do you think this is? How do you feel about this custom? How does this compare with similar customs in other countries?

4. Sometimes receiving gifts of a *giri* nature makes non-Japanese feel uncomfortable or uneasy. Why do you think this is? Discuss how to deal with such a situation.

5. In the West, people often prefer receiving gifts that have been made by someone with their own hands, rather than something that has been bought in a store, because it reflects a genuine feeling of friendship. Discuss these differences in relation to the concept of *giri* and the nature of gift giving in Japan.

腹芸

Haragei:
AN IMPLICIT WAY OF
COMMUNICATING IN JAPAN

Haragei is a well-known concept in Japanese culture, but it is generally unfamiliar to non-Japanese and is often misunderstood by them. *Hara* literally means "stomach" or "belly," and *gei* is "art." A Japanese dictionary (cited in Matsumoto, 1988, p. 20) describes *haragei* as follows: (1) the verbal or physical action one employs to influence others by the potency of rich experience and boldness, and (2) the act of dealing with people or situations through ritual formalities and accumulated experience. In other words, *haragei* is a way of exchanging feelings and thoughts in an implicit way among the Japanese.

Haragei is seen as both positive and negative in Japan. On the one hand, one can "read other people's minds" by using *haragei*, or guess what others are really thinking, allowing it to be used as a kind of social lubricating oil to avoid arguments. On the other hand, there is a negative side to this concept in which people hide their real thoughts and feelings, and it is often said that *haragei* is used in business and politics as a deceitful means of communication in which people hide their real motives in order to gain power and advantage.

There are a number of important concepts that are related to *haragei*. The notion of *amae*, for example, is contained within *haragei*, described by Matsumoto (1988, p. 17) as follows:

> *Amae* is a psychological dependence on the goodwill of others, sometimes understood as mutual help or sympathy. The kind of

symbiotic relationship that exists between parent and child for example, which does not seem to require any rational or logical justification or explanation, is often used as an example that imparts the feeling or atmosphere of this term.

On the basis of *amae*, a speaker in Japan allows him- or herself to become dependent on the sensitivity of the listener to "read between the lines" in order to catch the real meaning of the message in conversation. For example, if someone wants to go out to eat sushi and asks a friend to go along, and this friend actually does not want to go but thinks it rude to refuse the invitation, he or she may say yes hesitatingly, expecting that this reticence will be noticed. Thus, people depend on the sensitivity of others to understand the real messages in social interactions. The Japanese also count on the passing of time to help resolve problems in communication. In other words, they think that things can be worked out with time, and often wait for a consensus simply to be arrived at among participants without open discussion. In these ways, *haragei* is based on *amae*, being dependent on the goodwill and sensitivity of others, or on time, to solve problems.

Honne and *tatemae* are another related set of concepts that are linked to *haragei*. "These terms are often used as contrasting yet complementary parts of a whole, *honne* being related to the private, true self, and *tatemae* typifying the public persona and behavior. *Honne* then has to do with real intentions and sincere feelings, while *tatemae* conveys the face the world sees" (Matsumoto, 1988, p. 18). People in Japan are implicitly taught from a young age how to use *honne* and *tatemae* properly, and these concepts are important in maintaining face and not hurting the feelings of others; therefore, what a speaker says is not always what he or she really means. Conversation is not comfortable in Japan unless *honne* and *tatemae* are properly employed, and those who cannot use these concepts effectively are not considered to be good communicators, because they may hurt others or make a conversation unpleasant by revealing *honne* at the wrong moment. People have to be careful about situations in which *honne* should be hidden and *tatemae* used, and in order to do this, they need experience and sensitivity. Hence, it can be said that a person who can use *honne* and *tatemae* properly is good at *haragei*, resulting in *tatemae* being offered, *honne* hidden, and a comfortable and pleasant conversation being conducted smoothly and comfortably.

Ishin denshin is another Japanese concept that is similar to *haragei*, and can be defined as an "intuitive understanding, without the use of words or signs, a peculiarly Japanese form of telepathic communication, as a result of some intimate relationship or bond" (Matsumoto, 1988, p. 18). *Haragei* and *ishin denshin* are therefore both methods of exchanging thoughts and feelings in an implicit way. However, they differ in that *ishin denshin* happens unintentionally, while *haragei* is created by a person's will. Under the influence of *ishin denshin*, both a speaker and a listener can understand what the other is thinking and wants to say because they have similar experiences and backgrounds. In contrast, when *haragei* is used, people deliberately try to either transmit or catch hidden messages in conversation. *Ishin denshin* takes no effort, but *haragei* is a conscious attempt to communicate underlying meanings.

Although the Japanese accept *haragei* easily, most non-Japanese people have a hard time coming to terms with it. For Westerners, in particular, *haragei* is difficult to understand. One of the reasons for this is that Japan is a high-context culture, while many Western societies are low-context:

> In high-context cultures most of the information lies either in the setting or people who are part of the interaction. Very little information is actually contained in a verbal message. In low-context cultures, however, the verbal message contains most of the information and very little is embedded in the context or the participants. (Samovar & Porter, 1995, p. 102)

In a high-context culture, like that of Japan, people tend not to ask many questions and value silence. They are patient with regard to vagueness. On the contrary, in low-context cultures, such as those of the West, people often ask questions to try to make everything clear, because they are less tolerant about ambiguous situations. Due to this difference, *haragei* can be difficult to understand and accept, since it is very much part of high-context Japanese culture, and people need to function as part of this culture in order to acquire this ability to read between the lines.

There are many instances in which *haragei* is used in daily Japanese life; for example, long silences are readily accepted in conversation in Japan, a situation that often makes Westerners uncomfortable. The reason for this acceptance is that the Japanese believe that they can understand one another without words, and they do not like to argue openly. Silence, as a response, can be translated in many ways. It could be "yes," "no," or "I do not know," depending on the context. The Japanese evaluate silence using their experience and by assessing the atmosphere of the moment. Thus, as people understand and use *haragei*, silence can be just one more method of communication.

Another example of *haragei* can be seen in numerous Japanese expressions. When people give others a present, for example, they say something like "This is a trifling gift. . . ." The present may not actually be insignificant, but the giver shows modesty by using this type of expression. The receiver does not actually think that he or she is getting a trifling gift, but feels the modesty on behalf of the giver. *Haragei* is working here, because the receiver understands the feelings of the giver without direct expression. The Japanese use many similar expressions to that in this example that do not express their real thoughts and feelings, but they can "read other people's minds" because they are good at *haragei*.

DISCUSSION ACTIVITIES

Exploring Japanese Culture

1. In the West, the seat of the emotions is said to be the heart, whereas in Japan, it is the stomach, or *hara*. For example, to become angry is *hara ga tatsu* (literally, "guts stand up"), a scheming man is *hara ni ichimotsu aru otoko* (literally, "a man with an ulterior motive in his stomach"), and a person's trusted friends are called *fukushin*

(literally, "center of the stomach"). List other expressions in Japanese that contain *hara*, give their literal translations, and provide equivalent expressions in English.

2. Why did the actor Tora-san always wear a woolen *haramaki* in all his movies? What are the functions of *haramaki*?

3. Discuss the notion of *haragei* from the perspective of the Japanese saying "Words are the root of all evil."

4. Do you think the stereotype that the Japanese prefer intuition and feelings to cold logic is valid?

5. Are young people in Japan moving away from modes of behavior reflected by *haragei*?

6. Describe the positive and negative aspects of *haragei* in Japan.

7. Discuss the ways in which *haragei* is used in daily life in Japan. Is the term *haragei* still in current usage? If not, does this mean that the Japanese are losing *haragei*?

Exploring Cross-Cultural Issues

1. Westerners often feel the need to verbalize their thoughts and emotions, while nonverbal communication is more common among the Japanese. Discuss these differences.

2. Discuss the notion of *haragei* in relation to Hall's model of high- and low-context cultures.

3. The Japanese are often criticized for relying too much on implicit ways of communication (i.e., *haragei*) even in international relations. From the viewpoint of cultural relativism, however, this criticism may not be valid because the communication style of one culture is

no better or worse than that of any other. Therefore, the Japanese should not be ashamed of this communication style, nor feel that they have to change it when talking to people from other cultures. Do you agree or disagree? What is your viewpoint on this issue?

4. *Haragei* and *ishin denshin* are not unique to Japanese culture, but are seen in many societies in the world. Think about a conversation between married couples. They usually leave much unsaid (or implicit) between them and rely less on verbal communication with each other than with other people. This is *haragei*, or *ishin denshin*, is it not?

5. *Haragei*, as a means of hiding real thoughts and feelings, is not a uniquely Japanese concept. For example, it has been pointed out that *haragei* is used in business and politics as a deceitful means of communication in which people hide their real motives in order to gain power and advantage. However, politicians and businesspeople do this all the time in many cultures throughout the world. If this is the case, what makes *haragei* distinctly Japanese?

隔たると馴染む

Hedataru to Najimu:
JAPANESE PERSONAL SPACE

Personal space in Japanese human relationships can be symbolized by two words that describe both physical and psychological distance between individuals: *hedataru* and *najimu*. *Hedataru* means "to separate one thing from another, to set them apart," and it is also used in human relationships with such nuances as "to estrange, alienate, come between, or cause a rupture between friends." A relationship between two persons without *hedatari* means they are close. On the other hand, *najimu* means "to become attached to, become familiar with, or used to." For instance, if one says that students "*najimu*" their teacher, it means that they become attached to and have close feelings for the teacher. Relationships are established through *hedataru* and then deepened by *najimu*, and in this process, three stages are considered important: maintaining *hedatari* (the noun form of the verb *hedataru*), moving through *hedatari*, and deepening friendship by *najimu*. Underlying these movements are the Japanese values of restraint and self-control. In Japan, relationships are not built by insisting strongly on one's own point of view but require time, a reserved attitude, and patience. As a consequence, in Japanese society it is important to understand and use personal distance properly so as to build better human relationships.

In the following examples, relationships built on *hedatari* (maintaining distance) are described from both historical and modern perspectives in Japanese life:

- In any number of popular samurai dramas (*jidai geki*) that play nightly on television in Japan, a loyal retainer will often be seen sitting with his lord, but at a distance. There are two reasons for this: to show respect toward the lord and for the lord's own security through maintaining a distance well beyond sword length.

- In ancient times, retainers were taught the following saying: "*Sanjyaku sagatte shi no kage wo fumazu*" (Keep about ninety centimeters from one's master in order not to step on his shadow). Ninety centimeters and the shadow are the keys to this saying, which means that followers should respect their master and not forget propriety. According to Hall (1970, pp. 169–170), 90 centimeters is the limit for physically controlling others, or the distance from which one can maintain personal negotiations. Therefore, *sanjyaku* is the most appropriate distance for master-subordinate relationships. Similarly, to step on one's shadow indicates an infringement of one's personal space. For example, Japanese children often enjoy playing a game called *kage-fumi* (i.e., stepping on one another's shadows), illustrating in a symbolic way, this infringement of personal space.

- There was also an important convention in Japan that only disappeared recently whereby women were supposed to show their obedience to their husbands by walking a certain distance behind them. This practice may seem archaic to many Japanese today, but Americans who visited Japan right after the war were known to have commented on this custom.

- Students sitting in class keep a fixed distance from their teacher in Japan because they feel a strong psychological separation due to differing levels in social status.

- Yang Kim, a Korean scholar, compares Japanese greetings with those of Korea (1981, p. 74): "The Japanese have an ability to get on well together by keeping distance. In greetings, they say that they understand one another, even when bowing at a distance of one meter. Koreans, on the other hand, immediately shake hands because they do not feel familiarity unless they touch each other."

In fact, bowing at a distance of one meter is still a common form of greeting in Japan and creates a sense of familiarity for people by letting others know that one will not violate their privacy. This formal maintenance of distance is an important element in the communicative style of the Japanese.

The second stage, following the establishment of *hedatari*, is to move through it, and this is an important intermediate stage in going from *hedataru* to *najimu*. In terms of both ancient and modern Japan, there are basically three ways to move through *hedatari*. The first can be illustrated by returning to the above-mentioned samurai drama. When the lord is sure that he can trust his retainer, he says, "*Mosotto chikōyore*" (Come closer), reflecting the fact that the amount of distance between the lord and his retainer defines the nature of their relationship. Secondly, to invite someone to one's house in an effective way of moving through *hedatari*. Here the terms *uchi* (inside) and *soto* (outside) are important. *Uchi* is a space that indicates one's own world; *soto* has nothing to do with oneself. Therefore, a person who is invited to one's house has permission to enter one's personal space. A third and even more efficient way of moving through *hedatari* is to give presents. People in Japan believe that giving gifts shortens the distance between them, and they will give a gift saying, "*Ochikazuki no shirushini*" (As a token of getting acquainted). In short, *hedatari* is removed by giving the signal that others can approach or by showing an intention of becoming closer through offering a gift.

A relationship in which *hedatari* does not exist is called *najimu*, and such friendship can be deepened in two ways: staying together and becoming closer physically. Simply "staying together" is a concept that originated long ago, probably due to Japan's high population density, and creates a positive feeling because people know that they are not isolated. In Japan, even when individuals are in close proximity for long periods of time, people take care to protect their mutual privacy in this "cluster space." For example, "the Japanese family builds mutual trust by simply staying together rather than having conversations. Each person has his or her own privacy even though they are in the same room. They should not know what the others

are thinking even though they know what the others are doing"
(Hamil; cited in Condon, 1980, p. 369).

The physical senses also play an important role in the development of *najimu*, such as the kind of unity people feel sitting together
during the winter under a *kotatsu*, warming their legs (Hall, 1970,
p. 208). Hot springs have a similar function. Shedding one's clothes
prior to bathing with others in hot water requires the removal of one's
hedatari. Many elderly people go to hot springs not only for their physical health but also for a kind of psychological pleasure; it is a good
place for escaping from solitude and mixing with others as part of a
larger community in a warm atmosphere. In brief, spending time
together and feeling a sense of unity greatly contributes to promoting
human relationships in Japan through the development of *najimu*.

DISCUSSION ACTIVITIES

Exploring Japanese Culture

1. In Japan, drinking alcohol with others is thought to help get rid of
hedatari. What happens in this kind of situation?

2. When Japanese students want to make new friends in class, do
they make immediate advances or do they try to get closer to their
classmates little by little? How does this relate to the concepts of
hedataru and *najimu*?

3. Japanese people maintain relationships with their friends or colleagues for a long time, once *hedatari* has been eliminated. In fact,
many university students consider their best friends to be those that
they made in elementary school. What do you think about this?

4. As Japanese people start to get closer (*najimi-dasu*) to other people,
there are certain aspects of their interpersonal relationships that
change. What do you think they are?

5. In Japan, people reduce *hedatari* in *shūgakuryokō* (school excursions), at summer camps for clubs at university, and during *shain-ryokō* (company excursions). How is it that these occasions help remove interpersonal barriers (*hedatari*)?

Exploring Cross-Cultural Issues

1. In Japan, drunkenness is generally tolerated and is seen as a means of relaxing formal barriers that exist between people. In other societies, what happens when people get drunk at a party? Is it considered acceptable behavior? Are there differences between men and women in this regard?

2. In Japan, people consciously maintain distance (*hedatari*) from others and are cautious about becoming closer. Is this the same in the West? If not, why do these differences exist?

3. In other countries of the world, what strategies are used to reduce *hedatari*? Is it difficult to establish close relationships with others? How is this done?

4. When Japanese students go overseas to study, it is sometimes difficult for them to make friends with others. In fact, they sometimes view interpersonal relationships in Western countries as being rather superficial. Discuss this from the point of view of *hedataru* and *najimu*.

5. In Japan, many company employees feel obligated to go drinking after work with their colleagues almost every night as a means of reducing *hedatari*. People from other countries, however, often object to this practice and consider it an excessive obligation. Discuss this issue.

本音と建て前

Honne to Tatemae:
PRIVATE VS. PUBLIC STANCE IN JAPAN

The Japanese are coming into contact with people from other countries more and more these days and have to communicate with those who have cultural values that are markedly different from their own. In intercultural communication, the Japanese need to be familiar with the customs and attitudes of non-Japanese people, but they need to understand their own cultural values first and foremost, many of which operate at unconscious levels. One such set of concepts, which is fundamental to Japanese life, is *honne* and *tatemae*.

In Japan, the terms *honne* and *tatemae* are often used in conversation, but the concepts themselves are seldom fully understood. They can be defined as follows:

> These two words are often considered a dichotomy contrasting genuinely-held personal feelings and opinions from those that are socially controlled. *Honne* is one's deep motive or intention, while *tatemae* refers to motives or intentions that are socially-tuned, those that are shaped, encouraged, or suppressed by majority norms. (Honna & Hoffer, 1986, p. 94)

For many people, one's words and actual intentions do not always agree; in these situations in Japan, one's superficial words are called *tatemae*, while one's actual intentions are called *honne*. Although this distinction is not only found in Japan but is also prevalent in most other countries, the Japanese people make use of it extensively, taking *honne* and *tatemae* for granted in daily life because it is considered a virtue not to directly express one's real feelings and intentions. In intercultural affairs, however, this dichotomy can be a serious obstacle to communication because it creates confusion and misunderstandings.

In trying to understand *honne* and *tatemae* and how these contrasting concepts function in Japan, it is important to examine certain Japanese cultural characteristics, such as a dislike of direct expression and the importance of harmony and ceremony in Japanese life. The Japanese do not like to express themselves in a straightforward manner for fear that it might hurt others' feelings, so they are usually careful about what they say and often use *tatemae* in order to get along well with others. For example, when a person is visiting someone's house in Japan and it becomes time for supper, people will often say, "Won't you dine with us?" But this is not really an invitation; rather it is a subtle hint that it is time to go home. To those from other countries, this may seem confusing, but for the Japanese, it is a natural way to interact socially. So the correct response to "Won't you dine with us?" is "Thank you very much, but I am not hungry." This type of behavior is formulaic in Japanese life.

In Japan, there has also been, since ancient times, a great respect for harmony, called the spirit of *wa*. *Tatemae* is used to maintain this harmony and create a comfortable atmosphere. Thus, *honne* is used in one's personal space, but *tatemae* is used in more public forums such as business meetings, which are often rather ceremonial occasions, because *tatemae* agrees with commonly accepted societal standards. *Tatemae* is, therefore, like lubricating oil used to maintain harmony among people.

In Japan people can understand the differences between *honne* and *tatemae* because they have grown up with these dual concepts. People switch easily and skillfully between the two and are rarely aware that they can cause misunderstandings and confusion among people who are not accustomed to this way of interacting.

DISCUSSION ACTIVITIES

Exploring Japanese Culture

1. Describe some specific situations where *tatemae* is used in Japan, and explain why it is used in such cases.

2. In what situations in Japan is it acceptable to express one's *honne*? Why?

3. What are the advantages and disadvantages of using *honne* and *tatemae* in Japanese daily life?

4. Experts have pointed out that *honne* and *tatemae* form a unity in Japanese culture and that this dual structure plays a major role in maintaining psychic balance in Japan. Discuss how this might be so.

5. **Case Study**: Hiroshi is happy today at school because he has a new hairstyle he really likes. However, most of his classmates think his hair looks strange and make fun of him behind his back. Hiroshi comes up to Chie and asks, "How do you like my new hairstyle? Isn't it great?"
Question: Should Chie use *tatemae* and say, "I love it," or express her *honne* and say, "Actually, I think it strange." Why?

Exploring Cross-Cultural Issues

1. Generally speaking, Westerners feel that acting and speaking in accordance with one's innermost beliefs and convictions (*honne*) is a matter of personal integrity, whereas the Japanese tend to view the discrepancy between *honne* and *tatemae* as simply reflecting the way society works. In other words, individuals may hold their own personal views, but in the interests of group harmony, they should not express these views if they conflict with the opinions of others, and this is not seen as hypocrisy. In English, however, the idea of

hypocrisy is reflected in the expression "to be two-faced," which means to be sneaky or underhanded, and this has strongly negative connotations for most people in the West. How can these opposing points of view be reconciled?

2. Many non-Japanese have difficulty in adapting to Japan because the extensive use of *tatemae* makes it very difficult to find out what people really think. What can be done to help people from other countries adapt to Japanese society, from the perspective of *honne* and *tatemae*?

3. What are the advantages and disadvantages of exchanging opinions frankly and openly, as is generally the case in the West? Compare this approach to communication with the use of *honne* and *tatemae* in Japan.

4. When you are invited to go out drinking in the West, you can generally decline the invitation by explaining the real reason why you cannot attend (i.e., *honne*). But in Japan you usually have to tell a white lie as a form of politeness (i.e., *tatemae*). Why do such differences exist? Which approach is preferable? Why?

5. Is the use of concepts such as *honne* and *tatemae* more prevalent in Asian societies than in other parts of the world? If so, why? Compare the use of *honne* and *tatemae* in Japan with other nations in Asia.

The Japanese Ie System

Traditionally, the Japanese word *ie* has a variety of meanings: (1) a building that is used as a residence, (2) a family or household, (3) a group that consists of a family according to the old Japanese civil code, and (4) the family line that descends from one's ancestors and that will continue into the future. Hall and Beardsley (1965, p. 78) define *ie* as "a *patrilineage*, a network of households related through their respective heads, comprising main houses, branch houses, and the branches of branch houses traced down through generations." Though there are differences in the *ie* system among the various classes, and in the different regions or times, it has had a great influence on Japanese society and family life. It is said that the *ie* system disappeared after World War II because of the revision of the civil code, the increase in the number of nuclear families and the penetration of individualism in Japanese society, but it still remains strong among families in many parts of Japan as a long-standing custom or as a moral value with diminished but still significant social force.

THE FOUNDATIONS OF IE

The foundations of *ie* are thought to be based on the worship of ancestors. For most Japanese, except for the emperor and the aristocrats, the origins and names of one's ancestors were not usually known; nevertheless, all households had ancestors that they worshiped. These ancestors were perceived as a unity of souls of all the ancestors who had been part of the family line since the *ie* was founded (Takeda, 1981, p. 7). In addition, one's ancestors were believed to become *hotoke* (or Buddhas) after death, because in Buddhism, *hotoke* represents the supreme existence of a being that has reached the stage of spiritual enlightenment. Hence, the importance of ancestors in the *ie* system became absolute under the influence of Shinto and Buddhism.

In this system, people worshiped their ancestors because it was believed that they provided the foundations of the existence of *ie* and looked after the family and guaranteed its welfare, and if people did not honor their ancestors, it was thought that they would be cursed. Even today, Japanese houses have *butsudan* (family altars) for this kind of worship, and household members also respect their obligations to preserve the graves of their ancestors and to visit them periodically, such as in the Bon festival during the summer.

THE SYSTEM OF *IE*

Patriarchism is one of the main characteristics of *ie*. Under this system, the head of household, who was generally the senior male, decided on the actions of its members and had the absolute power of control over the family; for example, his consent was needed when family members married, and they had to obey his orders respectfully. People were trained to accept the system and were taught their position in the hierarchy of *ie* beginning in childhood. The head of the household was given privileged treatment and was normally served by other family members; for example, his meals had to be richer, he had to be welcomed when he came home, and his seat at the table had to be higher than that of other family members. In addition, the head of the household had complete control over the family property due to the right of single-heir inheritance, so he had significant economic power. However, as Kawashima (2000, p. 156) points out, these elements of patriarchism in the *ie* system were much stronger in the families of samurai than in those of farmers or artisans.

The succession of lineage was extremely important in the *ie* system. The notion that all family members belonged to the same lineage made them unite, cooperate, and support the *ie*. In particular, the *ie* of the samurai respected the blood relations of the head male's family, so high-class samurai had an official wife and many concubines in order to maintain the family lineage, and it was one of the main duties of wives to give birth to sons. For samurai, it was important how many famous ancestors they had in order to be promoted or dominate people in their fiefdoms.

The position of women was low in the *ie* system, since it was believed that they were inferior to men. Even if they married well, women were in a weak position because they could be sent away for any reason. They had to adjust themselves to the customs of their husbands' *ie* and work hard to satisfy their husbands' parents. Most important, they had the duty of bearing children, and if wives could not fulfill these obligations, they were often forced to divorce.

The succession to the future was also a characteristic of *ie*, and it was a duty of all family members to ensure the family line. Under this system, the family needed an heir to continue the *ie*, and one way of doing this was through adoption. Therefore, although lineage was important, the continuation of the family line was more important, and people had to maintain the family line even if the lineage ended. According to Kawashima (ibid., p. 37), the Japanese adoption system had two main goals: (1) to obtain an heir to succeed to the ownership of the land and property, and (2) to ensure the performance of proper rites for the sake of the family's ancestors. In this way, although adoption is normally a system of raising children who have lost their parents in most countries, it tends to have different characteristics in Japan. In the Edo era, for example, adoption was an effective means of obtaining an heir. At this time, people needed to limit the number of children because having too many offspring could also endanger the *ie*, as they would consume the resources of the household without contributing to its present and future existence. In those days, it was very difficult for people to plan how many children to have, and the death rates were high. Therefore, adoption was an important means of continuing the *ie*:

> Adoption . . . has long been recognized in Japan as an alternative way to obtain a successor, and thus a family could limit the

number of children without endangering the line. If there were no sons, a son-in-law could be adopted to marry the daughter; if none of the children survived to adulthood, a son or daughter could be adopted to carry on the line. (Hanley, 1997, pp. 138–139)

IE AND THE CLASS SYSTEM

Because the ie of samurai were strongly affected by Confucian thought, they had a fixed formal order that was influenced by a long history and tradition. Because patriarchism was strictly observed, the head of the household had great power and was obeyed voluntarily by other family members, who regarded his power as sacred and absolute (Kawashima, 2000, p. 15). It was also a characteristic of the samurai's ie to place great importance on maintaining the family line and the fame of the ie. Samurai always knew the origins and the names of their ancestors and took great pride in their family history, which was passed on to their offspring. It was believed that ending the family line was shameful for the family and a crime against one's ancestors—a samurai thus had to maintain the fame and dignity of his ie, which was descended from a long line of history. Expressions such as "for the ie" and "the shame till the last generation of the ie" showed this way of thinking among samurai.

The families of farmers, on the other hand, composed a unit of production, so all family members had a specific role, which was determined according to ability. Because it was economically difficult for farmers to live with a family member who did not work, everyone had to labor in cooperation in order to live, and family members had a position in the ie according to their role in this work. Therefore, some of the power in the family was not concentrated in the head of the household but existed separately in other family roles. In addition, although the power of the head of the household was the strongest, it was not generally despotic, because of the relaxed, familiar, and friendly atmosphere that existed in the families of farmers (ibid., p. 13). As Hanley (p. 138) states "the ie or family system that developed during the Tokugawa period was essentially a corporate unit for farmers; it was an economic unit, a unit of production, that existed as an entity apart from its membership."

IE IN FAMILY LAW

The family law section of the civil code, which was enacted in 1898 and which was valid until after World War II, had many characteristics of the *ie* system. The law regarded the *ie* system of ex-samurai as its model, because they became bureaucrats during the Meiji era. Therefore, although family law included elements that were not familiar to ordinary people, it had a great deal of influence on the Japanese *ie* in terms of its morals or ideology (Kawashima, 2000, p. 174).

First, according to this law, the head of the household was given legal power over other family members. He could decide on marriages, divorces, and adoptions into his family and could grant places of residence to his family members (ibid., p. 172). He could also exclude members from the family register if they went against his orders (ibid.). In this way, the power of the head of the household was prescribed in detail in family law.

Second, the law allowed parents to control the lives of their children because they needed the consent of their parents when they married, divorced, took part in adoption, or engaged in business or other occupations. Parents could choose where their children lived, and managed their children's property and that of their children's wives.

After World War II, when the old civil code was revised, the *ie* system was abolished, and as a consequence, the power of the head of the household lost its legal foundation. The present civil code prescribes that a husband and wife have equal rights, and both marriage and divorce need only the consent of both partners, with inheritances also divided equally. The family register was also revised to reflect these changes in individual rights. These revisions in the civil code have promoted the disappearance of the *ie* system in modern Japan.

CONCLUSION

In past the fifty years, the Japanese people have worked hard to create great economic growth, and in the process, the structure of industry has changed and many young people have moved from farm villages to the cities. As a result, the form of the family has changed and the number of nuclear familes has increased dramatically. The *ie* system still affects Japanese society, but its influence has been gradually lost in the younger generation. According to a public opinion poll (Prime Minister's Office, 1997), while 44 percent of people think that a married couple should have the same family name, 33 percent think that it is permissible to have different names. This shows that the belief that a wife goes into her husband's *ie* has been changing. Though marriage used to be between members of different *ie*, it is now seen in relation to the couple themselves. According to a public opinion poll (Prime Minister's Office, 2000), 51 percent of people think that men are treated better than women in the family, while 40 percent think that men and women are treated equally. This shows that patriarchism has gradually lost its power in the family. On the other hand, women still tend to avoid eldest sons when they marry, because the eldest son has to take care of his parents in the *ie* system. This shows that traditional ways of thinking are still strong in Japan; however, it is also certain that the foundations of the Japanese family have been shifting from the *ie* to the individual in modern times.

DISCUSSION ACTIVITIES

Exploring Japanese Culture

1. Some people have observed that as the *ie* system has collapsed in Japan, ties among family members have also become weak. What are your views on this observation?

2. Evaluate the validity of the opinion poll mentioned in the reading in which, even today, many people think that men are treated better than women in Japanese families. In what ways can this preferential treatment be seen in Japanese family life today?

3. Women in favor of the *fūfu-bessei* system, in which a married couple have different family names, claim that if they change their names at marriage, they will feel that they are being forced to

become a member of their spouse's family. Discuss this issue from the viewpoint of the *ie* system.

4. What are the advantages and disadvantages of the traditional Japanese *ie* system in the modern world?

5. Do you think that the weakened *ie* system is related to the recent increase in juvenile crime and classroom collapse at schools in Japan? In the past, children were often frightened of their fathers, who were sometimes severe in teaching them the difference between right and wrong. Along with the disappearance of the *ie* system, however, the authority of the father has also become weak, and it is said that this is one reason why children (especially boys) are not properly disciplined at home. Many people believe that boys need strong fathers in their families. If this is true, should we bring back certain aspects of the traditional *ie* system?

6. **Case Study**: Jun and Rie had promised to marry each other. Rie's family was well-to-do, and her father was the head of his own company. Since he did not have any sons, he expected Rie's future husband to become a member of his family and to eventually take over his company. However, Jun has other ideas about his career and is not happy about being adopted into his wife's family.
Question: Will they have to give up their marriage plans? How should Jun and Rie deal with this situation?

Exploring Cross-Cultural Issues

1. In Japan, it is important for one's spouse to be accepted by one's parents in order to maintain harmonious relationships within the family. Is parental approval necessary in other cultures? Discuss the pros and cons of such approval.

2. The eldest son is still expected to look after his parents in Japan, and this can be a great burden, especially in finding a wife. Compare

this role with the responsibilities of the eldest son in other cultures.

3. In Japan, it is still generally expected that a woman will take her husband's family name upon marriage. Compare this custom with that in other countries.

4. In many societies, contemporary social problems are being blamed on the breakdown of the family. Discuss this issue in relation to the importance of patriarchal authority in traditional family life.

5. Discuss the evolution of the family in various cultures of the world.

いいとこ取り

Iitoko-Dori:
ADOPTING ELEMENTS OF FOREIGN CULTURE

It is hard to imagine from the present state of industrialized Japan that Japanese society was controlled by samurai until about 150 years ago. It is said that the Meiji Restoration marked the start of modern Japan, but the connection between traditional Japanese culture and modern Japan is often a topic of intense debate. Many economists insist that developing nations can modernize by adopting technology from more advanced nations, much as Japan did in the past. However, it seems that mostly Asian countries (e.g., Korea, Taiwan, Hong Kong, and Singapore) have successfully modernized in this way, while many other countries have had considerably less success. Moreover, although countries like India and China had contact with Western civilization earlier and on a larger scale, Japan has achieved greater economic success, at least until recently. Therefore, the question needs to be asked why Japan was able to modernize more rapidly than most other countries. In response, it has been claimed that Japan had a good foundation for accepting Western technology because in the Tokugawa period both cottage industries and financial systems were quite well developed. In a sense, this is correct, but it is not enough to provide a complete explanation for Japan's rapid industrial development. In fact, there is another important reason: Japan has a long-established tradition of adopting elements of "foreign culture" and adapting them to Japanese use. The origins of this tradition can be found in Japanese religious beliefs, and in particular can be traced to the ability to bring into harmony two of Japan's earliest religions: Shinto and Buddhism.

THE PROCESS OF IITOKO-DORI

In Shinto, the concept of deity is found in aspects of nature, such as mountains, waterfalls, stones, and natural phenomena like thunder and typhoons, as well as in the worship of ancestors. This belief system is also found elsewhere in the world, where it is generally known as a form of animism. Of importance for Japan is the fact that Shinto contains no absolute sense of values, such as "the words and rules of God" in the Judeo-Christian tradition, and this has enabled it to coexist with other value systems that have entered Japan from the outside. In the sixth century, the Japanese encountered a more sophisticated religion, Buddhism. With time, however, people noticed that if they believed in Buddhism, the emperor system was denied, for it was through original Shinto myths that the emperor's family maintained its position of the highest status in Japan. This presented a serious problem not only for the royal family but also for the Japanese political system at the time. In the seventh century, Prince Shotoku, who was a nephew of Emperor Suiko, occupied the regency and discovered a way of permitting Buddhism and the emperor system to coexist, along with another belief system adopted from China, Confucianism. He stated that "Shinto is the trunk, Buddhism is the branches, and Confucianism is the leaves" (Sakaiya, 1991, p. 140). By following this approach, the Japanese were able to accept these new religions and philosophies, and the cultural values and advanced techniques that came with them, in such a way that they were able to reconcile their theoretical contradictions. In short, with the acceptance of the coexistence of Shinto and Buddhism, serious religious oppositions disappeared, a feature that was to have a great effect on the Japanese mentality in the coming centuries. Not only were the Japanese able to accept culture from other countries without any religious prejudices, but they also developed the habit of adopting only the most useful borrowings from other nations. This is the process of *iitoko-dori*.

THE CONSEQUENCES OF IITOKO-DORI

People in Japan often find themselves in the unusual position of believing in two or more religions simultaneously. Iitoko-dori, then, refers specifically to this process of accepting convenient parts of different, and sometimes contradictory, religious value systems, and this practice has long been widespread in Japan. In modern times, Sakaiya (ibid., p. 144) notes that the number of Japanese people who do not admit to following some form of iitoko-dori is only about 0.5 percent of the population.

Iitoko-dori can be seen most easily in the way technology has been adopted into Japan, a process that has had both positive and negative aspects. A good example is the Tomioka factory. In 1868, Japan adopted a new spinning technique from France, and in 1873, a model factory in Tomioka was built. Everything was imported, not only the design and the machines but also the bricks for the buildings, desks, chairs, and so on. In addition, French technicians were employed, and the Japanese workers copied them. As time went on, they tried to "catch up and surpass" the creators of their adopted models, and forty years later, in 1910, the Japanese had improved on the French model and were able to export silk overseas.

The Tomioka factory is also a representative example of the transformation of the Japanese economy from agriculture to industry. Through the process of iitoko-dori, the most effective elements of Western technology were brought into Japan and made its own, and this contributed enormously to the modernization of the country. On the other hand, people seem to have thought little of the consequences of these technological adaptations, and as a result, destruction of the environment in Japan has increased so alarmingly that many critics are predicting serious impending catastrophes. So, although the Japanese were eager to adopt aspects of Western culture, especially in terms of science and business, they did not recognize that using technology blindly, a kind of unbalanced iitoko-dori, would also result in many of the environmental and social problems that the country is experiencing today.

The consequences of iitoko-dori can also be illustrated in the ethical values of Japan, which arise from the country's coexisting religious systems. On the one hand, there is very little religious conflict in

Japan, and even if the Japanese are exposed to new concepts, they do not reject them outright, because they have the ability of *iitoko-dori*, in which the best parts are adopted and used. Thus, when a new religion like Christianity was introduced into Japan, people were open to its precepts, rather than simply denying it out of hand.

In any discussion of ethical values, Christians and Muslims would probably refer to some concept of God in their arguments, and an absolute sense of values is usually the basis for their decisions. But in Japan, the sense of ethical values is relative, and it varies with changes in people's opinions and the context in which decisions have to be made. As a result of a long history of *iitoko-dori*, the Japanese are able to change their sense of values in a short time and with little difficulty, and in this way, it is possible for society to be productively efficient.

However, the process of *iitoko-dori*, which has given rise to relative rather than absolute ethical value systems, has also resulted in serious negative consequences. For example, many Japanese students will not oppose bullies and stop them from hurting weaker students. Even if they know that bullying is wrong, they are not willing to stand up for their beliefs, because they are afraid of speaking out individually without a group consensus to back them. In other words, in Japan, even if people know that something is wrong, it is sometimes difficult for them to defend their principles, because rather than being absolute, these principles are relative and are easily modified, depending on the situation and the demands of the larger group to which people belong.

CONCLUSION

To summarize, *iitoko-dori* appeared as a phenomenon very early in Japanese history, and it has greatly affected the Japanese way of thinking. This process means taking in the most convenient parts of other systems, and it is now part of the cultural identity of the Japanese. It has been one of the most important factors in the rise of Japanese economic power, because new technologies and their underlying value systems are implemented easily. Unfortunately, however, the impact on the environment and on people's lives is often not properly considered. In terms of ethical values as well, the results of *iitoko-dori* are evident in contemporary Japan: there are few major religious conflicts among the Japanese; on the other hand, it is often difficult for people to stand up against injustice. Hence, we can see that, at least in part, *iitoko-dori* is responsible for the flexibility of the Japanese people, but perhaps what is needed is a closer examination of the consequences of "adopting the best parts of foreign culture" on the lives of people, both within Japan and in the world itself.

DISCUSSION ACTIVITIES

Exploring Japanese Culture

1. In Japan, wedding ceremonies generally follow a Shinto style, while funerals are Buddhist. How does this reflect *iitoko-dori*?

2. Many Japanese celebrate Christmas, although most people are not Christian. What is your opinion of this kind of practice?

3. Today, Japanese pop music is greatly influenced by American music, and many English words are borrowed and used in Japanese songs. How do you think this is related to *iitoko-dori*?

4. Japanese homes often have both traditional Japanese rooms with *tatami* (*washitsu*) and Western-style rooms with carpeting (*yōshitsu*). Is this an example of *iitoko-dori*? List other similar examples.

5. Most modern Japanese have a secular attitude toward life even though they observe religious rituals at certain times of the year, such as at *O-bon* and on New Year's Day. In light of this secular orientation, what is the future of *iitoko-dori* in Japan?

Exploring Cross-Cultural Issues

1. Give some examples of *iitoko-dori* in other countries. Are they similar to, or different from, the Japanese model?

2. In Japan, Shinto, Buddhism, and Confucianism have existed together in harmony for many centuries, whereas in many other countries, religious beliefs are the source of much bloodshed. Discuss this issue with reference to *iitoko-dori*.

3. Why do Japanese people feel that it is not contradictory to go to a Shinto shrine and then to a Buddhist temple on the same day? Can the same person pray to different gods or follow two or more religions in other countries of the world? Discuss this issue from the perspective of *iitoko-dori*.

4. According to Pinnington (1986, p. 22), "when we look at traditional Japanese arts—the No or Kabuki, kendo, waka, haiku, ikebana [sic]— all of them seem highly formal. All of them have their formal patterns which are learnt by watching and imitating the teacher and they all have their own complicated rules and conventions which must be learnt." Moreover, in many modern sports and hobbies in Japan, such as cycling and oil painting, "we find exactly the same attitude." This way of learning, "which emphasises rules, techniques and imitation," has long been "highly suitable for the quick assimilation and adaptation" of foreign elements from China and the West into Japanese culture (ibid., p. 23). As Reischauer (1988, p. 202) points out, in Japan, "scholarly activity has been largely devoted to absorbing large chunks of information from abroad and synthesizing it with what was already known." Industry has stressed the adaptation of already known technologies rather than the creation of new ones, although it must also be noted that many of these adaptations have been so imaginative that they should rightly be judged as creative (ibid.). Nevertheless, this approach to learning has led to widespread criticism of the Japanese as simply copying others, as well as to much stereotyping of the Japanese as being "intellectually not very creative" (ibid., p. 200):

> Japanese industrial triumphs have been based largely on efficient borrowing or ingenious adaptations of foreign technology rather than on independent scientific discoveries. Political thought, philosophy, and scholarship in the social sciences are to a large extent

the reworking or synthesis of ideas derived from abroad, rather than original creative work. . . . [Japan's past] is studded with prominent religious leaders, great poets and writers, outstanding organizers, and even distinguished synthesizers of thought, but not with great creative intellectual figures. (Ibid.)

Do you think such criticisms are valid and fair? How would you respond to them? Discuss these criticisms in relation to *iitoko-dori*.

5. Compare scholarly activity and the acquisition of knowledge in Japan with that in other countries of the world.

Ikuji:
CHILDREARING PRACTICES IN JAPAN

Childrearing practices reflect the cultures from which they arise in a kind of reciprocal relationship. Modern Japanese culture is derived from traditional agricultural society, in which people had to cooperate with one another in order to get by, so the main principles of childrearing focused on creating individuals who knew how to get along with others in the group. Cooperation was emphasized rather than individualism, and because people were protected within the group, self-assertion was considered a form of disobedience. This contrasts markedly with Western culture, especially American culture, which is based on a kind of pioneer spirit in which self-reliance and original thinking are required, resulting in childrearing practices that place much more emphasis on independence, creativity, and self-assertion.

According to Azuma (1994), Japanese parents tend to be of the "seep-down type" as far as discipline in the infant years is concerned. There are two main features of "seep-down" parenting. One is the tendency in Japan for behavior to be "learned by imitation of parents rather than by linguistic analytical explanation," as is the case in America (ibid., p. 123). In this regard, research reported by Azuma (ibid.) on the childrearing practices of Japanese and American mothers provides insights into differences between the two cultures. Mothers from both countries were asked to learn the task of classifying wooden blocks according to certain shapes and features, and then to teach their four-year-olds how to accomplish this task. Most of the Japanese mothers demonstrated how to build with the blocks first and then had their child imitate them. If the child got it wrong, they repeated the demonstration and let the child try again. In this way, they continued until the child succeeded. On the other hand, American mothers tended to explain systematically the reasons why each block should be placed in a certain position, confirming the child's understanding one block at a time before allowing the child to attempt the task alone. In other words, Japanese mothers let their expectations "seep down" to their children, while the American mothers were more verbally analytical.

The second feature of "seep-down" parenting is reflected in the fact that "Japanese mothers are not nearly as concerned with parental authority as American mothers" (ibid., p. 125). Azuma found that when children were disobedient, Japanese mothers tended to give in to them, whereas American mothers were more confrontational and placed more emphasis on parental authority. Japanese mothers seemed to change their policies depending on the circumstances in order to avoid creating any mental distance from their children. They also tried to maintain affection suitable for "seep-down" upbringing rather than being consistent in their discipline, which was quite dissimilar to the behavior of the American mothers.

Contrary to popular belief in the West, Japanese parents rarely discipline their children in an authoritative manner or punish them harshly in order to force them to be obedient (ibid.). In addition, according to Lewis (1984, p. 85), nursery school teachers in Japan use many strategies to help develop children's ability for self-control, such as "minimizing the impression of teacher control" or "delegating control to children." Children belong to small fixed-membership groups and do various cooperative tasks with the other members of the group and this group cooperation functions as a sort of control mechanism. In other words, it minimizes the pressure to force obedience while providing opportunities to develop a "good-child identity," which maximizes the internalization of children's norms of behavior. The same childrearing practices can be seen with Japanese mothers, who "apparently do not make explicit demands on their children and do not enforce rules when children resist. Yet, diverse accounts suggest that Japanese children strongly internalize parental, group, and institutional values" (Vogel; cited in Lewis, 1984, p. 82). American mothers, on the other hand, tend to regard it as a collapse of parental authority necessary for effective childrearing to concede to their children's egoism or to show weakness. Azuma (1994), for example, refers to the kind of instructions American and Japanese parents give when their children are disobedient. Taking as an example the case of children not eating their vegetables, American mothers tend to demand compliance even if the children do not understand the reason. If their children do not obey, "American mothers tend to state 'Eat it,' or 'You must eat it,' and then 'EAT IT, please.' In this way, they use an increasingly compulsory tone, whereas Japanese mothers tend to concede gradually, as in 'Eat it,' and 'Eat a little,' and then 'You can eat it tomorrow, can't you'" (ibid., p. 77). Although it would seem that Japanese mothers spoil their children when compared with American mothers, this strategy derives from the practice of developing a "good-child identity." With time, it is difficult for children to go against their mothers' expectations, and they even consider it shameful to do so.

It is also interesting to note the differences in this concept of "good-child identity" between Japan and America. As far as expectations for children's mental development are concerned, Japanese mothers tend to place emphasis on manners, while with American mothers the stress is on linguistic self-expression. Japanese mothers' expectations for children's early development include control of their emotions, obedience, good manners, and an ability to look after themselves, whereas American mothers expect their children to have social ability and the ability to express their views verbally. In other words, the ideal of the "good child" in Japan is that he or she should not be self-assertive in terms of rules for living together in society, while American "good children" should have their own opinions and be able to stand by themselves.

When the Japanese are asked to judge the behavior of others, they often attach importance to the personal background behind the behavior rather than specifically on what the person has done. Azuma describes this as *kimochi-shugi*, a feeling-based way of thinking, defining it as "the tendency to put importance on other people's feelings, or to try to be sympathetic to other people's feelings and perceive

their intentions" (ibid., p. 94). In a group-oriented society, it is important to be considerate of other people, and the Japanese style of communication is dependent on this kind of "mind-reading." As an example, returnee students in Japan who have been brought up overseas
often find it difficult to cooperate with teachers or friends, because
they tend to keep asking questions until they understand completely.
Japanese teachers tend to regard them as self-assertive and disruptive
to their classes, because normal Japanese students hesitate to ask
questions, even if they do not understand, for the fear of disturbing the
class. *Kimochi-shugi* has an important effect on the daily life of the
Japanese. For example, people do not like to make difficult requests of
others, because of consideration for the other person's feelings. When
someone has to refuse a request, both parties will be embarrassed;
therefore, people take a long time to make a decision, considering the
feelings of others. Japanese mothers often bring *kimochi-shugi* into childrearing by explaining a child's naughty behavior through this concept. For instance, when a child kicks at a door and damages it,
Japanese mothers try to correct the child's behavior with an expression such as "The door will be crying in pain," whereas American
mothers might say, "You shouldn't do such a thing. It's naughty!" In
other words, Japanese mothers tend to refer to people's feelings, or
even to those of inanimate objects, to modify their child's behavior,
and this establishes the basis for making judgments for the child:

> Children who are taught that the reason for poor behavior has
> something to do with other people's feelings tend to place their
> basis for judgments, or for their behavior, on the possibility of
> hurting others. On the other hand, children disciplined by decisive
> parental attitudes tend to rely on things outside of human rela-
> tionships, such as rules, laws, and norms when they make deci-
> sions. (Ibid., p. 142)

As a result, there is a constant emphasis on other people's feelings in
Japan, and parents try to teach their children from a very early age to
be sensitive to this information. In Japan, people are expected to consider others first and foremost, and this is a prerequisite for proper
behavior in society.

It is difficult to discuss the relative merits of Japanese and American childrearing. From a critical point of view, the Japanese concept of "good child" places too much emphasis on adaptability to the society or group, resulting in adults who tend to be indecisive and leave problems to other people, often avoiding personal responsibility and giving in to others. As Japan is changing rapidly to meet the demands of an internationalized world, it is important for people to develop their own individual ways of thinking in order to be more independent. Perhaps, therefore, the Japanese should reconsider the concept of a "good child." It is of little value to simply copy Western ways in this regard, however, because too much self-assertion and individualism can also be destructive and is difficult for the Japanese to accept. It is necessary to establish childrearing practices in Japan that enable children to develop real independence, having their own brand of self-assertion, as well as a cooperative spirit, rather than a sense of blind and unthinking obedience.

DISCUSSION ACTIVITIES

Exploring Japanese Culture

1. Who is the most influential figure in childrearing in Japan, the mother or the father? What forms does this influence take?

2. Children in Japan, especially the eldest son and his wife, often take care of elderly parents. Should this responsibility lie with the child?

3. Does childrearing in Japan suffer because of the demands of companies for employees to work long hours? Do fathers put company expectations first, ahead of the family?

4. Are boys raised differently from girls in Japan? If so, in what ways? How do expectations and values placed on children differ in terms of gender?

5. When children misbehave in Japan, parents usually say, "People

will laugh at you," instead of saying, "You should not do that." How does this kind of practice affect children's moral education?

6. It is said that Japanese children today are spoiled, that parents and grandparents buy them too many expensive toys, and that children have little sense of self-discipline. Discuss this aspect of childrearing in Japan.

7. In Japan, what are the differences between being an eldest child, second child, youngest child, and so forth? How is family life different if you are an only child?

8. The number of Japanese children is rapidly decreasing, and one of the most important reasons for this trend is that it is so expensive to raise a child in Japan. Moreover, many women want to work but cannot do so after having a child. What can be done to solve this problem?

Exploring Cross-Cultural Issues

1. Which cultures have stricter childrearing practices, Western societies or Japan? Discuss this with relevance to moral and social education.

2. How do career-choice expectations for children differ between Japan and the West? Discuss this in terms of gender.

3. Many female university students in Japan still have curfews (*mongen*) and are often closely supervised by their parents. How does this differ from the treatment of young women in other countries?

4. Japanese fathers generally play a minimal role in childrearing. How does this compare with other countries?

5. In Japan, many mothers are described as *kyōiku mama* ("education mothers"). What are the characteristics of *kyōiku mama*? Compare Japanese mothers with those in the West.

6. What are the most important qualities that parents try to teach their children in Japan (e.g., being considerate of others, making good friends, being disciplined)? Compare this with other countries.

7. Japanese children generally sleep with their parents, but children in the West usually sleep alone. Why? Discuss these differences.

8. In Japan, parents normally pay for their children's education, and many young people continue to live at home well into their thirties. However, in most Western societies, children are thought to become independent between the ages of eighteen and twenty-one, are usually responsible for paying for their own education, and rarely live at home later in life. Why does this difference exist? At what age are children thought to become adults, economically and socially, in other countries of the world?

謙虚

Kenkyo:
THE JAPANESE VIRTUE OF MODESTY

Modesty or humility is one of the most important aspects of proper behavior in Japan. In Japanese society, people are expected to be modest regardless of their social position; that is, they must learn to modulate the personal display of talent, knowledge, or wealth in an appropriate manner. Self-assertiveness is more or less discouraged, while consideration for others is encouraged. This attitude is illustrated in a famous Japanese proverb "The nail that sticks up gets hammered down" (*Deru kui wa utareru*), which means that those who display their abilities too openly run the risk of being crushed by others. On the other hand, there are other old sayings that extol the virtues of humility, such as "A rice plant's ears grow ripe and hang low" (*Bosatsu miga ireba utsumuku*), which is to say that rather than being proud and haughty, it is desirable to be modest and polite, even when one is more mature, experienced, and refined than others. The spirit of these sayings is effective in maintaining the group ideology of the Japanese people, and the attitude they represent will remain in society as long as honorific and humble forms of speech (*keigo*) exist in the Japanese language. As far as intercultural communication is concerned, the importance of modesty in the Japanese way of thinking often causes confusion and mixed messages because it results in too much self-deprecation or self-effacement by the Japanese when communicating with people from other nations.

THE VERTICAL SOCIETY

Japanese society is structured along fine lines of vertical hierarchy corresponding to degrees of power and distance in interpersonal relationships. For example, although company employees may be similar in terms of ability, they are always ranked according to age, year of entry into the organization, and length of continuous service. A senior or an elder is called a *sempai;* one who is younger or subordinate is a *kōhai.* This *sempai-kōhai* dichotomy exists in virtually all Japanese corporate, educational, and governmental organizations.

Until children graduate from elementary school, they are generally not completely conscious of these vertical relationships. However, as soon as they enter junior high school, they are expected to conform to this rigid system. This is particularly true in extracurricular activities, which are conducted with little adult supervision in Japan and which take place within a rigid hierarchical system. *Sempai* are allowed to "put on airs" with *kōhai,* but if *kōhai* pass *sempai* without greeting them courteously, they are thought of as insolent (*namaiki-na yatsu*) and are given the cold shoulder, or sometimes much worse. Students are educated in Japanese group dynamics and learn how to get along with one another in this vertical system.

Sempai-kōhai relationships are prevalent not only at Japanese schools or universities but also in companies and even in *ikebana* (flower arrangement) groups. Once people enter society, there are not only many *sempai* but also many customers and business connections, all of whom have to be treated carefully. This is the beginning of Japanese modesty.

Although a sense of egalitarianism seems to be growing today, people are still conscious of these hierarchies. In fact, even the seating arrangements and order of speeches at weddings and banquets are done strictly according to rank. In Japan, well-educated people are supposed to know their position; to abide by the tacit rules of society, which designate "superiors first"; and to show their modesty in a natural way. Honorific and humble forms of the language exist for this purpose.

THE FUNCTION OF *KEIGO*

The Japanese language has one of the most complicated honorific (keigo) systems in the world. There are basically three types of keigo: teineigo (polite speech), sonkeigo (honorific speech), and kenjōgo (humble speech).

Teineigo is used in both polite and normal conversation and is marked as such by the copula desu and -masu forms of other verbs. This is in contrast to the use of da as the copula and dictionary forms (kihonkei) of other verbs chosen for speaking to those with whom one is on more familiar terms (i.e., ordinary speech or futsūgo):

DICTIONARY FORM		-MASU (POLITE) FORM
kaku (to write)	»	kakimasu
yomu (to read)	»	yomimasu

Honorific forms of the language, known as sonkeigo, are used to describe the actions of a superior. The honorific or respectful forms of ordinary verbs are made by inserting the verb stem into the pattern o ~ ni naru:

kaku	»	okakininaru
yomu	»	oyomininaru

A second way of transforming ordinary verbs into their honorific forms is to attach the suffix -reru or -rareru. These forms may sometimes be mistaken by the listener (or reader) for passive or potential forms, so the correct meaning must be determined from the context:

kaku	»	kakareru
yomu	»	yomareru

Humble forms of the language, called kenjōgo, are used to describe one's own actions when talking to a superior, particularly actions undertaken for the benefit of that person or requiring his or her permission or cooperation. Some ordinary verbs have special humble forms, others are transformed by inserting the verb stem into the pattern o ~ suru:

iku (to go)	»	mairu
iu (to say)	»	mōsu
kaku	»	okakisuru
yomu	»	oyomisuru

Although *keigo* is used to address superiors or those whom one deeply respects, it is also widely employed in talking to people one does not know well, or who are simply older than oneself. Moreover, it is common for company employees to use *keigo* in addressing their bosses, whether or not they feel any respect for the other on a personal level. As such, the use of *keigo* is a matter of form, regardless of one's actual feelings, and there is a strong tendency to speak on these levels as a kind of social etiquette.

Recently, it has been said that the younger generation cannot use *keigo* properly. In fact, children do not use it in addressing their parents at home, nor do students in addressing their teachers in modern Japan. Furthermore, humble forms seem to be disappearing in colloquial language and can be found today only in formal speeches, greetings, and letters. Passin (1980, p. 16) addresses the significance of these changes as follows:

> In general, it is my feeling that the changes reflect Japan's shift from traditional social and ethical norms to greater individualism and egalitarianism. If, as so many commentators and scholars note, formal usage, or *keigo*, is falling into a state of confusion, it would not be unreasonable to suspect that the status relations that *keigo* reflects must be changing in some way. If we find that within the family unit there is an increase in the use of symmetrical terms and a decline in vertical terms, while we cannot conclude with absolute assurance that egalitarianism is growing, we surely want to look into this matter.

THE EXPRESSION OF HUMILITY

It is often said that the Japanese people are poor at displaying their strong points and are sometimes overly humble. When they receive a compliment, they usually feel awkward and will often seem to refuse to accept it in ways that may appear inappropriate in other languages:

A: "Your English is excellent."
B: "No, not at all. Far from it." ("*Iie, iie. Tondemonai.*")
A: "You must be very hardworking."

B: "No. I'm very ordinary, just the same as everyone else." ("*Iie, iie. Futsu desu.*")

Moreover, when Japanese people give presents or introduce themselves they commonly add modest expressions:

"This is just a trifle." ("*Tsumaranai mono desu ga . . .*")
"Health is my only strong point." ("*Kenko dake ga torie desu.*")

Although there are humble expressions in English as well, such as "Here's a little something for you" or "This is just a token of my gratitude," there is a difference from Japanese in the principles underlying these forms of modesty. The expression of humility in English is a kind of understatement, within the spirit of "you and I are equals." Japanese modesty, on the other hand, carries the connotation of "I'm your inferior" through the expression of negative self-images.

SELF-EFFACEMENT

Dictionaries usually suggest *kenkyo* as the equivalent of modesty. One Japanese dictionary states that *kenkyo* means *sunao to hikaeme*. *Hikaeme* gives the impression of being reserved, and *sunao* has a variety of meanings, including "gentle, mild, meek, obedient, submissive, docile, compliant, yielding," and so on. Many of these adjectives in English connote a weak character, but in Japanese *sunao* is always seen as a compliment. Teachers often describe good students as *sunaona iiko*. This means that they are quiet, listen to what the teacher says, and ask no questions in class. As Fromm (1988, p. 36) states, "the Japanese are not given to questioning authority however slight, while English-speaking people treat all authority with a certain amount of skepticism." The attitudes of students is one of the most evident differences between the cultures. In Japan there is an old saying, "The pheasant that keeps its mouth shut is least likely to get shot" (*Kiji mo nakazuba utaremai*), and Japanese students learn the spirit of "silence seldom does harm" throughout their school lives, pretending to be *sunaona iiko*. This can be contrasted with Western-style *sunao* as follows:

> The Socratic principle of 'Know thyself' is the essence of Western style *sunao*. One should question accepted ideas and beliefs . . . , [for] only in this way can one come to grips with one's own existence, and so create a firm, pure set of principles by which to live. As long as one is true to those principles, one can learn a life of 'justice' and 'humility.' (Ibid., p. 38)

The Japanese style of *sunao* is to be passive toward authority and has strong connotations of self-effacement. People do not have firm principles, and this is very effective when one is involved in a group-oriented society. People's "humility" is a kind of social etiquette used not to harm the feelings of others, or sometimes to provide others with a sense of superiority, and has nothing to do with one's own identity.

CONCLUSION

Today, Japanese society is rapidly changing. The traditional seniority system in companies is under attack, meritocracy through education is growing, and egalitarianism is being accepted more readily. Living in an information-oriented society, people tend to make more of *what* they communicate to others than *how* they do so. These are some of the reasons that *keigo* is in a state a confusion. As the educational system places more importance on students' individuality, self-assertion, and self-reliance, rather than on adaptability or *sunaosa*, these tendencies will become inevitable and will involve a rather creative process.

The sense of modesty in Japan originally arose from the assumption that a person's honor was as good as everyone else's. In other words, everyone has the right to have his or her honor respected. These attitudes have long reinforced the group ideology and harmony of life in Japan. However, when viewed from an international perspective, the Japanese too often present themselves in a rather negative or passive light. Will the Japanese be able to maintain their characteristic modesty in the future? If they hope to do so, they will have to consider carefully its origins and its value in the modern world, and try to help non-Japanese understand *kenkyo* as one of the virtues of Japanese culture.

DISCUSSION ACTIVITIES

Exploring Japanese Culture

1. Television programs in Japan these days often make fun of the younger generation's inability to use honorific and humble expressions properly. Do you think that this way of communicating is necessary for Japanese people in the modern world, especially the young?

2. How did the virtue of modesty enter Japanese culture? Why is it still important?

3. What is the real meaning of the *keigo* systems used in Japanese? Do these expressions really convey respect and self-deprecation, or is it simply a matter of *giri* in the form of *honne* to *tatemae*?

4. Many older people view those who cannot use *keigo* expressions properly as uneducated or lacking in manners. Do you think this is valid? Discuss this issue.

5. How does the use of *keigo* differ according to the person one is speaking to? For example, should honorific and humble expressions *always* be used with older people? What about within the family? How about between *sempai* and *kōhai*?

6. There is a saying in Japanese that is related to the use of modesty: "Nō aru taka wa tsume wo kakusu," or "A clever hawk conceals its talons"; i.e., genuinely capable people do not make a show of their abilities. In other words, in Japanese society, it is not good to parade one's knowledge, culture, and ability; in fact, it can be dangerous, because students who show their abilities too openly in school or people who excel in society are often bullied or ostracized by others. What are your views on this matter?

7. Older people in Japan sometimes dislike younger people expressing

their views in an open, objective, and matter-of-fact fashion. The same applies to the relationship between *sempai* and *kōhai*. In fact, in Japanese schools, many students are afraid to ask their teachers questions openly. How do you feel about this situation, and do you think changes need to be made?

8. How should one properly display one's personal talents and abilities in Japan?

9. **Case Study**: Tomoko Inoue, a housewife living in Japan, once received a letter from the old tailor who made her husband's suits. He was writing to inform her that his shop was closing and described the situation as follows: "I decided to close my shop because my *gusoku* [a Japanese word for referring to one's son in a humble way, literally meaning "my stupid son"], who is a graduate of Tokyo University, now works for Toyota and has no intention of joining my business." Tomoko enjoyed this letter, but wondered if the old tailor was really sad.

Question: How do people in Japan feel about modest expressions like *gusoku* ("my stupid son") or *gusai* ("my stupid wife")? Do you think that there is any hypocrisy in expressing oneself modestly in this way?

Exploring Cross-Cultural Issues

1. Communication depends the social context in which it is taking place. Do you think that the use of *keigo* is appropriate for Japanese people who are communicating in international settings?

2. Do you think that the use of *keigo* should be emphasized for non-Japanese people who are learning to speak Japanese? Is it necessary for them to have a good command of honorofic and humble expressions when communicating in Japanese?

3. Compare the following Japanese and English expressions in terms of the use of *keigo* and what they mean for communication in the two cultures: "*Deru kui wa utareru*" ("The nail that sticks up gets hammered down") vs. "The squeaky wheel gets the grease."

4. How do people from other cultures view the Japanese virtue of modesty?

5. Are honorific and humble forms of expression used in other cultures? What forms do they take in English? For example, do titles and other polite forms of speech in Western societies have the same role (i.e., respect and distancing) as *keigo* in Japanese?

6. Japanese people sometimes feel uncomfortable when they are praised too openly, so modest expressions are generally preferred and it is not uncommon for people to completely deny the praise they are receiving (cf. *Ie, ie, tondemonai*). In cross-cultural communication, how do people from other countries feel about this kind of response?

7. Given the fact that language not only is used to communicate but in the modern world also links people from different cultures, do you think that it is necessary for Japan to reevaluate *keigo* and its accompanying social requirements?

8. Isn't the concept of *keigo* just another superficial tradition in Japan, i.e., hasn't the underlying meaning been gradually eroded because of Japan's internationalization and contact with other cultures? If so, should Japan reassess its language structure in order to accommodate foreign nationals and companies?

9. **Case Study**: Hiromi Nakamura was surfing the Net one day and came across an "E-pal Corner" with some messages written in Japanese that caught her attention because they were quite different from the normal Japanese way of introducing oneself. One of them read as follows: "I'm an attractive, 35-year-old man, who is handsome, well educated, intelligent . . ." Hiromi wondered if this man was really Japanese and whether she should contact him.
Question: What effect does this way of expression have on Japanese people? Is it normal in other countries? Should Hiromi believe his statements and contact him?

季節

Kisetsu:
THE JAPANESE SENSE OF THE SEASONS

Japan has four well-defined seasons consisting of spring, summer, fall, and winter, as well as a rainy season called *tsuyu*, which prevails from June to July throughout most of the country, except for Hokkaido; and from August to October, typhoons spawned in the South Pacific arrive, often spreading havoc and destruction in affected areas. Thus, if the rainy season and the typhoon season are included, it can be said that Japan has six seasons (Kawazoe & Kuwabara, 1972).

Japan also has abundant rainfall, which has brought many blessings to the country, permitting a sophisticated system of wet rice farming to develop in ancient times. In this process, seeds are sown in the spring, and the rice seedlings are then transplanted to paddies in the early summer. They grow rapidly under the summer sun and bear grain, which is harvested in the fall. This cycle was repeated in exactly the same way for many centuries, and as a result, agriculture was the center of all life in ancient Japan and people were greatly concerned with the seasons and the climate, living throughout the year in accordance with rice-farming schedules. The modern Japanese have inherited these attitudes from their ancestors, which is why the seasons are still closely connected with contemporary Japanese life, and this sense of the seasons has had a great influence on Japanese lifestyles, annual events, and literature.

LIFESTYLES

Because the rainy season brings soaring temperatures and very high humidity from June to July, Japanese architecture is designed to protect people from these elements. Floors are raised to keep houses away from the damp ground, and dwellings are made airy and open by limiting the number of partitions between rooms as much as possible. Sliding latticework doors covered with translucent paper, called *shōji*, and heavier paper doors on wooden frames, called *fusuma*, are used to separate rooms instead of solid walls and are usually left open, creating airy dwelling spaces. Traditionally, the Japanese display seasonal flowers and scrolls in a *tokonoma*, an alcove in the wall of one of these rooms, to enjoy the beauty of the seasons, while in the hot and humid summer, they feel cool by listening to the tinkling of wind chimes (*fūrin*) hung at a window.

In addition, most modern Japanese wear Western-style clothing these days because traditional Japanese kimonos are more expensive and less functional. The *yukata* is an exception. It is the most informal type of kimono and can be worn not only as pajamas or for relaxing after taking a hot bath but also for going out on hot summer evenings, and many people look forward to wearing this type of clothing when summer arrives.

Furthermore, although people eat a wide variety of fruits and vegetables throughout the year in Japan, they also enjoy eating special dishes that are associated with the seasons. For example, bamboo shoots (*takenoko*) are a favorite in the spring, eels (*unagi*) are eaten in the summer, and mackerel (*saba*) are representative of the autumn season.

Finally, most letters in Japan begin with some form of seasonal greeting—in the spring, "It's the time when fresh grass sprouts" or "In this season of fragrant breezes," and in winter, "The cold gets more severe with each passing day" or "In this time of piercing cold." It is important to express the feelings of the seasons in these expressions, and many books are published in Japan that provide "set phrases" for accomplishing this goal.

ANNUAL EVENTS

There are many annual events in Japan that are also closely connected with the seasons; for example, *hanami* (flower-viewing) in the spring, *tanabata* in the summer, various autumn festivals, and ōmisoka (New Year's Eve) in the winter.

Cherry blossoms are the national flower of Japan and are seen as a harbinger of spring. Cherry trees usually begin to blossom from late March through the beginning of May, depending on the latitude of the region. When the cherry blossoms are in full bloom, colleagues and friends go out all over the country to parks for flower-viewing parties, where they eat box lunches (*bentō*) and drink under the cherry trees. Hanami lasts hardly a week, however, as the life of the cherry blossom is short, a fact that many Japanese poets throughout history have had cause to lament.

In Japan, the Tanabata Festival is traditionally celebrated on the night of July 7. According to legend, once a year the Star Weaver and her lover, Altar, who are separated from each other in the heavens by *Ama-no-Gawa* (the Heavenly River, or Milky Way), come together and meet. On this day, in accordance with Chinese ritual, the Japanese observe the custom of hanging oblong sheets of paper (*tanzaku*) on bamboo branches, which are used for writing poems that express one's wishes and heartfelt desires.

In autumn, a variety of festivals are celebrated in Japan that are based on old religious rites that have been passed on from generation to generation in the form of festivities to pray for a bountiful harvest. In the past, these autumn festivals were held to thank the gods for the harvest, but with the changing times, they have taken on a different meaning. Today, people who participate in these festivities regard them as a sort of recreational activity or tourist attraction. On these festive occasions, men parade through the streets of their towns, carrying portable shrines, sometimes jostling with other shrines to demonstrate their high spirits.

Ōmisoka is a family event in which people are busy all day preparing to welcome in the New Year. On the last day of the year, Japanese families clean the whole house and decorate their doorways with sacred ropes and tufts of straw or pine branches. Some families also put up gate decorations known as *kadomatsu*, while many households still observe the time-honored custom of pounding steamed glutinous rice to make rice cakes (*mochi*) using mortars (*usu*) and pestles (*kine*). These rice cakes are used as a New Year's decoration with one round *mochi* placed on top of a larger one (*kagamimochi*), or they are served in a soup (*zōni*). Many people also stay awake far into the night on New Year's Eve with other members of their family to share the joy of having spent the outgoing year in good health, as they listen to shrine or temple bells ringing just before the arrival of the New Year. Then they eat *soba* or buckwheat noodles, called *toshikoshi-soba* or year-passing noodles.

LITERATURE
In the not-too-distant past, almost all Japanese people were engaged in agriculture; as a result, they were very sensitive to the seasons because the climate was of crucial importance to their livelihood. Today, this is the basis of the Japanese sense of the seasons, which has also had a great influence on literature in Japan, especially with regard to haiku, the 17-syllable Japanese poem that has attained international popularity. When poets create haiku, they often use *kigo*, which are special words for expressing the seasons, such as *kachōfūgetsu* (a term meaning "flowers, birds, winds, and moon"). For example, an *uguisu* (a nightingale, or bush warbler) sings in spring, *asagao* (morning glories) bloom in summer, a full moon is most beautiful in autumn, and the wind turns cold in winter. And although the moon and the wind remain fundamentally unchanged, they are perceived differently in each season: a hazy moon in spring vs. a clear moon in autumn, or a spring breeze vs. a chilly winter wind. In addition, a haiku poem describes various personal discoveries in that the writer describes the coming of spring through the faint odor of a *ume* (plum) blossom or the approach of autumn by the sounds of the chirping of insects (Takaha, 1976). It may therefore be said that a delicate sense of the seasons is the basis of Japanese haiku.

CONCLUSION
It is sometimes said that the Japanese sense of the seasons is disappearing as modernization, industrialization, and urbanization are changing the national landscape. People do not feel severe heat or cold in their homes, do not see spring flowers on the roadside, and can eat fruit all year long. Buildings are air-conditioned, roads are paved, and nature is something that many young people only

read about in contemporary Japan. To experience the beauty of the seasons, to see flowers in full bloom, to watch fireflies darting above the water, to enjoy the beautiful colors of autumn, most people have to go to the outskirts of their cities. On the other hand, the Japanese still have a strong sense of the seasons, and this feeling is important in their daily lives because it connects them to their history and the culture of the nation, though sadly, all too often in modern Japan, this sense of the seasons is more metaphorical than directly experienced.

DISCUSSION ACTIVITIES

Exploring Japanese Culture

1. Present evidence supporting the claim that the Japanese have a strong sense of the seasons.

2. What are the most important seasonal events in Japan? Why are they important? What occurs during these events?

3. In Japan, what kinds of food do people eat during seasonal festivities (e.g., traditionally, people eat *mochi* on New Year's Eve)?

4. In the past, how did the Japanese build their homes so that people could be comfortable during the different seasons (e.g., during the rainy season or during the hot and humid summer)? What changes occurred in the architectural design of houses in different regions of Japan?

5. It is sometimes pointed out that modern Japanese are losing their sense of the seasons. If this is true, in what phenomena are these changes reflected?

Exploring Cross-Cultural Issues

1. Describe the most important seasonal events in other cultures of the world.

2. Does *koromo-gae* (i.e., a time for the official change of clothes) occur in other countries? If so, how many times a year do students, for example, change the type of clothes they wear in accordance with the change of seasons?

3. What kinds of food do people eat during seasonal festivities in other countries? What is the meaning of these foods? Why are they eaten at these times of the year?

4. The Japanese sense of the seasons is celebrated in traditional literary forms such as haiku through the use of *kigo*. In other cultures, how is the sense of the seasons expressed? What defining characteristics do the seasons have in other countries?

5. In Japan, there are distinct changes between the seasons, whereas in some other areas these changes are less clearly marked (e.g., Hawaii) or there is simply a transition between dry and rainy seasons. Which of these climatic conditions is preferable for living? Why?

根回し

Nemawashi:
LAYING THE GROUNDWORK IN JAPAN

The Japanese are not accustomed to the Western system of communicating and negotiating, which lets both sides present conflicting interests and ideas before reaching a conclusion. They prefer to reach a solution as amicably as possible, and there is a tendency to compromise with others by laying groundwork, referred to in Japanese as *nemawashi*, before reaching a final agreement.

Nemawashi was originally a gardening term meaning "to dig around the root of a tree a year or two before transplanting it"; however, it is widely used in Japan today, especially in business circles, to mean "groundwork laid unobtrusively in advance." The following example illustrates the importance of *nemawashi* in Japanese business practices:

A company in Japan held a meeting of section chiefs in order to make a decision on a change in models for their product. The chief of the planning section who was responsible for this plan was sure of the new model's surpassing the old one, so he was full of confidence at the meeting. However, contrary to his expectations, the other chiefs reacted negatively to his plan. The chief of the designing section criticized the new design severely because he and the chief of the planning section did not get along well. Then the chief of the finance section said it was too soon to change the model because of financial problems. Actually, there was no financial problem, but the chief of the finance section's superior was against the plan. Two section heads supported the new model, but five others remained noncommittal. As a result, they had to turn down the plan because of the supposed financial problems. Although the chief of the planning section usually expressed his ideas clearly and strongly, he sensed that he should not insist on an agreement at this time; otherwise, he might lose a second chance to present it. So he decided to postpone the proposed model change. (Naotsuka, 1980, pp. 201–202)

This is a clear example of a business situation lacking *nemawashi*. What should the planning chief have done before the meeting?

First, he should have met members individually, explained his ideas, and asked for their support. Then, if the chief of the finance section disagreed, the planning chief could have looked into the real reason why he had done so, which would have given him the opportunity to make some changes acceptable to the manager of the finance section. In addition, since he and the designing chief did not get along well, he should have asked the latter to go out drinking together, a common business practice in Japan, to talk about the plan with him beforehand.

As a rule, it is necessary to have a consensus before reaching decisions in Japan. Naotsuka (ibid., p. 202) points out that "this is a different principle from that of democracy: decision by majority." It is very hard to decide on something in Japan when there is no unanimity, and consideration of relationships with coworkers is crucial to the success or failure of important projects. Thus, maneuvering behind the scenes is very important for the Japanese before proceeding, and this is called *nemawashi*.

There is a similar type of behavior in other countries, which is called "spadework." According to Naotsuka (ibid., p. 205), in many countries outside of Japan, such as the USA, Germany, and the UK, *nemawashi*-like behavior takes place. For example, in Britain or America, spadework is needed in the political world in order to work smoothly with opposition parties or those who have great power in making decisions. However, although it is obvious that *nemawashi* takes place elsewhere in many different forms, Japan seems to be the only place where it has been completely systematized and plays a dominant role in the corporate world.

In addition, although they are similar in some ways, differences between *nemawashi* and spadework can be observed in terms of three main points: the decision-making process, the meaning of the meeting, and certain other characteristics. First, the Japanese generally decide things by unanimous agreement. Although the boss has nominal decision-making power, in fact, everyone must agree. Therefore, when a person would like to make certain that a proposal is acceptable, it is essential to sound out how others think in advance—not only opponents but also supporters. If one neglects to do this, others may say, "We didn't know about it." Then, believe it or not, this will be reason enough to go against the plan. In most Western countries, however, the boss keeps decision-making authority, and he or she can turn down any decision, no matter what the results of the discussion. As a result, people tend to do spadework mostly on those who have decision-making power. Secondly, the Japanese tend to make most decisions *before* discussing them at a meeting because people attending meetings often feel uncomfortable being too open and forthright or find it difficult to state their own opinions frankly. It is particularly difficult to take a totally opposite stance in Japan since opinions and emotions are often taken together as a whole. So if one presents an entirely opposing point of view, no matter how logical or effective it might be, it will be seen by others as losing face and insulting, and such behavior in public is generally avoided. Furthermore, even if one's ideas are not critical, to speak up at a meeting often makes others irritated. As a result, meetings in Japan are more like ceremonies, and often, important decisions have been made well in advance through the process of *nemawashi*. In contrast, in most Western countries, a meeting is a place to discuss matters and reach a conclusion. However much spadework has been done, one never knows what will happen at the meeting. The conclusion can be based on the discussion, or in some cases, can be decided on by the boss despite the discussion. Third, the main characteristic of *nemawashi* is notification, while that of spadework is effective advertisement. The former is aimed at reaching a unanimous conclusion and avoiding conflicts at the meeting, while the latter is aimed at effectively letting others know the merits of one's plan.

Nemawashi is widely used in Japan, but it often has a dark and negative image since it takes place behind the scenes. It is sometimes regarded as crafty, and according to Naotsuka (ibid., p. 217), many non-Japanese people think of it as cheating, lobbying, and politicking. However, nemawashi is indispensable when making decisions in Japan, and in fact, it can be a positive force, depending on the situation. In order to work harmoniously in Japanese society, nemawashi is very useful in reducing unnecessary friction, and when people do it effectively and achieve something of worth, they will develop good reputations and are soon promoted.

DISCUSSION ACTIVITIES

Exploring Japanese Culture

1. What are the advantages and disadvantages of nemawashi in the business world in Japan?

2. In Japan, before starting a meeting, those who have suggested a new proposal generally try to do nemawashi in order not to create conflict. Do you think this is really necessary? Why, or why not? In Japan, what happens when nemawashi does not take place?

3. Nemawashi also has some rather dark connotations in Japan and is considered by some to be a form of "backroom dealing." Is this a valid criticism? Why, or why not?

4. Discuss the relationship between nemawashi and the importance of arriving at a consensus in decision-making in Japan.

5. Explain specifically the ways in which Japanese-style meetings are often like ceremonies in which most important matters have already been decided.

Exploring Cross-Cultural Issues

1. Are there customs in other countries that are similar to *nemawashi*?

2. To what extent is arriving at a consensus important in decision making in the business practices of other cultures? What happens when a consensus is not achieved?

3. In the West, transparency (i.e., clarity) is considered to be a key element in the decision-making process. To what extent is transparency evident in decision-making in other countries? In what ways does the absence of transparency create problems in business practices?

4. Which style of decision-making do you think is more effective and efficient, the top-down management style of the West, or *nemawashi*-based decision-making, as in Japan?

5. One of the main functions of *nemawashi* in Japan is to provide a means for avoiding confrontation between individuals with opposing points of view. How is confrontation dealt with in organizations in other countries? What values (i.e., positive or negative) are associated with confrontation in other cultures?

お見合い

Omiai:
ARRANGED MARRIAGE IN JAPAN

Today, nearly 40 percent of Japanese women are still unmarried at the age of 29, while the divorce rate, though low by Western standards, is more than four times that of the 1950s and is continuing to rise (Rauch, 1995, p. 14). According to research conducted by the Asahi Life Insurance Company, by the year 2015, 58.2 percent of all Japanese men between the ages of 20 and 39 are expected to be bachelors ("Is one Japanese man," 1995, p. 12). Not so long ago, people thought that men should work and women should stay home to care for the family, but today a large number of women are able to find jobs and make a living. In fact, many Japanese women are much more selective in choosing a marriage partner, and large numbers are deciding not to get married. As a result, as the above statistics show, the rate of marriage in Japan is reaching alarmingly low levels. When the Japanese do get married, they generally choose one of two methods: "love marriages" or *miai-kekkon* (arranged marriages). Because this latter form of marriage, known as *omiai*, continues to be surprisingly popular in Japan, it will be examined from three main points of view: the origins of *omiai*, the process of *miai-kekkon*, and the reasons for agreeing to an arranged marriage in present-day Japanese society.

Minami (1983, p. 208) states that the method for choosing a spouse has changed throughout Japanese history. In ancient times, marriage was *mura-*, or community, centered, and people gave priority to the order and profit of the whole village. As a result, people generally married those who lived close by and whom they already knew well. As time went on, marriage became ie-, or family centered, and the head of the family decided on the choice of spouse for all the other family members. Selection criteria emphasized the social status of the family of the prospective spouse, which in turn promoted the long-term prosperity of the family. The wishes of the people who were getting married were most often ignored, and sometimes the couple did not even meet each other until the day of their wedding. Nowadays, marriage is individual-centered, and the wishes of the prospective bride and groom are respected, although family background is still an important consideration in modern omiai.

To begin the process of omiai, a nakodo (go-between) helps make an initial exchange of information between two individuals and their families (Motona & Beitz, 1983, p. 172). This information is normally exchanged in writing in a document called a tsurisho, and photos are always included. Then, if both parties agree to go on to the next stage, the nakodo introduces the prospective couple to each other along with their parents. After this initial meeting, called omiai, the couple see each other periodically until they decide to get married or not, giving proper consideration to each other's suitability as a partner. If they decide to get married, an engagement called yuino takes place, at which time it is then customary for the man to send gifts, usually an engagement ring and a certain amount of money, generally amounting to three months' salary, to his prospective bride and her family. In most cases, a few months later the wedding takes place, conducted Shinto style, or less commonly, in a Buddhist or Christian ceremony.

Omiai has a number of advantages, and according to the Japan Arranged Marriage Association, these benefits are as follows (Omiai-Kekkon Suishin-Kai, 1996, pp. 117–147):

- Through omiai, people can learn in detail about a large number of prospective partners.

- It costs less money finding a marriage partner through omiai than using a marriage agency.

- Women who do not want to marry an eldest son and live with their husband's family can find other suitable partners.

- *Omiai* includes parents in the process of selection, thus avoiding later conflict.

- People can determine whether or not a prospective partner meets their standards and can get to know something of one another's character and sense of values through the *tsurisho*.

- People do not have to suffer many of the negative consequences of dating, such as finding opportunities to meet others or suffering face-to-face rejection. Japanese people are often very busy and do not have the time or energy to meet and date a variety of prospective partners, so *omiai* provides a means of overcoming this obstacle.

Although the frequency of *omiai* has been decreasing, many modern Japanese young people still follow this practice. This is due to traditional Japanese views concerning marriage, which is still a matter of *ie* (family) or *mura* (village) rather than the individual for many people, creating a lot of public pressure to marry. Therefore, although the rate of marriage is falling to increasingly low levels in Japan, *omiai* continues to be a popular method for choosing a spouse.

DISCUSSION ACTIVITIES

Exploring Japanese Culture

1. In Japan, which type of marriage do you think has a better chance of enduring, *omiai* or a love marriage? Why? What are the advantages and disadvantages of *omiai*, when compared with a love marriage?

2. In *omiai*, the family background, educational status, and financial situation of the other person are extremely important in getting

married. What do you think of this? Are there differences in this regard between men and women?

3. These days in Japan, there is a flood of information about *omiai* on the Internet. How will these new technologies change the process of *omiai*?

4. *Omiai* is still very popular in Japan, even among young people. Why?

5. **Case Study**: As a woman, which person would you prefer to marry? Mr. A: You have been going out with him for five years now. He does not have a stable job, likes gambling, and does not have much money. However, you really love him.
Mr. B: You recently had an *omiai* meeting with him because your father pushed you to see him. He is a good-looking gentleman and is now working for a prestigious company. He has a bright future and you can probably make your parents happy if you marry him, but you do not have strong feelings for him.

Exploring Cross-Cultural Issues

1. When Japanese people choose a spouse and get married, they tend to think about their parents' wishes, as well as the people around them, such as whether their friends have become married yet or not. Compare these attitudes with those in other countries.

2. Do arranged marriages still take place in other countries of the world? Where, and why?

3. In other cultures, what are the most important factors in choosing a spouse (e.g., money, love, family)?

4. In the West, arranged marriage is very rare, yet the divorce rates are

extremely high. Do you think that some of the traditional values reflected in arranged marriage should be retained in Western cultures?

5. What role does love play in *omiai* and in Japanese marriages in general? Compare this with other cultures.

おとぎ話

Otogibanashi:
FOLKTALES OF JAPAN

Most people throughout the world are familiar with the folktales of the country they grow up in. Folktales are special because they contain morals and reflect the ways of thinking and the character of a people; as a result, they are an important means of transmitting cultural values from generation to generation. In Japan, as well, there are many folktales that are still popular among the people and that illustrate certain key cultural values, especially in terms of the Japanese sense of beauty, the concept of nature, and the ideal of perfect human beings.

THE JAPANESE SENSE OF BEAUTY

Japanese folktakes portray two kinds of beauty: one is visual; the other is emotional. Typically, these folktales are known for their portrayal of the physical beauty of the seasons, as well as their in-depth descriptions of the emotional lives of the hero and/or heroine. The following story, which illustrates these two features of folktales in Japan, is called "*Uguisu no Sato*" ("A Bush Warbler and the House"), and it is regarded as one of the most representative of Japanese folktales.

Once upon a time, a young woodcutter made his way into a grove of *ume* (plum) blossoms and discovered a house that he had never come across before. He went into the house, and he saw a beautiful young woman inside. She said that she had to leave and asked him to take charge of the house during her absence. However, before going out, she gave him the following warning: "Never look in the other reception rooms." But he did not heed her advice and looked in some of the other beautiful rooms. Surprisingly, each room had a set of fine furniture and paintings of scenes of the four seasons. At last, he reached the last room and found three little eggs. He picked them up and dropped them by accident. Just then, the beautiful young woman came home, complained to him about his insincerity, and, weeping bitterly, transformed herself into a bush warbler. She took wing, singing, "I miss my children!" Suddenly, the woodcutter found himself alone in a field, and the house and everything in it had disappeared.

As we read this story, we cannot fail to notice the beauty of the four seasons, and this is a common feature of many folktales in Japan in which the seasons, *uguisu*, *ume* blossoms, and golden ears of rice plants are described in detail. Moreover, in all these kinds *ume* tales, a bush warbler is expected to come onstage along with *ume* trees and blossoms. In Japan, this is natural because the bush warbler and *ume* trees constitute a unit that represents spring beauty; indeed, there is the common phrase *ume ni uguisu*, which means "talking of *ume* trees" in describing bush warblers in Japan. The beauty of this folktale becomes complete only when the three elements of *ume* trees, *uguisu*, and a beautiful woman make up a set. In other words, "*Uguisu no Sato*" illustrates the Japanese sense of beauty visually.

Second, in these folktales, we can discover a sense of emotional beauty, or a feeling of *aware*, which is embodied in feelings such as patience and pity. The beautiful young woman in this story was very patient and compassionate. Many readers may wonder why the woman (the bush warbler) took no revenge on the woodcutter for killing her children (i.e., by dropping the eggs). According to Kawai (1982, pp. 13–16), the woman felt shame at having her true nature exposed, and her shame was stronger than her anger, perhaps indicating the importance of shame in Japanese culture and the fact that patience has long been regarded as a virtue in Japan, especially for women. However, the principal feeling that readers are left with at the end of this story is pity, and although the woodcutter had broken his promise and killed the bush warbler's children, she did not seek revenge. In fact, Japan has many folktales such as "Uguisu no Sato" in which the heroines are tragic figures, reflecting the feeling that beautiful women who have an aura of sadness are graceful in a sense. As described in this story, Japanese heroines are often tragic figures and have to endure grief. At the end of our tale, we are left with nothing but the image of the man in the empty field, although the sadness of the uguisu remains. In other words, a woman's sadness plays an important role in finishing these stories, and this sadness is an important element in the Japanese sense of beauty. This feeling is called aware, and when the Japanese see a woman in grief bearing it with patience, they feel this sense of aware.

Thus, in a folktale like "Uguisu no Sato," there is both visual beauty in the form of ume trees, the uguisu, and the woman, as well as emotional beauty in the sense of aware. In reading such folktales, we can experience nature's beauty indirectly and enjoy the feeling of aware more directly. This sense of beauty is depicted in many similar folktales in Japan.

THE CONCEPT OF NATURE

Japanese folktales often contain animal characters that take the form of human beings, and these elements help explain the Japanese concept of nature in which people are thought to coexist with nature in a rather vague way (ibid., pp. 194–195). This is illustrated in folktales based on the notion irui-kon; that is, a person (usually a man) marries an animal that has transformed itself into a human being. Many kinds of animals appear in Japanese irui-kon folktales, including birds, foxes, mud snails, fishes, and frogs.

The plot development of Japanese folktales also reflects the concept of nature in Japan. Generally, these stories all develop in the same basic way. One day, a man meets a beautiful woman (an animal in reality) by accident. In the first stage of these folktales, she asks him to marry her, which he does, although he has no idea of her true nature. In the next stage, he discovers her true form by breaking a promise to her or ignoring some kind of prohibition. As a result of this act, she takes on her true form as an animal and inevitably leaves him. In the last stage, each of them lives in their own separate worlds as if nothing has happened. In terms of the interpretation of this plot, the first stage describes a situation in which the man is thought to have a deep, though vague, sense of unity with nature; as proof of this, he gets married without thinking at all about where his wife has come from. However, after he begins to feel doubtful because of some event, generally a prohibition of some kind, he starts to feel that human beings are different from nature. He then tries to understand the real character of nature by breaking his promise in the second stage of the folktale. However, as Kawai (ibid., p. 199) states, on the whole, it is impossible to truly grasp the reality of nature because it does not like its true form to be understood. As a result, "nature returns to nature"; that is, although animals can live in the human world for a time, they cannot stay there permanently and will eventually have to return to their own world. In the final stage, humans return to their normal lives as described in the beginning of these tales, without doing anything for the animals. In general, people rarely make active approaches to nature in these stories; they have no sense of revenge and do not hunt the animals. However, the relationship between themselves and the animals is not clearly defined, and in the end, they choose a way of living in harmony with nature, but in a rather vague fashion, which means maintaining some kind of distance.

THE IDEAL OF PERFECT HUMAN BEINGS

Although there are many tragic folktales in Japan, there are also wonderful tales with happy endings. The Japanese ideal of the perfect human being is illustrated in these folktales, and this is generally a person who has a very strong will. In examining a folktale called "Sumiyaki-chōja," this characteristic clearly emerges. "Sumiyaki-chōja" is a representative example of a tale about marriage in Japan with a happy ending. In Japanese, sumiyaki means a "charcoal burner, or the act of burning charcoal," and chōja means "a rich man." The following is an outline of this folktale.

Once upon a time, a poor charcoal burner lived deep in the mountains. One day a fine woman who came from a wealthy family visited him and asked him to marry her. He rejected her proposal at first due to his poverty, but she did not mind and still wanted very much to marry him. In the end, they were married, and the next day, she gave him a *koban* (formerly a Japanese oval gold coin) in order for him to buy food. Since he had never seen gold and did not know the value of a *koban*, he said to her, "What is it? Why can I buy things with this?" After listening to her explanation, he informed her that there was a lot of gold around the charcoal kiln, and because what he said was true, the couple became rich.

In this folktale, the woman is very active, in striking contrast to the tragic woman in the bush warbler tale. In "*Sumiyaki-chōja*," there are two reasons why the heroine is a wonderful figure: one is her bravery in marrying a poor man; the other is her intelligence in guiding him. First, she is very brave to become the wife of a poor charcoal burner, because in traditional Japanese society, the status system greatly affected people's marriages; therefore, it is very surprising to see a woman marry beneath her station. In so doing, she challenges feudal customs and turns her desire into reality. Second, she guides the charcoal burner, who did not know much about the real world. He is an honest man in this tale, although he does not have enough knowledge to create a good life for himself. She is able to make him great through her wisdom. In brief, we find many admirable people in Japanese folktales with happy endings. These are people who act in accordance with their own wills and who become happy through their intelligence. This is the ideal of the person that many Japanese long to become.

CONCLUSION

When people read folktales, they become connected to the history, traditions, and spirit of their culture. Folktales also reflect the national characteristics of a people, and in Japanese folktales, we can discover the Japanese sense of beauty, both in nature and in the form of emotional beauty, or *aware*, in which patience and pity are seen as virtues. Moreover, through these tales, we can understand the Japanese concept of nature and the desire of people to live in harmony with it, as well as the ideal of the individual in Japan as a person with a strong will and decisive judgment.

DISCUSSION ACTIVITIES

Exploring Japanese Culture

1. The heroine of the story "*Uguisu no Sato*" (i.e., the bush warbler, or *uguisu*) did not get angry with the woodcutter when he dropped the eggs and killed her children. Do you think this is a reflection of the Japanese virtues of compassion and patience? Why, or why not?

2. In what specific ways do you think the heroines of Japanese folktales represent Japanese women? What characteristics do they have in common?

3. What plants often appear in Japanese folktales (e.g., *ume*, *sakura*)? What do they represent or symbolize?

4. What are the names of some of the best-known Japanese folktales? Why are they popular?

5. It is said that young people in Japan read folktales less frequently than in the past; instead, they watch TV and read comic books. What changes can be expected in their cultural values in the future?

Exploring Cross-Cultural Issues

1. What are some of the most popular folktales in other cultures? What messages or lessons do they convey?

2. Describe the heroes and heroines of well-known folktales in other countries. Compare them with those of Japan.

3. What animals often appear in the folktales of other countries? What roles do they play? Compare them with animals in the folktales of Japan.

4. Folktales are a means of passing on important cultural values from one generation to the next. Do these values differ from culture to culture, or even among different ethnic elements of a given society? If so, how do they differ?

5. What are the best-known folktales in Japan that have been imported from other countries? Why are these tales popular among the Japanese?

良妻賢母

Ryōsaikenbo
"GOOD WIVES AND WISE MOTHERS":
The Social Expectations of Women in Japan

In Japan, as elsewhere, the sense of being a man or woman not only is determined by biology but also is formed by culture and social conditioning, and gender is determined through social, political, cultural, mental, and physical processes. These influences on gender appear in language, fashion, the workplace, politics, and so on. Japanese women today, however, are troubled by the social expectations of females in Japan, because a great many working women have the additional pressure of doing housework and are expected to be "good wives and wise mothers" as well as pursuing their careers.

HISTORICAL BACKGROUND
The term *ryōsaikenbo*, which means a "good wife and wise mother," was often used in relation to women in the past. It is not used so much today, but it remains an important unconscious concept among the Japanese. In the Edo period, the upbringing of females was designed to develop "good wives" who would be responsible for the household and produce many children. The concept of *ryōsaikenbo* did not yet exist, because women were not responsible for their children's formal education (Koyama, 1991, p. 14).

The social expectations of women changed in the Meiji era with the advent of a formal system of education for all children. The term *ryōsaikenbo* was introduced at this time, and in addition to their roles as wives, women became responsible for directing the education of their children (ibid., p. 33). To be a "good wife" in Meiji times meant to *support* one's husband, while in the Edo period women simply had to be *obedient* to their spouses. The educational system of the Meiji era emphasized schooling for girls as well as boys because it was considered that they would all become mothers in the future and thus have a formative influence on their children's education. In addition, females could become good teachers. As a result, women played a significant role in the Japanese people becoming a well-educated and cultivated people, and it is widely believed that schooling for females was an important factor in Japan achieving such rapid industrialization.

In the Taishō period, women were encouraged to engage in business because it was considered useful for socialization purposes and in deepening their comprehension of their husbands (ibid., p. 150). However, the concept of *ryōsaikenbo* was preserved, and women were not allowed to be superior to men. In fact, even though more than half of married women today are working, the ideal of *ryōsaikenbo* continues to be very influential.

In addition to expecting women to be "good wives and wise mothers," Japanese society has a long tradition of separate roles for males and females, such as men working and women doing housework. According to Takumi (1992, p. 23), for example, "boys like to play outside in [a] lively way; on the other hand, girls like to play quietly in the home." Such discriminatory stereotypes come from a long tradition of division of labor in which men worked outside and women stayed inside to look after the home. Although this way of thinking is still prevalent in Japanese consciousness, women's attitudes are changing. For example, women who have children often leave them in nursery school and go to work outside the home today. Furthermore, more and more women are working without getting married because they know that it is hard to do both a job and housework well. These attitudes are also responsible for the rising divorce rate, as well as a reduction in the birthrate.

CHILDREN'S SOCIALIZATION

Children are socialized in the cultural values of the community in which they live, and if they do not acquire these values, society will not recognize them as true members. In Japan, it is still believed that boys and girls should be brought up in different ways. In particular, discipline toward girls is much stricter than with boys, and the stereotype of "girlishness" is seen in every home that has female children. This powerful stereotype takes many forms. First, almost all little girls have dress-up dolls called *rika-chan ningyō*, which have ideal proportions, reflecting the Japanese image of the feminine. Therefore, girls tend to yearn to be like these dolls and identify with them. In addition to dress-up dolls, there are various kinds of toys that symbolize women's roles: miniature models of items such as sewing machines, kitchen appliances, and household items. Furthermore, many Japanese mothers like to dress their daughters in pink or red skirts and lace blouses. They expect their daughters to be "girlish," and these female children also try to be feminine, as society expects.

Female primary school students also read more books than their male counterparts. They read fairly tales, biographies of famous women, or stories for young girls, and long to be like the characters in these stories. Sewing, cooking, or knitting clubs are also popular with young girls, and many of them learn the piano or calligraphy after school. There are some clubs, however, in which females cannot take part, such as sports clubs for baseball, soccer, and so on. All female students can do is act as "managers" of these club activities or cheer on the male members.

Children's sense of identity is also an important factor in their socialization. This sense of identity is greatly influenced by parents, because children are closest to their mothers and fathers and spend the most time with them from early childhood. Children learn how to behave as men or women and how to act in personal relationships by modeling their parents (Takada, 1975, p. 3). Moreover, they learn sex roles, such as men working outside the home and women doing housework. This is reflected in *mamagoto*, or children playing house. As they grow up, humans develop more complicated relationships and begin to pattern their sense of identity on models other than their parents. They may identify themselves with TV personalities or famous people in history. TV programs have a surprisingly strong influence on young people, as Inoue (1992, pp. 30–31) points out:

Popular animation programs such as Rupan III or Ultraman have stories in which a smart young hero fights evil persons in order to protect women and children from danger. Women appear in supporting roles with long hair, big eyes, ideal proportions, and glamour, as the hero's girlfriend or to nurse the weak. Men's expectations of women, that they should be obedient, kind, and pretty are directly reflected in these TV programs. The image of manliness and womanliness is conveyed to children by such media.

In addition to such identity roles, mothers have a great influence on children's socialization in Japan. In particular, mothers' expectations of their daughters are rather special. For example, in fashion, as mentioned above, mothers try to make their daughters attractive, and even in ceremonies such as Coming-of-Age Day or weddings, they often arrange their daughters' dresses even though these young women are no longer children. Inoue (ibid., pp. 64–65) points out that *furisode* (long-sleeved kimonos), which Japanese women wear on Coming-of-Age Day, are "traditional and expensive, but parents buy *furisode* because this kind of kimono sets off their daughters' beauty and shows the economic power of the family. Daughters wear these dresses to meet social expectations, especially their mothers', even though they are only worn for one day."

In addition to paying attention to fashion, mothers expect their daughters to do housework but rarely force their sons to do these chores, because they want their daughters to be "good wives" who serve their husbands. The social expectations of women, for example, that they should be beautiful, kind, sensible, do housework well, and be obedient to their husbands, reflect mothers' attitudes toward their daughters.

WOMEN'S MAGAZINES AS CONVEYORS OF SEX ROLES

There are numerous magazines that are published for females in Japan, such as those that deal with fashion, childrearing, fortune-telling, marriage, show business, cooking, leisure. These magazines have a great influence on women.

Some of the most influential types of publications as conveyors of sex roles for women are fashion magazines. About 50 percent of women in their twenties read these magazines in order to keep up-to-date with the latest styles or to coordinate their clothing. These kinds of magazines also include information on cosmetics, accompanied by advertisements for perfume, nail polish, and so on. As a result, many women are extremely conscious of beauty and want to be attractive and fashionable. Inoue (1989, p. 6) argues that "women's magazines have added beauty to female roles by emphasizing youth and attractiveness. Such women must always have ideal proportions, wear make up and fashionable clothes, and be attractive sexually."

Photographs of fashion models published in these magazines also influence readers. Most women long to be like these models, who are beautiful and well proportioned. This is why many Japanese women are afflicted with a "diet syndrome," pursuing an ideal image of beauty through intensive dieting, exercise, or taking drugs in order to lose weight, though most of them actually have balanced proportions. According to a recent survey, 82 percent of women think that they are fat and wish to be thin, while 22 percent of women think they are normal but wish to be thinner (Morohashi, 1993, p. 143). In addition, not only fashion models but also advertisements in fashion magazines cause women to diet excessively. These advertisements publicize plastic surgery, ointments, teas, medicines, and so on, and try to convince women of the merits of their products through various forms of propaganda:

> Women become aware of their defects by looking at these advertisements, but what these advertisements suggest is that women will be able to get good results without any effort. They sell how-to techniques or manuals so that women can become beautiful or thin without effort in order to meet the social expectations of women in society. (Inoue, 1989, p. 139)

> Young women's neuroses or suicides are an SOS from those who are damaged by social expectations. Anorexia nervosa, or binge eating, which young women especially suffer from, would not be exist if it were not for the womanliness which advertisements exemplify and men require. (Miya; cited in Morohashi, 1993, p. 167)

CONCLUSIONS

In summary, this article has considered three points of view with regard to the social expectations of women in Japan, exemplified in the expression *ryōsaikenbo*: historical background, children's socialization, and women's magazines as conveyors of sex roles. Children acquire social expectations through the process of growing up and reflect them in their attitudes and behavior. As a result, traditional role models for women are creating many problems today. These issues are now being discussed, and solutions to sexual discrimination, such as the Convention for the Elimination of All Forms of Discrimination against Women or the Equal Employment Opportunities Law, have recently been introduced in Japan. However, women still experience many problems related to Japanese society's changing expectations of their roles.

DISCUSSION ACTIVITIES

Exploring Japanese Culture

1. The number of men who do household chores and help in the raising of children is reported to be increasing these days in Japan, but many women complain that they are still expected to do most of the work around the house even if they also have a job. In other cases, many Japanese men are said to do absolutely nothing around the house and are described as *sodai gomi* ("big garbage"). What should the role of men and women be in modern Japanese society?

2. It is true that there are few women in important political and economic positions in Japan. But do you think that all Japanese women aspire to these roles? Perhaps women do not want to work and would prefer being *ryōsaikenbo*, or perhaps they welcome having the free time to deepen their knowledge in areas that interest them. Discuss this issue.

3. Japanese men sometimes complain that their wives have an easy time, staying at home all day instead of having to face the pressures

of the workplace. They have lots of free time that they can spend pursuing their personal interests, going to the gym, or dining with friends at restaurants. In addition, they generally look after the family finances and have almost complete control over family life at home. Do you think that these men have a valid complaint?

4. Given the declining birthrate in Japan, do you think it will be necessary for companies to reevaluate their gender workplace and recruitment practices and to provide child-care facilities for working mothers?

5. Do you think that there is blatant discrimination against women in Japan, or is it simply an extension of the importance that Japan places on traditional family values and a sense of national unity?

6. Many Japanese recognize the need for business practices to change so that women can have equal employment opportunities. Yet people also worry about taking care of children and raising them in a proper way. Discuss this issue.

7. Are there any pressure groups or women's groups in Japan that have been fighting for women's rights in the workplace? How successful have they been?

8. Girls are said to be raised in a much stricter fashion than boys in Japan. For example, girls are often expected to do housework and help their mothers, while boys are exempted from these tasks in order to study for exams. Even at university, many young women still have curfews (*mongen*), whereas this kind of restriction is rare for young men. Do you think these kinds of practices are fair?

9. How is the concept of a "good wife and wise mother" changing in modern Japan?

10. **Case Study:** Kiyomi Tamai is a Japanese woman of the older generation who was forced to learn tea ceremony, sewing, cooking, and so forth before getting married because it was felt that knowledge

in these areas was expected of all women. This practice is called *hanayome-shugyō*, or "good wife training." In later life, she says that these skills have become the basis of her hobbies, which contribute greatly to her enjoyment of life. With all the changes that are occurring in Japanese society, she wonders if there is anything wrong with this. **Question**: How would you answer Kiyomi? Is *hanayome-shugyō* still practiced in modern Japan? Should it be?

Exploring Cross-Cultural Issues

1. A great many foreign firms are entering Japan these days, and this influx is expected to increase in the future. These companies are reported to be particularly interested in hiring young Japanese women, who generally work harder than young men at university and who often have superior communication skills, especially in foreign languages. Moreover, these firms will usually give these women the opportunity to have a genuine career if they have the necessary qualifications and abilities, in contrast to traditional Japanese companies, which generally force young women into "office lady" positions in which they spend most of their time serving tea and making photocopies. Discuss this issue.

2. More women in Western countries work outside the home, but the divorce rate in these countries is also much higher than in Japan, where women traditionally stay at home and raise their children. Which system do you think is better?

3. How do women in countries other than Japan cope with the responsibilities of work, household tasks, and childrearing?

4. Compare maternity-leave practices and equal employment opportunity laws in Japan with those in other countries.

5. What are the social expectations of women in other countries? How do they compare with those in Japan? Are there stereotypes that women are expected to conform to? What is the image of a "good wife and wise mother" in other countries?

先輩/後輩

Sempai-Kōhai:
SENIORITY RULES IN JAPANESE RELATIONS

There are many special aspects to Japanese culture, and in particular, human relationships are quite different from those in the West. Many scholars in social anthropology have discussed these differences, a typical example of which is Nakane (1967, pp. 70–71):

> Human relationships can be classified into vertical and horizontal hierarchies. The vertical includes relationships between parents and their children, while the horizontal involves classmates or colleagues. In Japanese society vertical rankings of human relationships have developed to a great extent and a seniority system is prevalent in Japan.

Horizontal relationships in Japan are expressed by words such as *dōryō* and *dōkyusei*. The former is used by businesspeople and refers to colleagues or those who are in the same position in a company, while the latter is a term used by students for classmates or those who are the same age. Such horizontal relationships are not the norm in Japanese society, however, and vertical hierarchies dominate. *Sempai-kōhai* relationships exemplify this kind of hierarchy. Seniors are called *sempai* in Japanese, a term that has a long history, first appearing in ancient Chinese texts, where it referred to people who are older or superior in ability. In contemporary Japanese, *sempai* is also used to refer to those who graduated earlier from the same school. *Kōhai* is the opposite of *sempai*: *kō* means "later" or "after-wards," and *hai* signifies "fellows" or "mates." So people who are junior or who entered the same school or company after oneself are called *kōhai* and are considered to be inferior to *sempai* because of their lack of experience. This expression can also be found in ancient texts and is used in the same way today.

Nakane (ibid, pp. 82–83) argues that "the Japanese tend to make too much of rank even in daily life; for example, people can neither be seated nor talk without considering the status and seniority of the other people around them." At schools and companies, seniors believe that it is natural to be respected by juniors because they are experienced in their jobs or other activities. In Japanese companies, in particular, people put more emphasis on age than ability because the system of wages and promotions is based on seniority rules. The older people become, the more they earn or the greater their chances for promotion. Such seniority rules have deeply permeated all aspects of Japanese life.

THE HISTORY OF SEMPAI-KŌHAI
Sempai-kōhai relationships have existed since the beginning of Japanese history, but three main formative influences on this ranking of human relations need to be considered: Confucianism, the traditional Japanese family system, and the former civil law.

Confucianism was originally imported to Japan from China from the sixth to ninth centuries but had its greatest impact on the Japanese way of thinking as neo-Confucianism, which became the official doctrine of the Tokugawa shogunate. At this time, the precept of *chō-kō*, or loyalty and filial piety, dominated Japanese thinking:

> Confucianism's concern with social conduct within a concrete human nexus fit well with Japanese values which placed primary importance on particularistic human relationships within a strictly-defined social hierarchy. Filial piety, respect for one's elders, and reverence for one's ancestors also suited native Japanese preferences. The present-day emphasis in Japanese life on education, diligence, and historical precedent (i.e., accumulated knowledge from the past as opposed to intellectual debate) all owe much to

Confucian influences. Nevertheless, as with other imported traditions, the Japanese adopted Confucian ideals and institutions
selectively; thus, 'loyalty' in the Confucian sense became synony-
mous with loyalty to one's lord and later to the emperor. (Davies,
1998; after Reischauer, 1988; Nakamura, 1971)

The *ie*, or family, system also had an influence on the development
of seniority rules. The family system, which was largely based on
Confucian codes of conduct, had two main principles: the father, as
chief male, had absolute power in the family, and the eldest son
inherited the family estate. The father was considered the family
ruler because he had received an education and had superior ethical
wisdom. Paying reverence to superiors was considered a virtue in
Japanese society, so his wife and children had to obey him. Moreover,
in the inheritance system, only the eldest son had the right to inherit
at that time—neither the eldest daughter nor any younger children
could succeed to the father's estate.

In addition to Confucianism and the family system, the former civil
law, which was brought into effect in 1898, strengthened seniority
rules and reinforced the traditional Japanese family system, as hierarchical values within the family were given a clear definition. This was
called *koshu-sei*, meaning "the system of the head of a family," which
stated that the master of the house had the right to rule his family and
that the eldest son succeeded to this position and to his father's estate.
These statutes were overturned in 1947 but continue to have a powerful psychological influence on the Japanese way of thinking.

SEMPAI-KŌHAI AND THE JAPANESE LANGUAGE

Seniority rules are reflected in certain grammatical forms in the
Japanese language. When people talk to superiors they use *keigo*
(honorific) language, which includes three types of language: *sonkeigo* (respectful or honorific language), *kenjōgo* (humble language), and
teineigo (polite language). *Sonkeigo* and *kenjōgo* involve particular sets
of expressions, while teineigo is used in a more general sense. People
make proper use of these forms as the situation dictates.

Sonkeigo is used when a speaker expresses respect toward an
addressee or someone who is being talked about. In this kind of

speech, the position of the addressee is raised by the speaker through the use of particular honorific expressions. In *sonkeigo*, there are many special verbs. For example, people use the verb *ossharu* instead of *iu* to show respect, although both are translated as "to say"—the former carries honorific connotations, while the latter is simply the plain or neutral form of the verb. In addition, terms of respect or titles of honor such as *-san*, *-sama*, and *-sensei* are added to people's family names or occupational titles in *sonkeigo*. The use of *-san* is neutral and can be translated as "Mr.", "Ms.", "Mrs.", or "Miss", while *-sama* has exactly the same translational meaning but is more formal or polite. *Sensei* is used for professionals such as teachers, doctors, or lawyers. In general, people can express their respect to others directly by using *sonkeigo*.

Kenjōgo is a type of speech that lowers the status of the speaker, who is thus able to communicate with humility. Speaking in this modest way thus indicates respect for one's addressee, because to humble oneself before superiors or seniors indirectly represents high regard for them. In this kind of speech, there are also special terms such as the expression *mōsu* or *mōshiageru*, humble forms of the verb *iu*, both of which also mean "to say," but with connotations of humility.

In addition to *sonkeigo* and *kenjōgo*, *teineigo* is a polite level of speech, using the prefixes *o-* or *go-* with nouns (e.g., *cha* is a neutral form of the noun "tea," while *o-cha* is its polite equivalent), or the verb forms *-desu* and *-masu* (e.g., *iu* is the plain or dictionary form of the verb "to say," and is conjugated as *iimasu* in its polite form). *Teineigo* is somewhat different from the other two types of *keigo* in that it is used not only with seniors but also with people around oneself as a way of expressing respectful politeness in a general sense. *Teineigo* is therefore commonly used in relationships among all kinds of people.

THE CURRENT STYLE OF *SEMPAI-KŌHAI*

Vertical hierarchies have existed since the beginning of Japanese history and are still prevalent in daily life, especially in schools, where seniority rules are important:

> The relationships between *sempai* and *kōhai* are very stable among students because everyone will sooner or later be a *sempai*, *kōhai*,

or both. Spending more time and having more experience at
school gives students *sempai* status. (Okazaki, 1989, pp. 190–191)

For example, third-year students have great power in junior high
and senior high schools, and especially in clubs, these relationships
are important. It is common in sports clubs for *kōhai* to clean the
rooms, collect balls, and manage the equipment for *sempai*. They
must also give a small bow or say hello respectfully to their *sempai*
when greeting them. In general, students put much more emphasis
on age than ability in Japanese schools, and seniority rules also
influence relationships between teachers and students. Although
schools are rapidly changing today, in most classes students would
never criticize or talk back to a teacher. They think that teachers
should be respected because of their age, experience, and ability, and
what teachers say is always considered to be right. Therefore, there
are few opportunities for students to have real discussions with
teachers in Japanese schools.

In universities, changes in relationships among students start to
take place. They express their respect and use polite expressions to
seniors, but *sempai-kōhai* relationships are not as strong, because
there is more variety in age among classmates. The differing status
between teachers and students remains the same as in high school,
but there are important differences that separate professors in terms
of rank and power, and vertical hierarchies involving seniority rules
are seen more among faculty than students in Japanese universities.
Nakane (1967, p. 92) notes, for example, that "in London University,
professors, assistant professors, and lecturers are considered colleagues, and they use first names without thinking in terms of seniority. On the other hand, there are definite vertical hierarchies in
Japanese universities."

Seniority rules in Japanese relationships are not only important at
schools but also in companies in contemporary Japan. The seniority
system and the lifetime employment system are the bases of life in
Japanese companies, though it remains to be seen whether this
structure will survive the changes that corporate Japan is currently
undergoing. Status, position, and salary still depend largely on seniority, and older employees are generally in higher positions and are

paid more than their younger subordinates. Moreover, until recently, once people were employed, they never had to worry about their positions because their posts were guaranteed for life. In the business world, the *sempai-kōhai* system has a powerful influence on human relations, such as in meetings where a junior employee will take a seat near the door, which is called *shimoza*, while the eldest person (often the boss) will be seated next to any important guests in a position called *kamiza*. In most meetings, the majority of businessmen do not normally voice their opinions. They simply listen to their superiors, flatter them, or express opinions that were formulated behind the scenes by senior employees of considerable influence.

PROBLEMS IN THE SEMPAI-KŌHAI SYSTEM

Sempai-kōhai relationships have deeply permeated Japanese life, but they are starting to change in schools and business organizations. *Sempai* used to be respected by *kōhai* because of their experience, but lately *kōhai* do not express as high a regard to seniors as in the past. While they use polite expressions, respect toward seniors has become rather superficial, and today, people tend to consider age less important because there is beginning to be more variety in the student body of Japanese schools with returnee students, non-Japanese, and so on.

The breakdown of the seniority system in companies is a much more serious issue in modern Japan. The collapse of the bubble economy has caused high unemployment, and even senior executives have lost their jobs. Many companies have begun to adopt the principle of "ability first," and lay off older workers if they cannot fulfill their job responsibilities satisfactorily. There are great changes taking place in the whole structure of Japanese companies, especially in the salary system, with some companies opting for a pay system in which people who are talented and productive can earn more money, regardless of age. It is widely believed that most companies will have to reform their entire corporate structures involving salaries and promotion sooner or later, and this will inevitably lessen the influence of seniority rules in Japanese society as a whole.

DISCUSSION ACTIVITIES

Exploring Japanese Culture

1. What are the advantages and disadvantages of vertical hierarchies such as *sempai-kōhai* for Japanese society? Discuss this issue in relation to business, education, and family life.

2. In Japan, *sempai-kōhai* relationships are starting to change, and some companies are adopting the principle of "ability first," in place of seniority. How will these changes affect the Japanese corporate world?

3. In Japanese schools, especially in clubs, senior students (*sempai*) have great power over those who are younger (*kōhai*). In most cases, *sempai* exercise this power responsibly, but in some circumstances, it can lead to bullying, physical abuse, and even death. Discuss this issue and suggest remedies for the negative effects of *sempai-kōhai*.

4. Relationships in Japanese families are also based on a vertical hierarchy in which older siblings play the role of *sempai* and younger siblings that of *kōhai*. Discuss the advantages and disadvantages of this way of relating within the family.

5. **Case Study**: Yoshi Murata is the junior member of his company's section, and for three years since he graduated from university, he has been serving drinks to his colleagues at meetings, photocopying materials for his superiors, and generally doing all the low-level work in his office. He is not happy about this situation, but he believes that if he carries out his responsibilities well, in two or three years he will be able to do the kind of work he really wants.
Question: If you were Yoshi, would you accept this situation? Do you think that this is an appropriate way for a company to operate in the modern world? How are the expectations of younger employees changing in Japan these days?

Exploring Cross-Cultural Issues

1. In Japan, people are often ranked by age, which is a kind of hierarchy within society that is reflected in *sempai-kōhai* relationships. In what ways are people ranked in other countries?

2. Why does the concept of seniority seem to be less important in Western societies than in Japan? Discuss this notion in relation to other Asian societies.

3. In Japan, *kōhai* are expected to use polite language (*keigo*) when speaking to *sempai*, and if they do not, they will be severely reprimanded. Do other languages of the world have similar respect systems based on seniority? Compare this with ways in which politeness and respect are expressed to older people in other societies.

4. Do you think the concept of *sempai-kōhai* enhances or hinders Japan's international business practices? Discuss its ramifications for multinational companies.

5. In the West, especially in modern times, egalitarian modes of discourse have become widely accepted, and people are generally expected to communicate with one another as equals regardless of their actual status in society. Discuss this approach to communication in relation to vertical hierarchies such as *sempai-kōhai*, which continue to dominate in Japan.

集団意識

Shūdan Ishiki:
JAPANESE GROUP CONSCIOUSNESS

In Japanese society, people are primarily group-oriented and give more priority to group harmony than to individuals. Most Japanese consider it an important virtue to adhere to the values of the groups to which they belong. This loyalty to the group produces a feeling of solidarity, and the underlying concept of group consciousness is seen in diverse aspects of Japanese life. In Japan, group members create their own social codes of behavior, and group consciousness has become the foundation of Japanese society. The development of nonverbal communication, the distinction between *uchi* and *soto*, and emphasis on harmony, have all had an influence on the distinct group consciousness of the Japanese.

Nonverbal communication in Japan is a typical example. Unlike in Western countries, Japan is a society in which conciliatory, cooperative attitudes are more highly valued than strong, unyielding insistence. So Japanese people manipulate *honne* (what is intended) and *tatemae* (what is said), depending on the situation. Sometimes speech is unnecessary, and even silence can be seen as a means of communication. In contrast, if people carelessly and directly express what they really think, there is the probability of hurting the feelings of others, disrupting the group ambience, or destroying harmonious relations. Many Japanese proverbs admonish against speaking carelessly; for example, "Out of the mouth comes evil" (*Kuchi wa wazawai no moto*) or "Silence is golden" (*Iwanu ga hana*).

Japanese society is made up of numerous interdependent groups, each with its own common consciousness and tacit understandings, which are conveyed without words. People who share these understandings are involved in *uchi*, and those who cannot are treated as *soto*. In other words, Japanese make a clear distinction between *uchi* (insiders) and *soto* (outsiders). According to Nakane (1967, p. 111), *uchi* consists of two categories. The first refers to "a group which has very close connections and a strong exclusive character [in which] the members have had a significant relationship with each other for a long time." For most people, this would be the nuclear or extended family. A second category of *uchi* is often established around the first one and includes people known as *shiriai* (acquaintances), the family of one's wife or husband, their children's married family, old friends and classmates, and more distant relatives. People outside these categories, that is, *soto*, include those whom one comes only occasionally into contact with, such as people encountered in business, for example. These three categories, two *uchi* and one *soto*, are said to be formed by one's twenties and seldom change. The Japanese strongly distinguish *uchi* from *soto* and are said to be poor at getting along with those who are *soto*:

> Japanese in groups are usually indifferent to outsiders. However, when outsiders are invited to come with appointments, they are treated courteously as formal guests. If they should try to join one's group without any contact, however, they would never have a warm welcome and might secretly become people who should be refused admittance and excluded from the group. (Takeuchi, 1995, p. 213)

There is no doubt that the harmony of the group is vitally important in Japanese society. People often think and behave as a group, and what benefits the group is mostly regarded as the correct thing to do. As a result, an individual who is a member of the group cannot help conforming to the group's aims, sense of values, customs, and so on. In public, they try to maintain an attitude of support toward the group, even if their own personal ideas are at odds with group values, a typical example of *honne* and *tatemae* in Japan. Needless to say, loyalty to the group creates a strong feeling of solidarity, which can work for good or bad. For example, such feelings can sometimes make people more cooperative in the group; on the other hand, it is sometimes responsible for the entire group committing crimes because it is more important for members to follow group values and protect themselves than to stand up and oppose wrongdoing. In fact, group members run the risk of being excluded if they ignore the rules or disturb group order. As the proverb says, "The nail that stands up will be pounded down" (*Deru kui wa utareru*). Individuals within the same group have a tendency to act in a similar way, partly because doing the same thing makes people feel relaxed, but it also helps in protecting themselves from being ostracized (*murahachibu*). Such group protection also causes individuals to refrain from becoming independent, however, and there are many examples of groupism working negatively. As noted by Reischauer (1980), during World War II the Japanese people were forced to obey the military absolutely, and as a consequence, in the end, both within Japan and in other countries, many helpless civilians were brutally dragged into the conflict. On the other hand, one cannot overlook the fact that groupism has contributed greatly to the postwar economic growth of Japan. It would have been impossible to reorganize society and reconstruct the economy quite so quickly if it had not been for the strong group consciousness of the Japanese people.

DISCUSSION ACTIVITIES

Exploring Japanese Culture

1. Ohnuki describes the Japanese individual as "defined within a network of heavily and intimately involved human relationships" (1984, p. 216), while Lebra (1976) describes Japanese culture as "social preoccupation" in that the Japanese are very concerned with social interaction and tend to be preoccupied with their relationships to other people. Discuss this issue from the perspective of *shūdan ishiki*.

2. The Japanese are often said to be group-oriented, and this is one of

the main reasons why they place so much emphasis on *sekentei* (reputation). The group-self is like a composite entity made up of individual members, and these members take great care to maintain harmony within the group because the group-self is what they depend on for their sense of identity. As a result, within the group, most Japanese do not express their opinions directly and clearly but study the faces of the other members and change their attitudes accordingly. All the members of a group are required to come to one unanimous decision in Japan, although this usually takes a long time. The group also protects its members in many ways, but if one is judged as not respectable, the group-self can be severe, and the individual will be ostracized by the other members. This occurs not only when one is looked down upon but also when one is envied. As a result, it is comfortable and safe for people to behave in exactly the same way as others. Discuss this issue in terms of the recent spate of crimes committed by young people in Japan, and especially with regard to bullying in schools.

3. Today, young people in Japan say that they should be free to express their individuality. However, everyone seems to follow exactly the same fads in fashion and to act and think very much the same way as others. In fact, being a true individual in Japan can be dangerous, especially in schools. How can this be explained?

4. In a recent study, the Dentsu Institute reported that only 8 percent of Japanese people surveyed said that they would maintain their own opinion even if it meant falling out with others, which was the lowest percentage in all Asian countries ("Dour and dark outlook," 2001, p. 19). Discuss these findings in relation to the notion of *shūdan ishiki*.

5. **Case Study**: Takashi is a member of the university tennis club. As is often the case, his club has many drinking parties, but Takashi does not like to drink. However, the last time he avoided going to a party, he was accused of lacking group spirit.
Question: Is this kind of pressure fair? Should Takashi change his attitude?

Exploring Cross-Cultural Issues

1. Do you think that Japanese students have a weaker sense of individuality than students in other countries. If so, why?

2. A strong sense of groupism is generally associated with Asian societies in general. Is this a valid assumption to make? If so, describe the differences among Asian countries in terms of group consciousness.

3. In any culture, there are strategies employed for developing and maintaining group cohesion. Compare how these strategies operate in Japan with those of other countries in the world.

4. In the West, asserting one's individuality, even if it means standing up to group pressure, is a major theme of many novels and movies. Compare this attitude with approaches in other cultures.

5. The power of the group is especially strong during adolescence. Describe its negative effects at this time of life in various societies.

6. How is it possible to strike a balance between individuality and group harmony? How does this balance differ among cultures?

葬式

Sōshiki:
JAPANESE FUNERALS

Those who face death, or whose family or friends have died, tend to want supernatural explanations to ease their suffering, so answers to the question of death have been among the most important themes in all religions of the world. For example, "the idea of Heaven in Christianity and the Pure Land in *Jōdo Shin* Buddhism helps people accept the pain of death by creating the image of a beautiful world in the afterlife" (Miyake, 1980, p. 14). After a person dies, it is the custom of family, relatives, and friends to hold a funeral and send the deceased on to this next world smoothly.

According to a Japanese book of manners, about 90 percent of funerals held in Japan today are Buddhist, and such funerals have to follow a great many strict customs: "Because Japanese Buddhists think that the soul of the dead person does not separate from the body for a period of time, a large number of rituals developed for funerals in Japan" (Kanzaki, 1995, p. 120). However, Japanese funerals are also based on an ancient way of thinking derived from Shinto, which requires respect and honor for the souls of one's ancestors. Shinto is a religion indigenous to Japan that involves nature worship and a belief in the souls of one's ancestors. In AD 538, Buddhism was introduced into Japan, and the Japanese people came to believe in Buddhism as well, mixing it with Shinto beliefs. Because Shinto did not have strict doctrines, and because there were many points in common between the two religions, the Japanese were able to

combine Shinto and Buddhism without much difficulty. As a consequence, modern Buddhist-style funerals in Japan are still greatly
influenced by Shinto traditions.[1] Therefore, in this chapter, the
nature of Japanese funerals will be investigated by first explaining
the influences of Shinto and Buddhism, and then by examining many
of the modern customs and rituals associated with Japanese funerals
both *during* and *after* the event.

SHINTO

Shinto, which originated in Japan in ancient times, emphasizes the
importance of nature: "the ancient Japanese believed in nature worship and there were a lot of gods (*kami*) who were guardians in every
region: mountain gods, sea gods, tree gods, earth gods, fire gods,
water gods, and so on" (ibid., p. 15). However, "although animals and
plants could be gods, human beings could not become gods during
their lifetimes and had to wait until after death" (Toyota, 1994, p. 135).

Although the ancient Japanese believed in a great many gods,
"they believed in guardian gods the most. These guardian gods were
the souls of ancestors who had brought the land under cultivation
and were accorded considerable respect" (Kanzaki, 1995, p. 15). In
those times, people "did not have clear and fixed ideas of the world
after death" and believed that the dead simply went to join the souls
of their ancestors (Toyota, 1994, p. 134).

Shinto is also a surprisingly flexible religion, with few taboos and
restrictions; as a result, "it has readily accepted foreign ideas, beliefs,
and customs" (ibid., p. 130). One of the most important taboos in
Shinto has to do with purity, and the Japanese have long been very
sensitive about anything that is considered impure. However,
because "Shinto is lacking in fixed doctrines, there are few rules that
clearly define what is impure, so the ancients simply divided the living world into two—the pure and the impure—though purity and
impurity were not contrasting concepts like good and evil or truth
and falsehood, as in Western thinking" (ibid., p. 116). In fact, people
did not think of impurity as permanent; instead, "it was thought of
as a period of transition, so that people tried to purify the impure by
using water or other purifying elements as quickly as possible" (ibid.).
The kind of impurity that people were most afraid of was death, but

they seemed not to know how to go about purifying such terrible impurity. In fact, in ancient times "the palace was simply moved to another place when an emperor died because it is thought that the impurity of his death influenced the people" (ibid., p. 131). Thus, though Shinto had traditional customs for purifying what was impure, it was thought that the great impurity of death could not be purified by human beings, so people often just waited for it to disappear. In general, a dead person was placed in a coffin for a while so that the impurity of death would become diluted, and this was followed sometime later by a burial.

BUDDHISM

When Buddhism was introduced into Japan, it flourished under the protection of the nation's rulers in the Nara period, and today it is one of the nation's most widely followed religions. Buddhism is divided into two types: the Hinayana, or Lesser Vehicle, and the Mahayana, or Greater Vehicle. "Japanese Buddhism is a branch of Mahayana Buddhism which teaches that everyone has the possibility of becoming a Buddha; that is, spiritually awakened" (Tsuchiya, 1988, pp. 21 & 24). One of the reasons why Buddhism became so successfully implanted into Japan is that Mahayana Buddhism and Shinto held common beliefs about respecting the souls of ancestors. Most modern Japanese follow both religions, at least nominally. Today, Buddhist rituals for funerals, the Bon festival, and the equinoctial week have become firmly established in Japan, and many of these rituals involve the idea of worshipping one's ancestors.

In Mahayana Buddhism, "there is also the belief in *samsara*: the transmigration of the soul" (Sadakata, 1989, p. 14) and that "this world where humans live is but one of six worlds, though it is the second highest" (Tsuchiya, 1998, p. 131). It is believed that a person goes on a journey after death, so the deceased is dressed in special clothes in order to travel safely (ibid., p. 127). In addition, in Mahayana Buddhism "it is thought that the deceased will be reborn in one of the six worlds according to his or her behavior during life [and] it takes forty-nine days after death to be judged" (ibid., p. 129), so the bereaved family holds special services for the departed soul during these forty-nine days.

With the coming of Buddhism, cremation, which originated in India, was introduced into Japan (Haga, 1996, p. 35), and in AD 702, the Emperor Jito was the first ruler to be cremated. Before cremation, people simply waited for the impurity of death to disappear by setting out the dead body in a coffin; however, they thought that cremation was a better way to purify death and accepted it readily (ibid.). Thus, although Shinto did not have specific ways of purifying the impurity of death, Buddhism offered a sophisticated, ceremonial means for easing the transition of the deceased to the afterlife, and the two sets of customs became combined (Tsuchiya, 1998, p. 320).

MODERN CUSTOMS DURING THE FUNERAL

The following descriptions of customs for Japanese funerals are taken from three principal publications, known as "manner books" in Japan. They include *Osōshiki no Manā* (Manners in Funerals), *Sōgi Hōyō Manā Jiten* (Dictionary of Manners in Funerals and Buddhist Services), and *Sōsō Bunka Ron* (A View of Funeral Culture).

Deciding on the Date of the Funeral

When a person passes away in Japan, the bereaved normally contact a Buddhist priest from the family temple, as well as undertakers, before deciding on the date, the place, and the chief mourner for the funeral. The Buddhist priest comes to the wake and to the funeral itself to hold a service for the departed soul, and the undertakers assume duties for caring for the deceased person's body on behalf of the bereaved family.

There is usually a *karitsuya* (a temporary wake) for close relatives on the day that the person dies, and on the next day there is a *hontsuya* (the wake itself). The funeral is then held two days later. However, if this event occurs at the beginning or the end of the year, or a day of *tomobiki*, the funeral is postponed. The term *tomobiki* is one of six basic labels printed on traditional Japanese calendars that indicate the auspiciousness of a given day: *sensho, tomobiki, senbu, butsumetsu, taian,* and *shakkō. Tomobiki* is a day on which it is thought that the bad luck of the family could affect their friends, so it is avoided in the scheduling of funerals. When the funeral takes place, it is usually at the home of the deceased, a Buddhist temple, a public facility, or at a funeral hall that is managed by the undertakers. In most cases, the chief mourner is usually the closest relative of the dead person.

Matsugo no Mizu to Yukan: *The Water of the Time of Death and Cleaning the Deceased*

The first thing that the bereaved family does for the deceased is to attend the deathbed. This ritual is called *matsugo no mizu* (the water of the time of death) or *shini mizu* (water of death). The bereaved family wets the mouth of the dead person with water using chopsticks that are bound with absorbent cotton and soaked in water. Those who have the deepest blood relationship with the deceased do so first, then other people in the same kinship order.

Next, the dead person is cleaned in a process called *yukan*, in which the body is washed with hot water in preparation for burial. Gauze or absorbent cotton with alcohol is used to clean the deceased; the mouth, nose, and anus are stuffed with absorbent cotton; and the eyes and the mouth are then closed. Generally, members of the bereaved family perform these actions under the direction and guidance of the undertakers.

Kyōkatabira to Shini Geshō: *Clothes and Makeup for the Deceased*

In the next stage, the dead person is dressed by members of the bereaved family in a *kyōkatabira* (a white kimono) before being laid out. The white kimono is always put on with the right side overlapping the left, then a covering for the back of the hand and wrist and a pair of sock gaiters are put on, followed by straw sandals, prayer beads in the hands, a cloth sack with *roku mon sen* (six old coins) as a shoulder bag tied around the neck, and a white triangular cloth around the head. The color white is associated with Buddhist pilgrimages, and there is the belief among Buddhists that people go on a kind of pilgrimage after death.

The bereaved family then applies makeup to the dead person's face. If the face is wasted, cotton is put into the mouth and the face is arranged so that it looks like it did during life. Then the nails of the fingers and toes are clipped; in the case of a man, his mustache or beard is shaved, while for a woman, light makeup is applied.

Laying out the Dead Person

After the the white kimono and makeup are put on, the deceased is laid out in a family Buddhist altar room or in a Japanese-style room in the dead person's house. At this time, it is important to keep the head pointed toward the north and the face to the west, like the Buddha when he passed away. After the dead person is laid out, the palms of the dead person are joined together on the chest as if in prayer. A quilt is put over the body, and the face is covered by a white cloth. An upside-down folding screen is then placed at the side of the pillow.

Sakasa Goto: Upside-down Things

The upside-down folding screen is used in accordance with a Buddhist custom for funerals called sakasa goto (upside-down things). Following this practice, people do things in reverse during a funeral; for example, putting on the white kimono with the right side over-lapping the left, pouring hot water into cold water to make it luke-warm, and putting a quilt over a dead person in reverse. People do not want death to give unhappiness to those who are still alive, so they do sakasa goto during the funeral, though these practices are taboo in daily life.

Makura Kazari: Pillowside Decoration

The next stage in this process is called makura kazari, or pillowside decoration, when a small table covered with a white cloth is placed at the pillowside of the deceased. A single stick of incense is then burned and a candlestick and flowers are arranged on the table, usu-ally white chrysanthemums or shikimi (an evergreen tree of the mag-nolia family), and it is necessary for the bereaved family to keep the incense and candle burning at all times. A rice bowl that the dead person used during life is then heaped with rice, and a chopstick is placed vertically in the rice. In addition, dumplings made of rice pow-der are placed on the table on a piece of white paper.

Kaimyō: A Posthumous Name

In Japan, people ask a Buddhist priest from their family temple to give a name to the deceased, and this posthumous name is called kaimyō, which originally meant a name for those who become

Buddhist priests. Dead people are regarded as becoming pupils of Buddha, so they are given a kaimyō, which is decided on according to their name during life and their achievements and character. Kaimyō also have ranks related to the amount of remuneration given to the priests. After the appropriate kaimyō has been selected, the priest writes it down on a mortuary tablet made of white wood.

Hitsugi: The Coffin
Before the wake, the dead person is placed in a coffin. A one-meter square of white cotton is laid on the bottom of the coffin, and the dead person wearing the white kimono is placed on top of it. Next, the favorite things of the dead person are put into the coffin, except for items made of metal and glass because the dead body will be cremated later. The coffin is then covered with a gold brocade cloth.

Tsuya: The Wake
During the wake, the bereaved family and relatives spend the night watching over the deceased in the coffin, and they must keep sticks of incense and candles burning all night. They hold a karitsuya (a temple wake) on the day that the person dies; the next night they hold a hontsuya (the wake), and during this time, they receive callers who come to express their sympathy. The hontsuya usually starts at about six in the evening and generally takes about an hour. In the beginning, a Buddhist priest comes to the hall and reads a sutra aloud. Then, the chief mourner performs a ritual called shōkō, which involves burning incense for the soul of the deceased; thereafter, others continue this practice in order of their blood relationship. Finally, the chief mourner entertains callers with food as an expression of thanks for their visit.

Sōshiki: The Funeral
On the day after the wake, the funeral takes place. At first, an altar and the coffin are arranged in the assembly hall. Before the funeral begins, the bereaved family, relatives, and others attending the funeral enter the hall, then a Buddhist priest comes in, and all of the mourners stand up if they are sitting on chairs, or make a bow if they

are in a Japanese-style room. After giving an opening address, the
Buddhist priest offers a candle on the altar, burns incense, and chants
a sutra, which takes about thirty minutes. Next, a number of mourners give eulogies to the deceased, and the funeral organizer reads
telegrams of sympathy. Then, the Buddhist priest performs shōkō
(burning incense for the soul of the deceased) and begins to chant a
sutra again, after which the chief mourner also performs shōkō, followed by other mourners in turn, while the priest is chanting.

During funerals, there are also some important customs that must
be followed involving clothes for mourning, prayer beads, shōkō,
items for the altar, and kōden (a monetary offering). At the funeral,
the bereaved family and relatives must wear special, formal clothes,
and the mourners are also expected to come in appropriate clothing.
Among family members, men generally wear a haori hakama, which
is a kind of black kimono with a half-length Japanese coat and a long
pleated skirt worn over the kimono. Women wear black kimonos
without patterns. Mourners usually dress in dark suits, black ties,
and black socks for men, and black kimonos or black suits for
women. Women's belts and handbags are also black, and women do
not wear accessories, except for pearls.

People normally bring prayer beads when they participate in
Buddhist services such as funerals and other memorial services
related to death. The prayer beads are made of transparent rock crys-
tal, coral, incense wood, and so on. They hold the prayer beads with
the tassel side down in their left hands. When they pray, they join
their palms together, putting the fingers of both hands in a loop
around the prayer beads and supporting them with their thumbs and
index fingers.

During a funeral, mourners always perform shōkō and burn
incense for the soul of the deceased. In this practice, they first bow
to the altar and join their palms together. Second, they pinch
incense in the form of brown powder with their thumb, index
finger, and middle finger. Third, they hold the incense above their
heads while bowing, and put it into an incense burner. Finally, they
join their palms together and bow to the altar again, and go back to
their seats.

The altar for the funeral is composed of a Buddhist mortuary tablet, a light, and offerings such as flowers. During the wake and the funeral, a Buddhist mortuary tablet, made of white wood on which the posthumous name of the deceased is written, is displayed on the altar. After the funeral, the mortuary tablet is taken to the crematorium with a photograph of the dead person.

Mourners also bring *kōden* for the departed soul to the wake or the funeral. The money is wrapped in a piece of paper specially used for *kōden*, and the names of the mourners are written on it. There are strict rules for wrapping the paper, including folding it with the right side overlapping the left in the front and with the bottom side overlapping the top in the back. The amount of money given is in relation to the degree of closeness with the dead person, the customs in the area, the social standing of the deceased, and so on. According to recent research, the average amount of money for *kōden* is 100,000 yen when a parent dies, from 30,000 to 50,000 yen when a brother or a sister dies, 5,000 yen when a neighbor dies, and from 5,000 to 10,000 yen when a close acquaintance dies. When mourners bring *kōden*, they put it in a square silk wrapping cloth of quiet colors about the size of a handkerchief, and at the funeral, mourners present the *kōden* at the reception desk.

Sōretsu: *The Funeral Procession*

After the funeral, the bereaved family and undertakers take the coffin down from the altar, and take off the lid. Then the family members and mourners who were close to the dead person have a last meeting with the deceased and put the flowers that were displayed on the altar and the favorite belongings of the dead person in the coffin. Next, they put the lid on the coffin, and the chief mourner drives in a nail, followed by other mourners in the same kinship order. It is the custom for a person to hit the nail twice with a large pebble.

About six male mourners carry the coffin out of the hall with the deceased's feet first and put it in a funeral car. Undertakers then drive to a crematorium, and the bereaved family follows after the hearse, carrying a picture of the dead person and the mortuary tablet. If the Buddhist priest goes to the crematorium, he shares the car with the bereaved family.

Kasō: *Cremation*

After the funeral, the bereaved family carries the mortuary tablet and the picture of the dead person to the crematorium, and undertakers prepare a cinerary urn. In the crematorium, undertakers put the coffin, the mortuary tablet, the picture of the dead person, flowers, and an incense burner on a small table in front of the furnace. Then, if the Buddhist priest comes to the crematorium, he reads a sutra aloud. The chief mourner, the family members, and other mourners perform shōkō in kinship order, and the undertakers then put the coffin in the furnace and ignite it. Finally, all the mourners go to a waiting room and spend some time remembering the dead person.

After the cremation, a pair of mourners put the ashes of the deceased into the urn with chopsticks that are made of bamboo, starting with the bones of the feet and finishing with bones of the head. The urn is put into a box of white wood and covered with a white cloth, and the chief mourner carries it with both hands back to the house. In the house the box is put on the family altar until forty-nine days after death.

MODERN CUSTOMS AFTER THE FUNERAL
Shijūku Nichi Hōyū: A *Buddhist Memorial Service Taking Place Forty-Nine Days After Death*

In Japanese Buddhism, it is believed that the soul of a dead person wanders between this world and the next for forty-nine days after death. As a result, the relatives hold a service so that the departed soul goes to Paradise after this period. The soul is said to be tried by the judge of the next world seven times every seventh day, so Buddhist memorial services are also held on these occasions.

After the funeral, a Buddhist service is held on the seventh day after the person dies, which includes the bereaved family, other relatives, and people who were close to the deceased, during which time a Buddhist priest reads a sutra aloud. On the fourteenth, twenty-first, twenty-eighth, and thirty-fifth days, a Buddhist service is held within the family circle, but these days are now sometimes omitted.

Condolences end on the forty-ninth day, and a big Buddhist service is held by the bereaved family, close relatives, and friends. It is customary to bury the ashes of the dead person in a grave on this day. The mortuary tablet made of white wood is exchanged for one made of lacquerware, and it is put on the family Buddhist altar. The bereaved family returns to normal life after the forty-ninth day, at which time they give presents in return for *kōden*, distributing mementos to mourners.

Butsudan: *The Family Buddhist Altar*

In Japanese Buddhism, a family altar is built in each house in order to pray to Buddha and for the soul of departed ancestors. Mortuary tablets, an incense burner, an incense holder, a candlestick, a bell, Buddhist tableware, tea utensil offerings, and flowers are put on this altar. Those who do not have an altar at home put the mortuary tablet inside a small case that is a model of a shrine instead.

When people pray, they light a candle and put incense by the candle. They then ring a bell twice, join their palms together, and read a sutra aloud, although in practice, reading the sutra is sometimes omitted. After praying, they put out the candle with their hands or with a round paper fan; however, they must not blow it out, because it is thought that the mouth is impure.

Haka: *The Grave*

Graves serve two purposes in Japan: to bury the ashes of the dead person and to have a place to go for worship. A new grave is prepared by the first anniversary after death, and a temporary grave marker made of wood is put there until this time. When the grave is ready, the name of the dead person and the day of death are written on the tombstone and on a slab of stone beside the tombstone.

The tombstone is usually rectangular in shape and is built on a stand made of stone, which is composed of granite. An enclosure is built around the gravestone, and an incense holder and flower vase are put in front of it. A slab of stone, a garden lantern, a card tray, a stone basin, and garden plants are arranged around the graveside, depending on its size and the relatives' taste.

If the grave is in the family temple, the Buddhist priest holds a service for the departed soul on the anniversary of death, the Bon festival, and *o-higan* (the equinoctial week). People visit the deceased's grave on these days, and when they visit, they clean the grave, leave offerings, burn incense, add water, and pray.

Kamidana Fūji: *Closing the Household Shinto Altar*

A Buddhist family altar and *kamidana* (a household Shinto altar) are found in most Japanese houses.[2] Because it is thought that death is impure in Shinto, the Shinto altar is closed during the period of mourning with a strip of white paper to signify mourning. In the past, a third party performed this task because it was thought that the bereaved family was impure. Today, however, family members usually do this task themselves, and after the period of mourning is over, the white paper strip is removed. Though it is not thought that death is impure in Buddhism, the family Buddhist altar is also sometimes closed, depending on the sect the family belongs to. If the Buddhist altar is closed, the bereaved family holds services for the departed soul at a temporary altar in the house, which contains the ashes of the deceased until the forty-ninth day after death.

Kōden Gaeshi: *Presents in Return for a Monetary Offering*

The bereaved family gives presents to the mourners on the forty-ninth day after death, which amount to one-third to one-half of the *kōden*, called *kōden gaeshi*, with a letter of thanks in order to inform people that the end of the period of mourning has arrived and to express their thanks for the *kōden*. These gifts are usually daily necessities such as bedsheets, bath towels, handkerchiefs, green tea, soap, coffee sets, and sugar. Those who receive these presents do not need to send a letter of thanks for *kōden gaeshi*.

Fuku Mo: *Mourning*

The bereaved family is expected to be in mourning for the deceased for a specific period of time, called *ki chū*, which lasts until the forty-ninth day after death, and *mo chū*, which is for one year after death. However, the bereaved family and close relatives cannot usually be absent from school or their companies for such a long time, so the period that they are absent for mourning is predetermined: ten days for a spouse; seven days for a parent; five days for a child; three days for a grandmother, grandfather, sister, and brother; and one day for a grandchild, aunt, and uncle. During *mo chū* (for one year after death), the bereaved family does not participate in extravagant leisure activities, does not attend wedding ceremonies, does not worship at the shrine, and does not make New Year's calls. In addition, they do not send New Year's cards, so greeting cards that apologize for not sending New Year's cards are sent instead by early December.

Nenki Hōyō: *The Buddhist Memorial Services on the Anniversaries of Death*

Memorial services are held on the first, second, sixth, twelfth, six-teenth, twenty-second, twenty-sixth, and thirty-second anniversaries of the death of the deceased. In some cases, a memorial service is also held on the forty-ninth anniversary of the death. If there are more than two anniversaries in one year for a family, the memorial serv-ice is held in a combined fashion. Because the mortuary tablet of the dead person is thought to have the personality and worldly passions of the deceased until the last anniversary (the thirty-second or forty-ninth year after death), it is put in the family Buddhist altar, and memorial services are held by descendants of the deceased. On the last anniversary of death, it is said that the dead person loses his or her personality and is able to protect the house, so the last anniver-sary is the end of the condolences, and the mortuary tablet in the family Buddhist altar is taken to the family temple.

On the first and second anniversaries of death, family, other rela-tives, and friends of the dead person hold the memorial service in the house or the family temple. The Buddhist priest reads a sutra aloud and the mourners perform *shōkō* before visiting the grave. After the sixth anniversary, the memorial services are usually held within the family circle.

O-Bon: *The Bon Festival*

The Bon festival is a Japanese Buddhist event in which the souls of the dead are thought to return to their houses during this period. It generally begins on August 13 and ends on August 16. Before the Bon festival, the family altar and grave are cleaned, and vegetables, fruits, and the favorite foods of the deceased and other ancestors are prepared. Small fires are lit at the gate of the house in the evening of the first day to welcome back the departed souls, and they are lit again to speed the spirits back to the next world on the last day. The first Bon anniversary after a person's death is elaborate, with a white paper lantern put under the eaves.

O-Higan: *The Equinoctial Week*

There are two equinoctial weeks during the year, in spring and autumn. The middle day of the vernal equinoctial week is the vernal equinox, while the middle day of the autumnal equinoctial week is the autumn equinox. *Higan* means "the next world," and memorial services are held to wish the departed souls a safe journey to the next world during these equinoctial weeks. These events are held in temples, where people pray for the departed souls at the family altar and the grave.

CONCLUSION

In conclusion, most modern Japanese funerals are held Buddhist-style, and there are a great many strict customs to be followed both *during* and *after* funerals. These customs are based not only on Buddhist thinking, however, but also on Shinto beliefs, and many funeral rituals reflect a combination of these two belief systems. Today, the Japanese people continue to worship their ancestors and believe that they keep their eyes on the living.

NOTES

1. It should be pointed out that one of the most difficult problems in understanding Japanese cultural history is to determine from which particular historical layer specific religious practices are derived (Sansom, 1976, p. ix). Perhaps the most contentious of these issues involves the custom of ancestor worship. In fact, most mainstream scholars maintain that ancestor worship was an importation from China:

> During the most vigorous period of the T'ang Dynasty, the impact of Chinese civilization upon Japan reached such a climax that it marks the turning point in the evolution of Japanese

institutions. . . . China under the early T'ang rulers was one of the most highly civilized states in the world, as well as the most powerful, and in the Far East had no rivals for such a distinction. Throughout the seventh and eighth centuries the government in Yamato sent a succession of official embassies to the T'ang court [and] the result was a wholesale copying of Chinese techniques and ideas affecting almost every aspect of Japanese life and society. . . . The Chinese classics, especially the Confucian writings, were studied intently, since every well-bred person was expected to be familiar with them. . . . A new emphasis was placed upon family solidarity and filial devotion, including the duty of sacrificing to ancestral spirits. (Burns & Ralph, 1964, p. 337)

On the other hand, as Burns and Ralph (ibid.) add, "[s]ome Japanese scholars deny that the custom of ancestor worship was an importation; but in any case it was intensified by contacts with the Chinese."

2. Many Japanese homes contain both a miniature Shinto shrine and a Buddhist altar in their inner sanctums, and Shintoist ancestral mortuary tablets are placed beside the Buddhist altar during memorial observances. Most Japanese also choose Shinto ceremonies for their weddings, while Buddhist rites are reserved for funerals.

DISCUSSION ACTIVITIES

Exploring Japanese Culture

1. In Japan, the death of a person is treated Buddhist-style, while the birth of a baby is not. What is responsible for this difference?

2. Some people point out that because the main job (and means of making money) of Buddhist monks in Japan these days is to chant the Buddhist invocation for the dead at funerals and other related events, they have lost sight of their original religious mission. What do you think of this criticism?

3. Funeral rituals are extremely complex in Japan, and many people simply follow the outer forms without having much understanding of the deeper meanings of these rites. Discuss this aspect of Japanese funerals.

4. In Japan, death is considered the ultimate symbol of impurity. Discuss the origins of this concept and its relevance to life in modern Japan.

5. The grieving process for a deceased family member is very long and complicated in Japan. Discuss the notion of grief in relation to Japanese funeral customs.

Exploring Cross-Cultural Issues

1. There are certain set codes or customs for conducting funerals in all cultures. What are some of the important procedures for funerals in other countries of the world, and how do they compare with those in Japan?

2. Describe some dos and don'ts for funerals in other cultures (e.g., wearing black).

3. Are there annual events for the dead such as the Bon festival in other countries? What is the meaning of such events?

4. What religious meanings does death have in other cultures, and how are they expressed at funerals?

5. The *kōden* custom of giving money at funerals is widely accepted in Japan, but it is not customary in the West. How is this practice viewed in other cultures?

内と外

Uchi to Soto:
DUAL MEANINGS IN JAPANESE
HUMAN RELATIONS

The Japanese generally call people from other countries *gaijin* no matter how long they have lived in Japan or how well they speak the Japanese language. Some husbands call their wives *uchi no mono* (my wife), and people outside the immediate family are known as *soto no hito* (outsiders). These divisions reflect a basic dichotomy in the Japanese way of thinking known as *uchi* and *soto*. *Uchi* can be defined as (1) inside, (2) my house and home, (3) the group that we belong to, and (4) my wife or husband; in contrast, *soto* means (1) the outside, (2) outdoors, (3) other groups, and (4) outside the home (*Kokugo Jiten*, 1991, pp. 99 & 706). The Japanese clearly distinguish insiders from outsiders in daily life, depending on whether the others belong to an *uchi* or *soto* group. Although this distinction can be seen to some degree everywhere in the world, it is fundamental and widespread in Japan, where the dual concept of *uchi/soto* has had a great influence on Japanese society, especially in terms of human relations.

Contrasts between *uchi* and *soto* are prevalent at every level of Japanese life today, but the origins of this dichotomy can be found in the traditional *ie* system of Japan (Minami, 1980). Ie means "house," and the *ie* system was essentially a model of the extended family, headed by a senior male who had responsibility for the whole family. It was based on moral codes developed in the Tokugawa period and later reinforced by the Meiji government. According to Minami (ibid., pp. 62–72), in traditional Japanese society, there were three main characteristics of the ie system. First, it was male-dominated—the head of the family was always a senior male, and he had absolute power over other family members, who had to obey him. Second, the head of the household was in charge of the family business, including providing salaries or allowances for the other family members. Because the eldest son was destined to be the next head of the household, he brought his bride into the home, and the young couple lived with the groom's parents and grandparents. He became an apprentice in running the family business, in contrast to his younger brothers and sisters, who had other responsibilities. In this way, the head of the family succeeded to the family business through several generations. Third, the household itself was considered to be far more important than its individual members. Individual opinions were not valued, and every member had to consider the harmony of the family first and foremost. As a result, within contemporary Japanese families there still tends to be a strong sense of unity and a marked distinction between family members and others. The notions of uchi and soto can also be seen in the physical arrangement of traditional ie-style housing, which is still prevalent to a greater or lesser degree throughout Japan today. As Nakane (1970, p. 68) states:

> In the traditional Japanese pattern, each household is a distinctly isolated unit of its own, complete with walls and a high fence around the house to insure privacy. Yet inside, walls consist of sliding doors made of paper so that privacy is kept to a minimum. The family stays together most of the time and moves from one place to the next, depending on whether it is eating, relaxing, playing, or sleeping. Although this pattern tends to create family unity, it widens the gap between the family and outsiders.

The ie system thus had an important influence on present-day Japanese society in many ways and was the foundation on which the dual concept of uchi/soto was built.

The notion of uchi/soto also dominates human relationships throughout Japan, and people make strong distinctions between inside and outside in order to feel a sense of security within their groups. However, distinguishing between groups and group members is a dynamic process in Japan and not a fixed state of affairs. For most Japanese, group boundaries are in a constant state of flux, depending on the situation. Groups include one's home, school, and community, with the outermost boundary being that of the nation itself. As a result, the Japanese have long stressed the need for harmonious relationships within the same group (*uchi*) but are often not good at associating with those from other groups (*soto*).

This distinction sometimes causes problems within Japanese society itself, as well as in international relations. The distinction between *uchi* and *soto* is obvious in Japanese psychological exclusivism toward other peoples, and discrimination against minority groups such as *burakumin*, the Ainu, and ethnic Koreans is still widespread in Japan. As Collucut et al. (1988, p. 21) point out: "*burakumin* [are] the descendants of outcast communities of the premodern period. Although legally protected against overt discrimination, *burakumin* still face severe prejudice. They are often refused employment in any but menial jobs." In addition, "members of the Korean community, even those born in Japan and speaking fluent Japanese, are aliens. They face discrimination in education, job opportunities and marriage prospects" (ibid.). Even today, if a person's language, skin color, habits, or appearance are different, many Japanese will regard them as *soto*, or outsiders, and will ignore them in order to live more easily in harmony among members of their own *uchi* groups. In the international world, too, the Japanese need to develop relationships with people from other countries, but a major obstacle in achieving this goal has been a common tendency to group all such people together as *gaijin*, ignoring individual differences among them because they are all *soto*. Because such distinctions, which can be deeply hurtful to outsiders, are often unconscious among the Japanese, in order to truly internationalize and become effective members of the world community, it is most important for young Japanese, in particular, to become conscious and aware of such elements in their own culture.

DISCUSSION ACTIVITIES

Exploring Japanese Culture

1. Describe how the architectural features of Japanese houses illustrate the spatial classification of "inside/outside," and in particular, explore the notion of the *genkan* as "a circumscribed space where 'inside' meets 'outside'" (Ohnuki, 1984, p. 25).

2. What kind of language phenomena reflect the *uchi/soto* distinction (e.g., terms of respect for other *uchi* members often being deleted when talking to people who are *soto*)?

3. The *uchi/soto* distinction may be more clearly made by Japanese people living in rural areas than those in cities. Why do you think this is so?

4. **Case Study:** Ms. Takeuchi is working for a newspaper company. One day, she answered a phone call to Mr. Kato, her boss, from someone from a different company. Since Mr. Kato was not in his office, she answered, "*Kato-buchō wa gaishutsu-shite-orimasu*" ("Mr. Kato is out just now"). Ms. Takeuchi's senior colleague, watching this, criticized her, saying, "You should know better about the rules of politeness in Japanese."
Question: What was wrong with what Ms. Takeuchi said?

5. **Case Study**: Mr. Suzuki retired from Sony last year. He decided to leave Tokyo and spend the rest of his life in the countryside, so he bought a house in Tottori. When he arrived there with his wife, the village people seemed nice to him at first, but even after living there for a year, they made it clear that they did not accept Mr. Suzuki and his wife as true members of the community.
Question: Do you think the Suzuki family would face the same problems in other areas of Japan? Why, or why not?

Exploring Cross-Cultural Issues

1. If the rigid *uchi/soto* mentality prevents Japanese people from becoming international and communicating well with people from other countries, how can this be changed?

2. In the twenty-first century, Japan stands out as one of the most important economies in the world, with its products valued almost everywhere. Yet, as Reischauer (1988, p. 409) contends, the greatest single problem the Japanese face today is their relationships with other peoples:

> During the past century and a half they [i.e., the Japanese] have overcome truly mountainous problems, but they now find themselves struggling with the largely self-created psychological problem of their own self-image and the attitude of other nations toward them. Japan naturally is much admired, but it is not widely liked or trusted. It is feared both for its past military record and for its current unprecedented economic success. Its low political posture in world politics is looked on with suspicion as an attempt to avoid responsibilities and concentrate on its own narrow advantages. [It] is recognized as an economically dominant power, but it is not well understood and is felt to be uncommunicative and to hold itself self-consciously apart. Lingering feelings of separateness and uniqueness are still serious problems for the Japanese themselves, [and] the country's narrow emphasis on its own economic growth, which has been its chief policy ever since World War II, has become positively dangerous. Japan as a world leader must adopt broader aims, which embrace the other nations of the world. International understanding is not just a pleasantly innocuous catchphrase for Japanese policy but has become a practical necessity.

Do you agree or disagree with this statement? Support your opinion with reasons and facts. How are Reischauer's views related to the concept of *uchi/soto*?

3. The term *gaijin* is used to refer to Westerners only, not to other Asian people. Does this mean that the Japanese distinguish between different types of *soto no mono* (outsiders)? Is so, how and why do the Japanese make such distinctions?

4. In a recent survey of international students at the University of Tokyo ("International students seek interaction," 2000, p. 3), nearly half the population reported having been denied tenancy in apartments because they were foreigners, more than 90 percent found it difficult to have deeper relationships with Japanese students, and only 30 percent said that they had Japanese friends with whom they could seriously discuss life and the future. Discuss these issues from the perspective of *uchi/soto*. How do you feel about these problems, and what can be done to bring about changes?

5. In the past, calamities and epidemics were viewed in Japan as coming from the outside, and "often brought by strangers and foreigners," resulting in the need to "culturally control any outside force, lest it exercise the negative power" (Ohnuki, 1984, pp. 33–34). Discuss this concept in relation to the comments made by Tokyo governor Ishihara about the potential dangers of *sangokujin* ("Third World people") and other foreigners rioting after an earthquake, and the need to deploy Self-Defence Forces to protect the nation in such a situation. How are his views connected to the concept of *uchi/soto*? How do you feel about such comments?

6. Several recent letters to the editor in newspapers in Japan report that many non-Japanese are being turned away from Japanese blood banks. Various implausible reasons have been given for this kind of discrimination, such as "foreigners cannot read kanji," but most non-Japanese donors are still left with the feeling that they have "unwanted dirty blood." Discuss this issue from the perspective of the Japanese notion of *uchi/soto*.

侘び／寂び

Wabi-Sabi:
SIMPLICITY AND ELEGANCE AS JAPANESE IDEALS OF BEAUTY

Simplicity and elegance are often considered two of the essential aesthetic qualities of Japanese culture, and they have been important features of Japanese life since ancient times. Traditional Japanese architecture, for example, seems simple because of its emphasis on empty space, lack of ornamentation, and quiet, subdued colors; nevertheless, such buildings are said to possess an elegant beauty. Such qualities are also found in the Japanese arts and literature: the design of pottery is often simple and the color unobtrusive, while the structure of Japanese poems is spare and uncomplicated, yet both reflect a simple and elegant beauty. *Wabi-sabi* is the Japanese term that expresses this sense of beauty, but at the same time, it connotes certain other characteristics that are difficult to define. The aesthetic qualities reflected in *wabi-sabi* derive from Buddhist ideals of the medieval period, when the diffusion of Buddhism throughout the country brought the notion of *wabi-sabi* into the cultural domain as aesthetic values, which, even today, define the essential nature of many traditional Japanese art forms.

THE ETYMOLOGY OF *WABI-SABI*
Wabi-sabi is a compound expression composed of two distinct though related elements: *wabi* and *sabi*. *Wabi* is both an aesthetic and moral principle, originating in the medieval eremetic tradition,

which emphasizes a simple, austere type of beauty, and a serene, transcendental frame of mind yet also points to the enjoyment of a quiet, leisurely life, free from worldly concerns. In its archaic form, it expressed a quality of loneliness or sadness, but when used with reference to haiku or *sadō* (tea ceremony) it suggests a calm, quiet, austere state of mind (*Ohbunsha Kogojiten*, 1988; *Shinsen Kokugojiten*, 1992). *Sabi* also developed as a medieval aesthetic, reflecting qualities of loneliness, resignation, tranquillity, and old age while also connoting that which is subdued, unobtrusive, yet tasteful (ibid.).

Wabi is a noun form of the verb *wabu*. The adjective, *wabishi*, indicates good taste and refinement today, but such *wabi*-related expressions did not always have this kind of aesthetic value. Originally, they were used to describe unfavorable conditions, such as discouragement, anxiety, or being at a loss,[1] and were first seen in written form in the *Manyōshū* (The Collection of Ten Thousand Leaves), the oldest extant collection of Japanese poems, in situations in which people lamented the pain of unrequited love. In the later poetry of the Heian era, *wabi*-related terms were still being used to refer to the desolation of love but for the first time started to express the disappointed feelings of people who deplored their misfortune in general. Such expressions started to develop aesthetic qualities with the spread of Buddhism in the Kamakura period as a result of changes in attitude toward unfavorable conditions. At that time, wandering monks and poets found that solitary life was an attractive alternative to the materialism and strife of mainstream society because it provided them with an opportunity to cultivate a sense of unity with nature. By following such a solitary lifestyle, they began to value a simple and austere type of beauty and developed a transcendental attitude toward life in general, an attitude that is dominant in the literary works of the period. Typical of this view was their sense of the seasons, particularly with regard to late autumn and winter. They felt lonely and forlorn when looking at falling leaves and the coming snow, especially as they imagined the blooming cherry blossoms and green leaves of spring. However, this also inspired a positive attitude toward such desolation in treasuring the beauty that was out of sight. From this, they gradually developed an attitude in which the forlorn and desolate was thought to contain its own inherent beauty, and leading a simple, austere life came to be thought of as elegant and tasteful. Thus, although a basic sense of *wabi* had existed for a long time prior to this period, Buddhist values had a great influence on its development as an aesthetic quality.

Sabi is associated with the beauty of silence and old age, and today, *sabi*-related words, including the verb *sabu* and the adjective *sabishi* are used more to express quietude, loneliness, and the beauty of antiquity, but like *wabi*, they did not originally possess such aesthetic values.[2] *Sabi*-related words can also be seen in ancient literary works such as the *Manyōshū*, in which they were used to describe a lonely state of mind or the desolate conditions of nature. The first person to employ *sabi*-related expressions as a form of praise was Fujiwara no Toshinari, one of the major poets of the Heian and Kamakura periods. He used images such as "frost-withered reeds on the seashore" in a positive way to suggest aesthetic qualities involving tranquillity and desolation that were already in existence prior to the usage of the term. Since that time, many poets and writers have added further qualities, while in the Edo period, the notion of *sabi* was fostered by Matsuo Basho and his followers as a poetic ideal.

ZEN BUDDHISM AND THE DEVELOPMENT OF WABI-SABI

The ideals of Buddhism, especially those of the Zen school, contributed to the development of *wabi-sabi* as a Japanese aesthetic value because of the influence of Buddhist religious beliefs on Japanese culture. In particular, the notion of *mu*, "nonexistence" or "emptiness," a quality that is central to Zen, played an important role in the evolution of *wabi-sabi*.[3] There are many Zen kōans and sutras that address this concept of nonexistence, the most famous of which is "form is nothing but emptiness, emptiness nothing but form." As the monk Sotoba wrote in *Zenrin Kushū* (Poetry of the Zenrin Temple), Zen does not regard "nothingness" as a state of the absence of objects but rather affirms the existence of the unseen behind the empty space: "Everything exists in emptiness: flowers, the moon in the sky, beautiful scenery." The following poem by Fujiwara no Sadaie has often been cited as exemplifying the essence of the relationship between "nothingness" and *wabi-sabi*:

As I look afar
I see neither cherry blossoms
Nor tinted leaves
Only a modest hut on the coast
In the dusk of autumn nightfall

This poem is famous in Japan as a description of nothingness as an ideal form of beauty because in describing a deserted winter scene, the poet creates an image of its opposite in which cherry blossoms are in full bloom and the leaves are multicolored.

WABI-SABI IN THE TRADITIONAL ARTS

There are many examples of *wabi-sabi* as a representative form of beauty in the Japanese traditional arts, in particular, in the tea ceremony and in traditional Japanese poems. The tea masters Jo Takeno and Sen no Rikyu, for example, considered that the poem alluded to above depicts the ideal state of mind for the tea ceremony. They taught that a sense of beauty should not be explicit, and their emphasis on emptiness is reflected in the lack of ornamentation and austere simplicity found in the rituals of the tea ceremony, in which the quality of *wabi-sabi* is often emphasized as an ideal form of beauty. The tea ceremony derives from religious ceremonies performed by Zen monks starting in the Kamakura period, in which *wabi cha* (the tea of *wabi*) is served in rustic settings as the following description by the Portuguese missionary Rodrigues illustrates:[4]

It is a secluded and solitary exercise in imitation of . . . hermits who retire from worldly, social intercourse and go to live in thatched huts and give themselves over to the contemplation of the things of nature . . . to contemplate within their souls with all peace and modesty the things that they see here . . . to understand the mysteries locked therein. In keeping with this, everything employed in this ceremony is as rustic, rough, completely unrefined and simple as nature made it, in keeping with a solitary and rustic hermitage. (Plutschow, 1986, pp. 156–157)

From this description, it is clear that this type of ceremony was held to enlighten people's spirit, emphasizing contemplation and the simple, natural surroundings of tea-drinking activities. In fact, there has been a great influence of Zen Buddhism on the aesthetic of *wabi cha*, and many tea masters studied Zen and applied Zen practices to the tea ceremony in order to reach an ideal state of mind for enjoying tea. As Sen no Rikyu stated, "The essence of *wabi* is in the Law of Buddha." Simplicity, lack of polish, and asymmetry were all highly esteemed qualities in the performance of the tea ceremony, reflecting the Buddhist notion that the imperfect is the natural condition of nature that underlies all existence (Keene, 1988). A lack of ornamentation requires an effort on behalf of participants to complete their surroundings in their minds, and such mental movements are required during the tea ceremony. As such, the quality of *wabi-sabi* is not found in the features of manifest existence; rather, it is created in the mind of the beholder. Sen no Rikyu, for example, criticized the practice of deliberately creating utensils and settings that had the quality of *wabi-sabi* because for him the most important element was not found in the outward features of objects, but in the refined sense of being able to recognize the unseen qualities that exist in each of them. In short, *wabi-sabi* as an aesthetic of the tea ceremony represents a beauty of appreciation in the mind.

Wabi-sabi is also important in the field of Japanese poetry, especially haiku, and in this domain, it is necessary to note the contribution of Matsuo Basho, one of the great poets of the Edo period, known for leading the life of a wanderer in order to pursue this ideal, aesthetic quality. It is said that it was Basho who used the noun *sabi* for the first time, though the idea of *sabi* as an aesthetic value had already existed for some time, and *sabi*-related words such as *sabu* and *sabishi* had been used in earlier writings. According to Basho's disciple, Mukai Kyorai, *sabi* is very important for haiku, and it is a quality that cannot be acquired easily.[5] The following is an example of Basho praising his disciple, using the word *sabi*:

Yamei asked: "Tell me, what is the *sabi* of haiku like?"
Kyorai answered: "*Sabi* is the color of a poem. It does not depict desolation, but is the same as old age. For example, even if an old

man wears armor on the battlefield, or is present at a banquet wearing embroidered clothes, his age cannot be concealed. *Sabi* can exist in the lively poem, as well as the desolate one. Now let me compose one:

> *Two blossom watchmen*
> *With their white heads together*
> *Having a chat."*

The teacher [Basho] commented: "It is marvelous. The color of *sabi* emerges well." (Fukumoto, 1983, pp. 10–11)

The expression "blossom watchmen" makes us think of the splendid view of cherry blossoms in full bloom and perhaps alludes to the watchmen wearing colorful clothes. As a result, we have calm and quiet feelings through the image of the "white-headed" old men. What needs to be emphasized is that this quietude is not the mere negation of such beauty—it contains more than the loneliness of old age. By the synthesis of conflicting values, the beauty of the cherry blossoms and the white hair of the old men, these images affect each other and bring out deeper qualities, which are not described in the surface features of the poem. The aesthetic of *sabi* suggests such qualities and creates the appropriate atmosphere. People require mental discipline for real understanding of beauty because in this way of thinking, beauty emerges from inside objects. As a consequence, rejection of apparent beauty and affluence is the ideal condition for enjoying *wabi-sabi*, which does not indicate definite features but is a quality recognized by the heart.

WABI-SABI IN MODERN JAPAN

After the isolation of the Edo period, Japan underwent rapid industrialization in modern times. As a result, lifestyles began to change and the Japanese began to demand more affluence in life. The Japanese way of thinking changed because of this modernization, and these changes can be seen in people's attitudes toward the traditional arts. Many of the ancient customs are fast disappearing in modern Japan, and in the traditional arts, there are serious problems.

Although millions of people continue to learn calligraphy, tea ceremony, and flower arrangement, most do so not to develop their own
distinct inner sense of beauty but simply as an imitation of models.
Hisamatsu (1987, pp. 18–19) deplores this attitude in the modern
practice of tea ceremony:

> From the Muromachi to the early Edo period, the spirit of wabi
> showed its energy. Then gradually, the practice of tea ceremony
> and other traditional arts became inflexible and formalistic, and
> lacking in creativity. Such spirit is dead now, and for this reason,
> the practice of tea ceremony today does not have a 'now' or a
> 'future,' but only the glory of the past.

He understands that the disappearance of wabi-sabi in modern Japan
is the result of a lack of understanding of its essence. As stated previously, wabi and sabi can be recognized through the discipline of the
mind, but many people practice tea ceremony today without such
mental effort. As a consequence, it has become a form of entertainment, which only imitates past models. The main reason for this
vanishing sense of wabi-sabi is materialism. As opposed to the time
when wabi-sabi became established as an ideal sense of beauty in
people's lives and in the arts, as a result of modern materialism,
many Japanese today esteem only the surface value of things and
cannot recognize the unseen behind the outer world. Originally, wabi
and sabi were used to express the dissatisfaction of people with the
difficulties of their lives; however, attitudes toward such unfavorable
conditions changed under the influence of Zen. Such feelings were
transformed as people began to contemplate what exists beyond
manifest existence, and wabi-sabi began to play an important role in
the arts as an ideal sense of beauty. Wabi-sabi is not "apparent beauty"
or "atmosphere"—people can recognize these qualities only through
inner contemplation which is felt unconsciously in the heart. People
used to live simple lives free from materialism and had the opportunity to cultivate a sense of unity with nature. The modern Japanese
lead more luxurious lives but need to realize that these lifestyles
were built on other values that should not be forgotten.

NOTES

1. *Wabu*: to worry or be pessimistic, to feel lonely, to be perplexed, to be reduced to poverty, to enjoy a quiet and deserted state. *Wabishi*: lonely and unsatisfactory, deserted, hard and troublesome, shabby and poor, uninteresting, unbearable (*Ohbunsha Kogojiten*, 1988, p. 1254).

2. *Sabu* has two related sets of meanings: (1) to lie in waste or go to ruin, to feel lonely, to get old; (2) to rust, to become weaker or fade, to have an elegance that comes from aging. *Sabishi*: quiet and lonely, discouraging because of a lack of necessities (ibid., pp. 551 & 552).

3. The Zen school advocates the discipline of one's mind by practicing meditation, and the goal is to transcend one's mundane self. This state is called *jaku*, which derives from the Sanskrit *santi*. It is also called *ku*, which comes from the Sanskrit *sunya*, the word for zero. In Zen, this translates as the value of emptiness and silence.

4. It should be noted that *wabi cha* also embodies *sabi* as an essential aesthetic, although the latter is not included by name.

5. Because Basho himself did not mention *sabi* explicitly in his writings, the notion of *sabi* in Basho's haiku is often examined through his disciple's writings.

DISCUSSION ACTIVITIES

Exploring Japanese Culture

1. Do you think the younger generation in Japan still values the concept of *wabi-sabi*? Compare their values to those of the older generation, especially in relation to people's hobbies—for example, haiku, *ikebana* (flower arrangement), *sadō* (tea ceremony), *shodō* (calligraphy), and so forth.

2. How can the notion of *wabi-sabi* be reconciled with the fact that Japan is one of the foremost high-tech nations in the world?

3. According to this chapter, rejection of apparent beauty and affluence is the ideal condition for enjoying *wabi-sabi*, and people in Japan used to live simple lives free from materialism in which they had the opportunity to cultivate a sense of unity with nature. Discuss this with reference to young Japanese people today, most of whom buy and wear brand-name clothes and accessories, have mobile phones, and seem primarily concerned with making enough money to maintain their consumer habits. Why do young people prefer expensive brand-name goods rather than those that are simple and modest?

4. It is said that the Japanese sense of *wabi-sabi* is disappearing. Why is this so, and what can be done to preserve *wabi-sabi*?

5. Young Japanese women used to have lessons in flower arrangement and tea ceremony as a form of cultural training in preparation for marriage. What are the advantages and disadvantages of this kind of training in the modern world? Why is this custom disappearing, and does this have any relationship to the decline in people's sense of *wabi-sabi*?

6. It is said that tea ceremony has become very expensive in Japan and many people can no longer afford this practice. Is this not a contradiction in terms of the meaning of *wabi-sabi*? How can the aesthetic arts be maintained in modern Japan?

Exploring Cross-Cultural Issues

1. Do you think other cultures are now trying to embrace the concept of *wabi-sabi* as a way of escaping materialism? Discuss this issue with reference to growing trends in the West toward the practice of meditation, minimalist art, concepts such as "simple is better," and so forth.

2. Does the notion of *wabi-sabi* exist in other nations of the world? If so, what forms does it take?

3. Compare the sense of aesthetics in other countries with the notion of *wabi-sabi* in Japan.

4. When people practice *ikebana* (flower arrangement) in Japan, they do not arrange many gorgeous, colorful flowers in full bloom but prefer a few small flowers, wild grasses, and branches with a few buds. Why do people treasure this kind of aesthetic, and how does this compare with the way flowers are generally arranged in other countries?

5. Traditionally, nothingness and emptiness (i.e., *ma*) have been thought to reflect a sense of beauty in Japan. How are these concepts viewed in other parts of the world?

6. Writing haiku has recently become popular internationally, but as it is practiced in other countries, *kigo* (special words to describe nature that are traditionally used in haiku) have changed to reflect elements of nature in other countries. These changes are sometimes difficult for the Japanese to accept. Discuss the ramifications of the internationalization of haiku and why they have become popular abroad. Can the notion of *wabi-sabi* truly be shared with people beyond the borders of Japanese culture?

贈答

Zōtō:

THE JAPANESE CUSTOM OF GIFT GIVING

The Japanese give many gifts to each other throughout the year. On all traditionally important occasions, enormous amounts of goods and money are delivered to families and individuals all over Japan as gifts. For example, on New Year's Day, people generally receive hundreds of New Year's cards, and children are given money gifts, called *otoshidama*, from relatives and neighbors. Seasonal gifts, called *ochūgen* and *oseibo*, are also given to express feelings of appreciation, the former in July and the latter in December. Of course, gifts are not only seasonal; people receive gifts at all significant phases of their lives, such as at birth, entering and graduating from school, weddings, celebrating old age, death, and even anniversaries after death. Moreover, the Japanese are always supposed to bring gifts with them when visiting homes, expressing apologies, returning from trips, and so on.

According to Maruyama (1992, p. 2), there are forty-three kinds of seasonal and ceremonial gifts given in Japan, while Befu (1984, pp. 40–42) lists eighty-five occasions on which gifts may be given. From these data, we can understand that gift giving covers all events in Japanese life and is used to express a variety of feelings: congratulations, apology, appreciation, consolation, and so on. The Japanese give gifts each year on the following occasions: New Year's Day, St. Valentine's Day, Christmas, Girls' (Doll's) Festival, *Higan* (the equinoctial weeks in the spring and fall), Boy's Festival, Mother's

Day, Father's Day, Respect for the Aged Day, *Tanabata* (Star Festival), and Bon (the Buddhist summer festival) (Befu, 1984, pp. 40–42). The gifts for these events can be classified into three main types: seasonal gifts, ceremonial gifts, and gifts for other occasions. According to Maruyama (1992, p. 3), a typical Japanese executive working for a company spends an average of ¥228,860 each year on such gifts. These gifts are used not only to express personal feelings, however, but also to maintain social relationships. In other words, the Japanese give gifts when they do not particularly want to, a characteristic of gift giving that is rarely seen in other cultures, at least to the extent that it takes place in Japan. The custom of gift giving thus provides important insights into Japanese cultural values and lifestyles.

SEASONAL GIFTS

The New Year is the most important event of the year for the Japanese, when most people return to their hometowns to celebrate and spend a few days with their families and relatives. On New Year's Day, they traditionally receive New Year's cards (*nengajō*), not only from relatives and close friends but from old friends, bosses, business partners, colleagues, and almost all of one's acquaintances. All of these cards are kept until the end of the year so that people do not forget whom to send cards to the next year. Most of the cards are quite formulaic, containing statements such as "Thank you for your kindness last year. I hope we can keep a good relationship this year, too." Sending these cards is considered a duty for most Japanese because they are very important in Japan for maintaining relationships.

In July and December, gifts called *ochūgen* and *oseibo* are given and both represent the giver's appreciation toward others, especially, but not limited to, one's superiors. *Ochūgen* should be delivered between July 1 and 15, which is the duration of the Buddhist Bon holiday, during which people visit their family tombs and give homage to the spirits of their ancestors. Traditionally, the Japanese used to visit their parents, matchmakers, teachers, and superiors at work to thank them with some gifts during Bon, though nowadays a wide range of people can be the recipients of these gifts (Nagata, 1989, p. 48). In addition, people do not always give *ochūgen* in person today but just mail them instead. *Oseibo* are similar to *ochūgen* but are delivered between

December 10 and 20 each year. Most important, both *ochūgen* and *oseibo* must be sent every year continuously if relationships are to be maintained.

Another example of a seasonal gift is that given on Valentine's Day, which is not a traditional Japanese event but is nevertheless very commonly observed today. On Valentine's Day, February 14, women (especially young women) are encouraged to give chocolates to the various men in their lives. It is a rather commercial event in Japan and has become a day to consume tons of chocolates. Furthermore, a day was created for men to give chocolates in return, called White Day. Both women and men tend to give chocolates as a kind of duty, or social obligation, however, and these are called *giri-choko*, or "duty-chocolates."

CEREMONIAL GIFTS

From the day of birth to the moment of death, and even after death, the Japanese give and receive various kinds of gifts. According to Befu (1984, pp. 40–42), there are thirty-seven occasions for giving these ceremonial gifts, including getting pregnant, birth, the first new year of a baby, the first (boy's or girl's) festival, the first birthday, entering and graduating school, being promoted a grade, attaining adulthood (reaching twenty years old), getting a job, marriage, retiring, celebrating longevity (at ages sixty-one, seventy, seventy-seven, eighty, eighty-eight, ninety, and ninety-nine), vigils, funerals, *hōji* (a Buddhist memorial service), anniversaries after death, and so on. Some of these events are private and take place between individuals, while others are public and involve all of one's relatives. They may also take the form of celebration, appreciation, or consolation.

A typical example of a ceremonial gift can be found at weddings. Marriage is still considered one of the most important events for the Japanese, and since it is seen as the beginning of a new connection between two families, people often invite all their relatives and friends to their weddings in order to make the event a public occasion. Wedding parties have become increasingly large recently, and today marriage in Japan costs an average of more than eight million yen (Shiotsuki, 1993, p. 53). At these events, the new couple is presented with gifts, which can be either goods, such as tableware or other items for the house, or money. These days people tend to give money as a gift, and they consider carefully how much should be given, depending on their relationship and status with the couple and their families. It should not be too little, nor too much, but should accurately reflect the interpersonal relationships involved. The average amount of money given at a wedding, for example, is ¥30,000, but can vary from ¥20,000 to ¥100,000, according to the relationship (ibid., p. 90). This monetary gift must always be enclosed in a specially decorated envelope designed for the occasion. In return for these wedding gifts, the newlyweds provide souvenirs for their guests, each of which costs about ¥5,000 on average and usually take the form of items for daily use, which are exactly the same for all guests.

Another typical example of an event involving ceremonial gift giving in Japanese life is on the occasion of death, at which time there are a series of fixed and traditional Buddhist ceremonies to be observed, including the vigil and the funeral. As mentioned previously, participants at these events bring gifts, usually in the form of money, called *kōden*, to console the bereaved family. At the funeral, it is traditional for each guest to burn incense for the dead. People used to bring their own incense in the past, but this became money in modern times, and the meaning of the ritual changed from consoling the dead to consoling the family (ibid., p. 161). *Kōden* should also be enclosed in a special envelope designed for the occasion, and as with weddings, the amount should reflect the relationship between the guest and the deceased, with the average being approximately ¥5,000, but varying between ¥3,000 and ¥100,000, according to the relationship (ibid., p. 163). People also sometimes bring flowers, food, or incense, instead of money, and offer them to the dead, but this is becoming more uncommon. Forty-nine days after death, the family holds a ceremony called *hōyō* to pray for the soul of the deceased, and at this time the family gives gifts in return to people from whom they have received *kōden*. This gift, which is usually items such as sugar, soap, or tea, is carefully selected so that it costs about one-third to one-half of the *kōden*. On the other hand, if one is invited to attend the *hōyō* memorial event, one should also bring money as a gift for the family.

The Japanese also celebrate the birth of newborns by giving gifts.

These are more personal and informal than in the former two examples, and the givers are usually parents, relatives, and close friends. For this kind of gift, babyware is often chosen so that it can be used in daily life, but money is acceptable, too. Traditionally, the mother's family used to give a baby's kimono, but people tend to buy other things these days. After about one month, the baby's parents give presents in return, which should cost about one-half the cost of the gifts given, and are usually in the form of towels, sugar, soap, dishes, sweets, liquors, and so on.

GIFTS FOR OTHER OCCASIONS

The Japanese people give gifts in many other situations in addition to those mentioned so far. For example, when a baby is born, the parents give gifts to the doctor and nurses to thank them. In many other cases in which they want to express their appreciation, apology, consolation, or sincerity, the Japanese give presents; for example, they are known to spend a huge amount of money and energy buying souvenirs when they travel abroad. Long ago, if they wanted to visit famous shrines or temples far from their towns, one man would be chosen as the representative of his group, and the other members of the group provided him with money for the journey. So he had a duty to buy something for the others, such as talismans at the shrine or temple of his destination. This is the origin of the Japanese custom of buying souvenirs (Kato, 1975, p. 125). Even today, when a couple goes on a honeymoon, they have to buy plenty of souvenirs for their relatives, friends, colleagues, all those who have celebrated with them at the wedding party, and even those who have seen them off at the airport. Nobody would blame the couple if they did not buy souvenirs, but in Japan it is a kind of social obligation for them to do so, and most people would not neglect such duties.

CONTINUITY AND RECIPROCITY

It is very important to exchange gifts continuously and reciprocally in Japan. As mentioned above, *oseibo* and *ochūgen* must be given every year without interruption if relationships are to be maintained. Similarly, with gifts for ceremonial occasions, such as weddings or funerals, continuity and reciprocity are important considerations.

Every family experiences a series of such events throughout life, and other families make gifts on these occasions, which are reciprocated in return. For example, once a family gives a gift for the wedding of a son in another family, that family feels a duty to give something in return. In order to balance the relationship, they will give some kind present when the other family's daughter enters high school, for instance. Now, however, the situation of the two families is reversed, and the process continues. The reality is perhaps not this straightforward, but in the long term, these two families will give gifts to each other continuously and reciprocally in order to even out the unbalanced relationship due to debts or duties. This idea of social obligation in owing another, which is called giri in Japanese, underlies this process. The Japanese give gifts in order to carry out giri, and interestingly, some people call attending funerals "going to giri," and holding funerals is known as "receiving giri" (Ishimori, 1984, p. 270).

It is also very important that the value of the gifts reflect the relationship between the two parties; in other words, the gifts must be equivalent to the amount of giri recognized. Their value must not be smaller or larger than the amount of giri—if it were smaller, the receiver would be disappointed; if it were larger, the receiver would feel burdened. Thus, in the past, Japanese families traditionally kept a written record of celebrations and consolations in which the giver's name, date, and quality of the gifts were noted, so that their giri should not be forgotten.

SOMETHING FOR DAILY USE — PRACTICALITY

Another characteristic of Japanese gift giving is its practicality. Something that can be used is chosen for almost all kinds of gifts, and because money is the most practical of all, it is given on many occasions. When babies are born, for example, the event is celebrated with many types of gifts. The most common items are babyware, a small chest of draws, small blankets, and bibs. When the children grow up and enter high school, they are presented with something that can be used in school, such as pens, dictionaries, and calculators. Then, when they get a job after graduation, the gifts will be suits, neckties, bags, memorandum books, and other things for a new life. People then give gifts to their bosses, such as beer, cookies, canned foods, frozen fish, tea, or anything that can be consumed in daily living.

There is not a great deal of variety of choice in terms of proper gifts, especially for seasonal ones such as ochūgen and oseibo. An example of these stereotyped choices is salad oil, because it can be used in the receiver's kitchen without becoming spoiled and its value will be recognized by anyone. People choose practical goods because gift giving is a means of carrying out their giri. So the gift's value, as well as the giver's sincerity, must be clear to the receiver and others. For example, even if somebody made a present of expensive china for ochūgen, the receiver might not be familiar with its value; if so, the giver's giri would not be considered executed. In order to prove the value of a gift and that the giver has executed his or her giri, practical things for daily use are suitable because everyone can understand their value. Of course, highly personal gifts involving creativity and wit are acceptable, but only between close friends.

Money is the most practical of all gifts because its value is clear to everybody. By giving money, people can avoid searching through department stores to select gifts, and those who receive it do not have to be bothered with gifts they do not want. For these reasons, the Japanese frequently give money as a present, and this custom is one of the most characteristic features of Japanese gift giving.

In spite of their practicality, however, gifts are always wrapped neatly or enclosed in special envelopes in Japan. They must also be labeled to conform with a special set of manners. Shiotsuki (1993, pp. 378–418) lists 114 examples of such labeling in a book on ceremonial manners. Moreover, there are many special conventions for handling or sending these gifts. These imply that the gifts, which reflect the giver's sincerity, and at the same time his or her giri, are something important. As should be clear, however, these customs and attitudes contain an inherent contradiction. People regard sincerity as the most important factor when giving presents; nevertheless, a simple heart-to-heart message card is not usually enough because of the presence of giri.

A COMPARISON WITH THE WEST

In general, traditional Japanese gift-giving customs are highly formalized, but of course, people also make gifts that are more private and personal. In fact, according to Befu (1984, p. 29), 62 percent of Japanese gift giving is private, including situations such as giving an old doll to a little cousin, sharing soup with neighbors, giving birthday presents within the family. These gifts are given more frankly and privately and do not need to be practical. Since most Japanese consider "public" superior to "private," and *giri* more important than personal feelings, however, there are no formalized rules or manners for these private gifts, and as such, they are not considered as important, even though they often come more from the heart.

Such gifts are similar to ones given in America and Europe, for in the West, people usually give presents personally, such as at Christmas and on birthdays. They have a great deal of freedom in giving these presents, which should be something specially selected or made for the receivers, and not simply commonplace things. As a result, giving practical goods, such as soap and canned foods, which are appropriate for the Japanese, would not be considered a good idea. Gift giving is also a matter for the individual in the West; in Japan, on the other hand, gifts are more often seen as going from family to family. In addition, Western people often give presents without expecting anything in return, and do so simply because they want to. As a result, the notion of *giri* is not nearly as strong, though people do feel a sense of obligation when they receive a gift from others. On the other hand, suppose someone from the West gave a personal present to a Japanese person. The Japanese would give some gift in return that was of equivalent value. But if the original gift were worth more than their relationship, the Japanese person would feel burdened and subject to a heavy *giri*. In this case, the only way to return the *giri* would be to give an equivalent gift back to the Westerner. Thus, even private gifts are connected to *giri* in Japan, and the process can be much more complicated than most non-Japanese are aware.

One of the most distinct contrasts between Western and Japanese cultures in this regard is that money can be a proper gift in Japan but not in the West, where giving money may be looked upon suspiciously and even considered a form of bribery. Making gifts to one's superiors in the workplace is not common because of these connotations.

The one situation in which giving money is acceptable in the

West is tipping; however, this custom is not common in Japan, and the only times when people tip are at weddings, when moving house, or a few other celebrations. Otherwise, at a restaurant, for example, tipping is not appropriate, because it is felt that waiters and waitresses serve for their wages, and the customer pays a certain amount for the food and service. Here is a fair exchange of money and service, and also a balanced relationship between the customer and server. If the customer left a tip, the relationship would be unbalanced, and the waiter or waitress would own unexpected *giri* toward the customer.

For most Western people, "just giving" is a good thing to do. This may be influenced by religious beliefs, which state that it is better to give than to receive. People give but do not expect rewards in this world, and although this ideal is not always put into practice, it is an effective explanation of gift giving in the West. On the other hand, it is interesting to note that the Japanese often offer money to their gods or deities while praying, expecting *goriyaku*, or benefit and favor in return. This occurs in praying for a healthy baby, to pass an examination, to avoid traffic accidents, and so on. There exists a give-and-take relationship even between the gods and people in Japan, and this morality of balancing relationships has strongly influenced the Japanese custom of gift giving.

DISCUSSION ACTIVITIES

Exploring Japanese Culture

1. These days, some people in Japan have recommended a halt to the exchange of New Year's cards because this custom has become so highly ritualized that its real meaning has been forgotten. In fact, many people send the exact same formulaic message to everyone and often do not even include handwritten messages on their cards. In addition, an enormous number of cards are exchanged on New Year's Day, and this causes a massive waste of paper. Do you think the Japanese should stop sending New Year's cards or limit this exchange to those people they really want to send a message to?

2. Some people point out that the Japanese exchange gifts on so many occasions not because they wish to express gratitude or friendliness to others but simply because they are being unconsciously manipulated by the propaganda put out by those in the gift business, who actually create reasons for giving such gifts, such as major department stores (e.g., Valentine's Day and White Day). What do you think about this observation?

3. Do you think there is a relationship between recent widely publicized instances of governmental and corporate bribery (*wairo*) and corruption (*fuhai*) in Japan and the traditional custom of gift giving? What do you think about recent legislation that prohibits bureaucrats from accepting gifts?

4. Gifts are generally wrapped very extravagantly in Japan. Do you think this is necessary?

5. **Case Study**: Dr. Mitsuko Takeda is a Japanese professor at XYZ university and recently introduced Ms. Megumi Ueda, one of her senior students hunting for a job, to the principal of a Matsuyama high school. Partly because of her strong recommendation, Ms. Ueda successfully obtained a teaching position there. However, Dr. Takeda did not receive *ochūgen*, *oseibo*, or any other gift for her help.
Question: Do you think she has good reason to be upset with Ms. Ueda and her family? Why, or why not?

Exploring Cross-Cultural Issues

1. In Japanese culture, there are occasions when money can be an appropriate gift but other contexts in which it cannot. How do the Japanese distinguish between these occasions? What do you think about giving money as a gift? How is this practice viewed in other cultures?

2. What do you think about gift giving at Christmas? What kind of gift-giving occasions do you like? Which ones do you dislike? Compare gift giving in other cultures with that of Japan.

3. In Japan, if you give a gift, you usually expect to receive one in return. If you do not receive a return gift, you may feel slighted. Are these feelings similar in other societies?

4. In many other cultures, giving gifts "against one's will," rather than from a genuine feeling of affection or liking for someone, is often seen as hypocrisy. Discuss the relative merits of both points of view, and compare this aspect of gift giving with attitudes in other countries of the world.

5. **Case Study**: Madoka has just started studying at an American university. One day before the beginning of the semester, she visited her academic adviser with a present from Japan. She brought a Japanese doll as a gift, but her adviser, Professor Long, did not understand this custom and seemed a little embarrassed. Madoka was confused, because she had not had any problem when she gave the same present to her host family the week before.
Question: Why did Madoka and Professor Long experience this kind of miscommunication with regard to the gift?

References

Aimai

Aoki, T. (1990). *Nihonbunkaron no henyō* [Changes in critiques on Japanese culture]. Tokyo: Chuokoronsha.

Morimoto, T. (1988). *Nihongo omote to ura.* [Pretense and truth in the Japanese language]. Tokyo: Shinchosha.

Oe, K. (1995). *Aimaina nihon no watashi* [Japan, the ambiguous, and myself]. Tokyo: Iwatanimishinsho.

Peng, H. (1990). *Gaikokujin wo nayamaseru nihonjin no gengokanshu ni kansuru kenkyu.* [The study of Japanese customs that cause trouble with non-Japanese]. Osaka: Izumishōin.

Amae

Doi, T. (1973). *The anatomy of dependence.* New York: Kodansha.

Doi, T. (1974). Amae: A key concept for understanding Japanese personality structure. In W. Lebra & T. Lebra (eds.), *Japanese culture and behavior: Selected readings* (pp. 145–154). Honolulu: University Press of Hawaii.

Sahashi, S. (1980). *Nihonjinron no kensho: Gendai nihonshakai kenkyu* [The study of the theory of Japanese uniqueness: Modern research into Japanese society]. Tokyo: Seibundo Shinkosha.

Amakudari

Gibney, F. (1987; revised edition 1996). *Japan the fragile super power.* Tokyo: Charles E. Tuttle Company.

Hollerman, L. (K. Ozawa, trans.). (1996). *Senryō seisaku no kōisyō* [The aftereffects of the American occupation after World War II]. In F. Gibney (ed.), *Kanryōtachi no taikoku* [The bureaucratic superpower] (pp. 184–204). Tokyo: Kodansha.

Ikuta, T. (1992). *Nippon kanryō yo dokoe yuku* [Where are you going, Japanese bureaucrats?]. Tokyo: NHK Books.

Kuji, T., & Yokota, H. (1996). *Seiji ga yugameru kōkyōjigyō* [The government distorts the public works]. Tokyo: Ryokuhukan.

Kunimoto, R. (1991). *Kore de iinoka kensetsugyōkai* [Are you all right, builders?]. Tokyo: KK Best Books.

Lake II, C. (K. Ozawa, trans.). (1996). *Gosōsendanhōshiki wa kaitai dekiru ka* [Whether Japan's financial policies can be dismantled or not]. In F. Gibney (ed.), *Kanryō tachi no taikoku* [The bureaucratic superpower] (pp. 107–131). Tokyo: Kodansha.

Neff, R. (1998, May 18). "Why Japan won't act to save itself." *Business Week*, p. 44.

Omae, K. (1994). *Heiseikanryōron* [Heisei bureaucratic system]. Tokyo: Syōgakukan.

Special Reporters Group. (1996). *Jūsen no uso ga nihon wo horobosu* [*Jūsen* lies lead to a fall in Japan]. Tokyo: The Daily Mainichi Company.

Stern, J. (M. Tani, trans.). (1996). *Shijyōgenri ga hakai suru gyōkaidantai* [Industry destroys market principles]. In F. Gibney (ed.), *Kanryō tachi no taikoku* [The bureaucratic superpower] (pp. 252–272). Tokyo: Kodansha.

"The system to sustain monopoly through public corporations" [editorial]. (1996, December 16). *Nikkei Business News*, p. 34.

Wood, C. (R. Yamamoto, trans.). (1996). *Okurasyō no kauman no hana* [The haughty ministry of finance]. In F. Gibney (ed.), *Kanryō tachi no taikoku* [The bureaucratic superpower] (pp. 237–251). Tokyo: Kodansha.

Yamamoto, Y. (1992). *Nagatacho, kasumigaseki, otemachi.* Tokyo: Daiyamondosha.

Bigaku

Hirayama, I., & Takashina, S. (1994). *Japanese art in perspective: A global view*. Tokyo: Bijutsu Nenkansha.

Ishikawa, T. (1992). *Traditions—A thousand years of Japanese beauty*. Tokyo: The East Publications.

Keene, D. (1988). *The pleasures of Japanese Literature*. New York: Columbia University Press.

Bushidō

Beasley, W. G. (1999). *The Japanese experience*. Berkeley: University of California Press.

Burns, E., & Ralph, P. (1955). *World civilizations*, Vol. 1. (3rd ed.). New York: W. W. Norton & Company.

Bushidō. (1983). *Kōdansha Encyclopedia of Japan* (Vol. 1, pp. 221–223). Tokyo: Kodansha.

Bushidō. (1988). *Daijirin* [The great dictionary] (p. 2111). Tokyo: Sanseidō.

Davies, R. (1998a). Confucianism. Unpublished manuscript. Ehime University.

Davies, R. (1998b). Zen Buddhism. Unpublished manuscript. Ehime University.

Ikegami, E. (J. Morimoto, trans.). (2000). *Meiyo to junnō: Samurai seishin no rekishishakaigaku* [The taming of the samurai: Honorific individualism and the making of modern Japan]. Tokyo: NTT Shuppan.

Kogaku. (1993). *Japan: An Illustated Encyclopedia*. (pp. 808–809). Tokyo: Kodansha.

Nitobe, I. (1935). *Bushidō: The soul of Japan*. Tokyo: Kenkyūsha.

Nomura, T. (ed.). (1995). *Bushidō: Samurai no iji to tamashī* [The way of the warrior: Their pride and soul]. Tokyo: Shinjinbutsuōraisha.

Okuma, M. (1995). *Seppuku no rekishi* [The history of *seppuku*]. Tokyo: Yōzankaku Shuppan.

Ozawa, T. (1994). *Bushi kōdō no bigaku* [The warrior: The aesthetics of behavior]. Tokyo: Tamagawa Daigaku Shuppan.

Sagara, T. (1964). *Nihonjin no dentōteki rinrikan* [The Japanese traditional feeling of ethics]. Tokyo: Risōsha.

Shushigaku. (1993). *Japan: An Illustrated Encyclopedia*. (pp. 1426–1427). Tokyo: Kōdansha.

Suzuki, D. (1988). *Zen and Japanese Culture*. Tokyo: Charles E. Tuttle Company.

Tomikura, M., Fukawa, K., Ohama, T., & Miyata, N. (1975). *Kenshin* [Devotion]. Tokyo: Kōbundō.

Varley, H. P. (1986). *Japanese Culture*. (3rd ed.). Tokyo: Charles E. Tuttle Company.

Chinmoku

Akiyama, K. (1994). *Terebikōkoku kara mita nichibei bunka hikaku* [A comparison of Japanese and American culture from TV commercials]. Tokyo: Sanshusha.

Hall, E. (1970). *The hidden dimension*. Tokyo: Misuzu Shobō.

Ishii, S., & Bruneau, T. (1994). "Silence in cross-cultural perspective: Japanese and the United States." In A. Samovar & E. Porter (eds.), *Intercultural communication: A reader* (pp. 246–251). Belmont, CA: Wadsworth.

Lebra, S. (1987). "The cultural significance of silence in Japanese communication." *Multiligua*, 6 (4), 343–357.

Naotsuka, R. (1996). *Ohbeijin ga chinmoku suru toki* [When westerners are silent]. Tokyo: Taishukan.

Danjyo Kankei

Doi, T. (1975). *Amae zakkō* [Views on dependency relationships]. Tokyo: Kōbundō.

Kumata, W. (1992). *Onna to otoko* [Women and men]. Tokyo: Horupu Shuppan.

Research Group for a Study of Women's History (ed.). (1992). *Nihon josei no rekishi: Sei, ai, kazoku* [A history of Japanese women: Sex, love, and family]. Tokyo: Kadokawa Sensho.

Reischauer, E. (M. Fukushima, trans.). (1977/1990). *The Japanese today: Change and continuity*. Tokyo: Bungei Shunju.

Yuzawa, Y. (1995). *Kazoku mondai no genzai* [Present-day problems in Japan]. Tokyo: Nihon Hōsō Shuppan Kyōkai.

The Dō Spirit

Claiborne, G. (1993). Japanese and American rhetoric: A contrastive study. Florida: University of South Florida. Ph.D. diss.

Kotkin, J. (1997, April 4). *Daily Yomiuri*, pp. 7–8.

LaPenta, J. (1998, March 29). "Form in a teacup: Japan's most famous—and misunderstood—ceremony." *Daily Yomiuri*, p. 13.

Niki, K., Irie, K., & Kato, H. (1993). *Budō*. Tokyo: Tokyo-do Press.

Pinnington, A. (1986). *Inside out: English education and Japanese culture*. Tokyo: Sansyusha.

Reischauer, E. (1988). *The Japanese today*. Cambridge, MA: Belknap Press.

Sakaiya, T. (1994). *Nihon towa nanika* [What is Japan?]. Tokyo: Kodansha.

Sansom, G. (1963). *A History of Japan* (Vols. 1–3). Tokyo: Charles E. Tuttle Company.

Suzuki, D. (1964). *An introduction to Zen Buddhism*. New York: Evergreen Black Cat-Grove.

Watts, A. (1957). *The way of Zen*. New York: Pantheon.

Gambari

Amanuma, K. (1987). *Gambari no kōzō* [The structure of *gambari*]. Tokyo: Yosikawa Hirofumikan.

"Collapse of the Classroom" [editorial]. (1998, November 15). *Asahi Daily Newspaper*, pp. 16–17.

"Education in Relaxation" [editorial]. (1998, November 18). *Ehime Daily Newspaper*, p.1.

Kato, S. (1978). *Shūzoku no shakaigaku* [Social studies of customs]. Kyoto: PHP-Kenkyusho

Kawato, H. (1991). *Karōshi* [Death from overwork]. Tokyo: Sosha.

Kenbō, H. (eds.) (1989). *Sanshodo* [Japanese Dictionary]. Tokyo: Sanshodo.

Lee, O. (1982). *Chizimi sikō no nihonjin* [The Japanese being apt to look inside]. Tokyo: Gakuseisha.

Matsumoto, S. (1994). *Nichibeibunka no tokushitsu*. [Characteristics of Japanese and American culture]. Tokyo: Kenshusha.

Matsuoka, Y. (1989). *Amerika no jōshiki nihon no jōshiki* [Common sense in America; common sense in Japan]. Tokyo: Yomiuri Shinbunsha.

Miyazaki, O. (1969). *Nihonjin no seikaku* [Characteristics of the Japanese]. Tokyo: Asahi.

Sera, M. (1994). *Nihonjin no pasonariti* [Personality of the Japanese]. Tokyo: Kinokuniya.

Tada, M. (1972). *Shigusa no nihonbunka* [Behavior for Japanese]. Tokyo: Chikuma Shobō.

Tsuzino, I. (1993). *Nihon ha donna kuni ka* [What country is Japan like?]. Tokyo: Kinokuniya.

Velisarios, K. (1998, November 16). "Where Are the Children?" *Newsweek*, pp. 16-20.

Wagatsuma, H. (1983). *Encyclopedia of Japan 3*. Tokyo: Kodansha.

Giri

Gillespie, J., & Sugiura, Y. (1996). *Nihon bunka wo eigo de shōkai suru jiten* [Traditional Japanese culture and modern Japan]. Tokyo: Natsumesha.

Matsumura, A. (ed.). (1988). *Daijirin* [The Japanese dictionary]. Tokyo: Sanseido.

Minamoto, R. (1969). *Giri to ninjō* [Social obligations and human feelings]. Tokyo: Chuo Koronsha.

Ohshima, T., Ohmori, S., Goto, K., Saito, S., Muratake, S., & Yoshida, M. (eds.). (1971). *Nihon wo shiru jiten* [Encyclopedia for understanding Japan]. Tokyo: Shakai Shisōsha.

Yamane, A. (1997). "Marriage, funeral and events of the season," in T. Ishii, M. Suzuki, K. Hirakuri, & H. Hirose (eds.), *Asahi gendai yōgo chiezō* [The Asahi encyclopedia of current terms]. Tokyo: Asahi Shinbunsha.

Haragei

Matsumoto, M. (1975). *Haragei no ronri* [The logic of *haragei*]. Tokyo: Asahi Shuppansha.

Matsumoto, M. (1988). *The unspoken way.* New York: Kodansha International.

Samovar, L., & Porter, R. (1995). *Communication between cultures.* Belmont, CA: Wadsworth Publishing Company.

Hedataru to Najimu

Condon, J. (1980). (C. Kondo, trans.). *Cultural dimensions of communication.* Tokyo: Simul Press.

Hall, E. (1970). (T. Hidaka & N. Sato, trans.). *The hidden dimension.* Tokyo: Misuzu Shobō.

Kim, Y. (1981). *Nōmen no yōna nihonjin.* [Japanese as noh-mask]. Tokyo: TBS-Buritanika.

Honne to Tatemae

Honna, N., & Hoffer, B. (eds.). (1986). *An English dictionary of Japanese culture.* Tokyo: Yuhikaku.

The Japanese Ie System

Hall, J., & Beardsley, R. (1965). *Twelve doors to Japan.* New York: Mcgraw-Hill Book Company.

Hanley, S. (1997). *Everyday things in premodern Japan.* London: University of California Press.

Kawashima, T. (2000). *Nihon shakai no kazokutekikōsei* [The family constitution of Japanese society]. Tokyo: Iwanamishoten.

Prime Minister's Office. (1997). The public opinion poll about the family law [online], www8.cao.go.jp/survey/shakaiishiki-h10.html.

Prime Minister's Office. (2000). The public opinion poll about society where men and women participate equally [online], www8.cao.go.jp/survey/danjyo/y-index.html.

Takeda, T. (1981). *Nihon no ie* [The family constitution in Japan]. Tokyo: Kokushokankōkai.

Iitoko-Dori

Pinnington, A. (1986). *Inside out: English education and Japanese culture.* Tokyo: Sansyusha.

Reischauer, E. (1988). *The Japanese today.* Cambridge, MA: Belknap Press.

Sakaiya, T. (1991). *Nihon towa nanika* [What is Japan?]. Tokyo: Kodansha.

Ikuji

Azuma, H. (1994). *Nihonjin no shitsuke to kyōiku: Hattatsu no nichibe hikaku ni motozuite* [Socialization and education in Japan: A comparison between Japan and the USA]. Tokyo: University of Tokyo Press.

Lewis, C. (1984). "Nursery schools: The translation from home to school," in B. Finkelstein, A. Imamura, & J. Tobin (eds.), *Transcending stereotypes: Discovering Japanese culture and education* (pp. 81–94). Yarmouth, ME: Intercultural Press.

Kisetsu

Kawazoe, N., & Kuwabara, R. (1972). *Kisetsu to nihonjin,* in M. Tada & S. Umesao (eds.), *Nihonbunka to sekai* [Relations between Japanese culture and the world] (pp. 31–74). Tokyo: Kodansha.

Takaha, S. (1976). *Haiku no tanoshisa* [Enjoying haiku]. Tokyo: Kodansha.

Kenkyo

Fromm, M. (1988). *The culture of language.* Tokyo: Macmillan Language House.

Passin, H. (1980). *Language and cultural patterns.* Tokyo: Kinseido.

Nemawashi

Naotsuka, R. (1980). *Obeijin ga chinmoku suru toki* [When Westerners keep quiet]. Tokyo: Taishukan.

Omiai

"Is one Japanese man in five destined to be a bachelor for life?" (1995, November 18). *Shukan Asahi*, p. 12.

McLean, P. (1990). *Nihongo notes*. Tokyo: Macmillan Language House.

Minami, H. (1983). *Nihonjin no seikatsu bunka jiten* [Japanese life and culture dictionary]. Tokyo: Keisōsha.

Motona, N., & Beitz, H. (1983). *Nihon bunka wo eigo de hyōgen suru jiten* [An English dictionary of Japanese culture]. Tokyo: Yuhikaku.

Omiai-Kekkon Suishin-Kai [The Arranged Marriage Association]. (1996). *Omiai-kekkon no susume* [Recommendations for arranged marriage]. Tokyo: Iikurashō.

Rauch, J. (1995, January 9). "Facing up to Japan's quiet revolution. Review of *About face: How I stumbled onto Japan's social revolution*." *Daily Yomiuri*, p. 14.

Otogibanashi

Kawai, H. (1982). *Mukashi-banashi to nippon no kokoro* [Folktales and the Japanese heart]. Tokyo: Iwanami Shoten.

Ryōsaikenbo

Inoue, T. (1989). *Joseizasshi wo kaidoku suru*. [An examination of women's magazines]. Tokyo: Kakiuchi Shuppan.

Inoue, T. (1992). *Joseigaku heno shōtai*. [An invitation to women's studies]. Tokyo: Yuhikaku.

Kanda, M., Kimura, K., & Noguchi, M. (1992). *Shin gendai josei no ishiki to seikatu*. [New consciousness and the life of present-day women]. Tokyo: Nihonhōsō Shuppan Kyōkai.

Kasahara, M. (1996). *Asahi gendai yōgo*. [Encyclopedia of current terms]. Tokyo: Asahi Shinbunsha.

Koyama, S. (1991). *Ryōsaikenbo to iu kihan*. [Model of a good wife and wise mother]. Tokyo: Keisō Shobō.

Morohashi, T. (1993). *Zasshi bunka no naka no joseigaku*. [The culture of women's magazines]. Tokyo: Akashi Shoten.

Okamoto, H., & Tadai, M. (1990). *Gendainihon no kaizō kōzō.* [The structure of modern Japan]. Tokyo: Tokyo Daigaku Shuppankai.

Shimizu, T. (1989). *Onnanoko ha dō sodatuka.* [How are girls brought up?]. Tokyo: Shin Nippon Shuppansha.

Takada, K. (1975). *Oya to ko no rinshō shinri.* [Psychological relations between parents and children]. Tokyo: Sōgensha.

Takumi, M. (1992). *Seisa wo koete.* [Surmounting gender]. Tokyo: Shisensha.

Sempai-Kōhai

Davies, R. (1998). Confucianism. Unpublished manuscript. Ehime University.

Nakane, C. (1967). *Tateshakai no ningenkankei* [The ranking of human relationships in society]. Tokyo: Kodansha.

Nakamura, H. (1971). *Ways of thinking og eastern peoples: India–China–Tibet–Japan.* Honolulu, HI: University of Hawaii Press.

Okazaki, M. (1989). "*Naze sempai-kōhai ni kodawarunoka*" [Why do people stick to *sempai-kōhai* relationships?], in N. Hosaka (ed.), *Sempai ga kowai* [The fear of seniors] (pp. 190–191). Tokyo: Riyonsha.

Reischauer, E. (1988). *The Japanese today.* Cambridge, MA: Belknap Press.

Shūdan Ishiki

"Dour and dark outlook pulling Japan farther from neighbors." (2001, June 1). *The Japan Times,* p. 19.

Lebra, T. Sugiyama (1976). *Japanese patterns of behavior.* Honolulu: University of Hawaii Press.

Nakane, C. (1967). *Tekiō no jōken.* [Requirements for adjustment]. Tokyo: Kodansha.

Ohnuki, E. (1984). *Illness and culture in contemporary Japan.* Cambridge: Cambridge University Press.

Reischauer, E. (M. Fukushima, trans.). (1977/1980). *The Japanese today: Change and continuity.* Tokyo: Bungeishunju.

Takeuchi, Y. (1995). *Nihonjin no kōdō bunpō.* [Japanese social behavior]. Tokyo: Tōyō Keizai Shinpōsha.

Sōshiki

Asoya, M. (1989). *Shinto no shisei kan* [The view of life and death in Shinto]. Tokyo: Perikansha.

Burns, E., & Ralph, P. (1964). *World civilizations: from ancient to contemporary*. 3rd ed., vol. 1. New York: W. W. Norton & Company.

Haga, N. (1996). *Sogi no rekishi* [History of funerals]. Tokyo: Yuzankaku.

Inoue, S. (1984). *Reikyusha no tanjō* [The origin of funeral cars]. Tokyo: Asahi Shinbunsha.

Ishikawa, Y. (1994). *Sōgi hōyō manā jiten* [Dictionary of manners in funerals and Buddhist services]. Tokyo: Shufunotomosha.

Kanzaki, N. (1995). *Kami sama hotoke sama gosenzo sama* [Gods, Buddhism, and ancestors]. Tokyo: Shogakukan.

Miyake, H. (1980). *Seikatsu no naka no shukyo* [Religions in life]. Tokyo: Nihonhōsōshuppan.

Sadakata, A. (1989). *Butsuji bukkyō no kiso chishiki* [Fundamental knowledge of Buddhism]. In Y. Yamamoto (ed.), *Ideas of the next world in Buddhism* (pp. 14–15). Tokyo: Kōdansha.

Sansom, G. (1976). *Japan—A short cultural history*. Tokyo: Tuttle.

Shimada, K. (1993). *Osōshiki no manā* [Manners in funerals]. Tokyo: Sanseido.

Shintani, T. (1992). *Nihonjin no sōgi* [Japanese funerals]. Tokyo: Kinokuniyashoten.

Sōsōbunka Kenkyudai. (1993). *Sōsōbunka ron* [Funeral culture theory]. Tokyo: Kokinshoin.

Toyota, A. (1994). *Shinto to nihonjin* [Shinto and the Japanese]. Tokyo: Nesuko.

Tsuchiya, H. (1988). *Bukkyō essensu jiten* [Dictionary of Buddhist essence]. Tokyo: Sōkishuppan.

Uchi to Soto

Collucut, M., Jansen, M., & Kumakura, I. (1988). *Cultural atlas of Japan*. Oxford: Phaidon Press.

International students seek interaction (2000, April 20). *The Daily Yomiuri*, p. 3.

Kokugo Jiten [Japanese Dictionary]. (1991). Tokyo: Ohbunsha.

Minami, H. (1980). *Nihonjin no ningenkankei jiten* [Japanese human relations dictionary]. Tokyo: Kodansha.

Nakane, C. (1970). *Japanese society.* Berkeley: University of California Press.

Ohnuki, E. (1984). *Illness and culture in contemporary Japan.* Cambridge: Cambridge University Press.

Reischauer, E. (1988). *The Japanese.* Tokyo: Tuttle.

Wabi-Sabi

Fukumoto, I. (1983). *Sabi.* Tokyo: Haniwashinsho.

Furuta, S. (1970). *Zen to cha no bunka* [The culture of Zen and tea ceremony]. Tokyo: Yomiuri Shinbunsha.

Hisamatsu, S. (1987). *Wabi no sadō* [A tea ceremony of austere refinement]. Tokyo: Tōeisha.

Keene, D. (1988). *The pleasures of Japanese literature.* New York: Colombia University press.

Keene, D. (1990). *Nihon no bōshiki* [Japanese aesthetics]. Tokyo: Chuokoronsha.

Kumakura, I. (eds.). (1985). *Seikatsu to geijutsu: Nihon seikatsubunkashi* [Lifestyle and art: Japanese cultural history]. Tokyo: Nihon Hōsōsyuppan Kyōkai.

Kuriyama, R. (1981). *Bashō no geijutsukan* [Basho's artistic view]. Tokyo: Nagatasyobō.

Ohbunsha Kogojiten [Dictionary of Archaic Japanese Words]. 1988. Tokyo: Ohbunsha.

Plutschow, H. (1986). *Historical chanoyu.* [historical tea ceremony]. Tokyo: The Japan Times.

"Sabi." (1989). *Encyclopedia Nipponica 2001.* Vol. 10, p. 224.

"Sabi." (1993). *Japan, An Illustrated Encyclopedia.* p. 1289.

"Sabi." (1992). *Shinsen Kokugojiten* [Newly edited Japanese-language dictionary]. (6th ed.), p. 451. Tokyo: Shōgakukan.

"Sabishi." (1988). *Ohbunsha Kogogiten* [Ohbunsha: The dictionary of Japanese archaic words]. (4th ed.), p. 551. Tokyo: Ohbunsha.

"Sabu." (1988). *Ohbunsha Kogojiten* [Ohbunsha: The dictionary of Japanese archaic words]. (4th ed.), p. 552. Tokyo: Ohbunsha.

Sakaguchi, A. (1989). *Nihonron* [Essays on Japan]. Tokyo: Kawadeshobōshinsha.

Shimoyama, K. (eds). (1987). *Nihon no kokoro; Bunka, dentō to gendai* [Essays on Japan from Japan]. Tokyo: Public Relations Department, Corporate Secretariat Division. Nippon Steel Corporation.

Shinsen Kokugojiten [Newly-Edited Japanese Language Dictionary]. (1992). Tokyo: Shōgakukan.

Tanaka, S. (1982). *Chanobi nyūmon* [An introduction to the beauty of tea ceremony]. Tokyo: Gakushukenkyusha.

"Wabi." (1989). *Encyclopedia Nipponica 2001*. Vol. 24, p. 822.

"Wabi." (1993). *Japan, An Illustrated Encyclopedia*. p. 1677.

"Wabi." (1992). *Shinsen Kokugojiten* [Newly edited Japanese-language dictionary]. (6th ed.), p. 1243. Tokyo: Shōgakukan.

"Wabishi." (1988). *Ohbunsha Kogojiten* [Ohbunsha: The dictionary of Japanese archaic words]. (4th ed.), p. 1254. Tokyo: Ohbunsha.

"Wabu." (1988). *Ohbunsha Kogojiten* [Ohbunsha: The dictionary of Japanese archaic words]. (4th ed.), p. 1254. Tokyo: Ohbunsha.

"Zen." (1993). *Japan, An Illustrated Encyclopedia*. p. 1773.

Zōtō

Befu, H. (1984). "A study on gift giving as a cultural concept." In M. Ito & Y. Kurita (eds.), *Nihonjin-no zōtō* [Japanese people's gift giving]. Kyoto: Mineruva.

Ishimori, S. (1984). "Death and gift giving." In M. Ito & Y. Kurita (eds.), *Nihonjin-no zōtō* [Japanese people's gift giving]. Kyoto: Mineruva.

Kato, H. (1975), *Nihonjin no shūhen* [Around the Japanese]. Tokyo: Kodansha.

Maruyama, T. (1992). *Oiwai, okuyama, omimai tō no zōtō-jittai: nichibei-hikaku-chōsa* [Gift giving on celebration and consolation: A comparitive research between Japan and the USA]. Tokyo: Life Design Research.

Nagata, H. (1989). *Nenchu-gyōji wo kagaku suru* [History of seasonal events]. Tokyo: Nihon-keizai-shinbunsha.

Shiotsuki, Y. (1993). *Keichō-jiten* [Dictionary of celebration and consolation]. Tokyo: Shogkukan.

Glossary

Aimai: ambiguity; used as a way of avoiding open confrontation in Japanese communication; *aimai-na*: the adjective form of *aimai*; *aimai-na kotoba*: ambiguous language

Ama-no-gawa: the Heavenly River, or Milky Way

Amae: the state of being dependent on the benevolence or goodwill of others; *amaeru*: the verb form of *amae*; *amayu*: the literary form of *amae*

Amakudari: lit. "descent from heaven"; the process by which senior Japanese bureaucrats take important positions in private or semi-private companies after retirement

Asagao: morning glory flowers

Aware: the Japanese feeling of compassion, patience, and pity; felt especially towards the beauty of that which is transitory or ephemeral

Bentō: boxed lunches

Bigaku: aesthetics; the Japanese sense of beauty

Botaikō: a complex web of interlocking financial institutions that lie behind housing loan companies (*jūsen*)

Burakumin: the descendants of outcast communities of the pre-modern period

Bushi: the warrior class; also called samurai

Bushidō: morals having to do with the way samurai should live; characterized by absolute loyalty to one's lord and a strong sense of personal honor

Butsudan: the family Buddhist altar

Chinmoku: silence

Chōja: a rich man

Chotto / Demo / Kangaete-oku(ne): ambiguous expressions that serve to qualify or temporize a statement or question (see also *ichiō* and *maa-maa*)

Chū-kō: loyalty and devotion to one's lord

Dangō: collusive tenders for gaining orders; also known as "bid rigging"; *Danjyo*: men and women; *danjyo kankei*: male and female relationships in Japan

Dō: Tao, "the way"

Dōjō: practice room

Dōkyō: Taoism

Dōkyōsei: classmates

Dōraku: entertainment

Dōro: street or road

Dōryō: colleagues, or those who are in the same position in a company or institution

Dōtoku: morals

Enka: traditional Japanese popular songs

Enryo: restraint; *enryo-sasshin*: reserve and restraint; a custom in which people do not express their true feelings or intentions

Fūfu: husbands and wives

Fūfu-bessei: a system in which a married couple have different family names; in other words, the woman keeps her maiden name after marriage

Fuhai: corruption

Fuku mo: mourning

Fukushin: one's trusted friends

Fūrin: wind chimes

Furisode: long-sleeved kimonos that Japanese women wear on Coming-of-Age Day and at other formal occasions

Furo: bath

Fusuma: paper doors with wooden frames

Futsūgo: ordinary speech

Gaijin: abbreviated form of *gaikokujin*; lit. "foreigners," but used in Japan mostly to refer to Westerners

Gakkyū hōkai: classroom collapse; a situation in which the behavior of students in the classroom is beyond the teacher's control; at present, a serious problem in the Japanese educational system

Gambari: Japanese patience and determination; *gambaru*: the verb form of the noun *gambari*, or the act of doing one's best and hanging on patiently

Genkan: the entrance area of a Japanese house

Giri: a feeling of obligation to others

Giri choko: lit. "obligation chocolates"; chocolates that women give to their friends, colleagues, and superiors on Valentine's Day as a way of maintaining harmony in human relationships (cf. *honmei choko*)

Go-on to hō-kō: the custom of receiving favors and returning something for the goodwill of others, particularly in samurai society

Gokudō: lit. "the way of wickedness"; a term used for Japanese gangsters

Goriyaku: benefit or favor that people expect from offering money to gods or deities

Haiku: a type of Japanese poetry

Haji: shame

Haka: gravestone; graveyard; tomb

Hako-iri-musume: a term referring to daughters who are raised very carefully, as if they were family treasures

Hampuku: repetition

Hanami: flower-viewing; an annual event in Japan that occurs when cherry blossoms are in full bloom and people go out to parks to take part in flower-viewing parties

Hanayome-shugyō: "good wife training"

Haori hakama: a black kimono with a half-length Japanese coat and a long pleated skirt worn over the kimono

Hara: stomach

Haragei: lit. "belly art"; implicit, non-verbal, mutual understanding in Japanese communication

Haramaki: a strip of woolen cloth used to bind the midsection

Hedataru: a state in which one keeps a certain distance from
others; this term has many nuances, including to estrange,
alienate, come between, or cause a rupture between
friends; *hedatari*: noun form of the verb *hedataru* (cf. *najimu*)

Hikaeme: to be reserved in one's behavior

Hikikomori: withdrawal from the world; an increasingly common social problem in Japan

Hitsugi: coffin

Hōgaku: traditional Japanese music

Hōji: Buddhist memorial service

Hōkō: the act of serving one's superior honestly in the hope
of receiving his goodwill

Honmei choko: chocolates that women give to men whom
they really care for on Valentine's Day (cf. *giri choko*)

Honne: one's true feelings (cf. *tatemae*)

Hontsuya: wake held on the day after the death of the
deceased

Hotoke: a Buddha; after death, the deceased is believed to
become a Buddha after a certain period of time

Hōyō: ceremony a family holds to pray for the soul of the
deceased 49 days after death

Ichiō: an ambiguous expression meaning "tentatively" or
"for the present" (see also *maa-maa* and *chotto / demo /
kangaete-oku*)

Ie: the family system in which the father, as senior male,
had absolute power, and the eldest son inherited the
family estate

Iitoko-Dori: the act of adopting elements of foreign culture
into Japan without necessarily considering their underlying philosophies

Ikebana: the art of flower arrangement (see also *kadō*)

Ikuji: childrearing

Irui-kon: in folktales, when a person marries an animal that
has transformed itself into a human being

Ishin denshin: a state in which people can communicate with each other without using words; similar to "telepathy" in English

Jen: the principle of humanism in Confucianism

Jidai geki: samurai dramas commonly seen on Japanese television and in the movies

Jōdo Shin-shū: the True Pure Land sect of Japanese Buddhism

Jūsen: the name given to housing loan companies in Japan

Kachōfūgetsu: a term meaning flowers, birds, winds, and moon

Kadō: the art of flower arrangement (see also *ikebana*)

Kadomatsu: gate decorations for New Year's Day

Kagamimochi: rice cakes used as a New Year's decoration

Kage-fumi: the act of stepping on the shadows of others, symbolizing an infringement of personal space

Kaimyō: the act of giving a posthumous name to the deceased in Japanese funeral rites

Kami: god

Kamidana fūji: the act of temporarily closing the household Shinto altar during the period of mourning

Kamikaze: military pilots who committed suicide by crashing into enemy ships during World War II

Kamiza: the head position at a table or in a room where the most important person is supposed to be seated (cf. *shimoza*)

Kanai: lit. "inside house"; a term used by Japanese husbands to refer to their wives (cf. *shujin*)

Kanzen shugi: the principle of perfectionism

Karitsuya: a temporary wake held on the day a person dies

Karōshi: death from overwork

Kasō: cremation

Kata: pattern or form; *kata ni hairu*: to follow the form; *kata kara nukeru*: to go beyond the form; *kata ni jukutatsu suru*: to perfect the form; *kata ni hamatta hito*: a rigid and inflexible person

Keigo: morphologically marked, honorific language

Keishika: formalization

Kendō: swordsmanship

Kenjōgo: humble language in which one shows respect

towards the addressee through lowering one's own status (cf. *sonkeigo*)

Kenkyo: modesty

Ki chū: the 49 days after death during which the bereaved family is expected to be in mourning

Kigo: special words for expressing the seasons in haiku

Kimochi-shugi: a feeling-based way of thinking

Kine: a pestle; traditionally used in making Japanese rice cakes

Kisetsu: seasons

Kōan: enigmatic, paradoxical, non-logical sayings used as teaching tools in Zen Buddhism

Koban: old Japanese gold coins

Kōden: a monetary offering which mourners bring to the funeral; *kōden gaeshi*: presents given in return for these monetary offerings

Kogaku: schools established in the Edo period for the study of Confucianism

Kōhai: those who are younger and subordinate in schools, companies, and so forth (cf. *sempai*)

Koromo-gae: a time for an official change of clothes in accordance with the change of seasons

Koshu-sei: the former civil law which stated that the master of the house had the sole right to rule his family and the eldest son succeeded to this position and to his father's estate

Koto: a Japanese thirteen-stringed musical instrument

Kū: to eat

Kyōiku mama: "education mother"

Kyōkatabira: a white kimono worn by the deceased in Japanese funeral rites

Kyū: licenses and grades in the Japanese martial and aesthetic arts

Kyūdō: archery

Li: the principle of propriety in Confucianism

Ma: empty spaces that are full of meaning; important in Japanese literature and art

Maa-maa: an ambiguous expression meaning "so-so" in
   English (see also *ichiō* and *chotto / demo / kangaete-oku*)
Makura kazari: a small white-cloth table placed beside the
   pillow of the deceased at a funeral
Mamagoto: children playing house
Manyōshū: lit. "The Collection of Ten Thousand Leaves"; the
   oldest extant collection of Japanese poems
Matsugo no mizu: lit. "the water of the time of death," or
   "water of death"; a funeral custom in which members of
   the bereaved family wet the mouth of the deceased with
   water (also known as *shini mizu*)
Miai-kekkon: arranged marriages (as opposed to "love mar-
   riages"; see also *omiai*)
Mo chū: the mourning period, which takes place for one year
   after death
Mochi: rice cakes
Mokusō: meditative silence
Mondō: dialogues between Master and disciple in Zen
   Buddhism
Mongen: curfew
Mu: nonexistence or emptiness; a central principle in Zen
Mura: villages or communities
Murahachibu: the act of being ostracized from other members
   of the group
Mushin: "no-mind"; in Zen, the state of being free from
   worldly thoughts
Najimu: the act of becoming more familiar with, or closer to,
   others; *najimi-dasu*: to become closer (cf. *hedataru*)
Nakōdo: in arranged marriages, the go-between, who officially
   introduces the prospective couple to each other, along
   with their parents
Nemawashi: a Japanese style of negotiation, or decision making, in which people take care to lay the proper groundwork before a decision is made
Nengajō: New Year's cards
Nenki hōyō: Buddhist memorial services on certain anniversaries of a death

Neru: to sleep

Noh: a traditional form of musical drama in Japan

O-bon: Japanese Buddhist holiday in mid-August; a time in which the souls of the dead are believed to return to their earthly homes

O-chūgen: gifts delivered in July to show the giver's appreciation towards others

O-seibo: gifts delivered in December to show the giver's appreciation towards others

Okaeshi: sending gifts in return

Okāsan: mother

Omiai: arranged marriage

Omisoka: a family ritual cleaning of the whole house and decoration of doorways with sacred ropes and tufts of straw or pine branches, on December 31 of each year

Onna no ko: girl

Otenba: girls who are considered to be "tomboys"; i.e., healthy, vigorous, and difficult to control

Otogibanashi: folktales of Japan

Otoko-masari: a term used to describe women who surpass men physically and mentally

Otōsan: father

Otoshidama: monetary gifts that children receive from parents and relatives on New Year's Day

Roku mon sen: the custom of putting six old coins in a shoulder bag and tying it around the neck of the deceased

Ryōsaikenbo: lit. "good wives and wise mothers"; a term reflecting traditional societal expectations for women in Japan

Ryōtei / kappo: high-class Japanese restaurants

Saba: mackerel

Sabi: silence, loneliness, and antiquity as a Japanese ideal of beauty; *sabishii*: the adjective form of *sabi*; *sabu*: the verb form of *sabi* (cf. *wabi*)

Sadō: tea ceremony

Sakasa goto: upside-down things; the custom of doing things in reverse during funeral rites, such as putting on a white kimono with the right side overlapping the left

Sakoku: "closed country"; a term used to describe Japan during the Edo period

Sakura: cherry blossoms

Sangokujin: lit. "third world people"; a derogatory term usually used in Japan with reference to other Asian people

Sararīman: "salary man"; a white-collar worker

Satori: spiritual enlightenment achieved through meditation

Seishin shūyō: mental discipline

Sekentei: reputation

Sempai: seniors or elders in schools, companies, and so forth (cf. *kōhai*)

Sensei: a term of respect used for teachers, doctors, and so forth

Seppuku: suicide by self-disembowelment; regarded as the most honorable form of death for a samurai

Shain-ryokō: holiday excursions for company employees

Shakuhachi: a Japanese bamboo flute

Shamisen: a Japanese three-stringed, banjo-like instrument

Shijūku nichi hōyō: a Buddhist memorial service taking place 49 days after death

Shijyo: boys and girls

Shikimi: an evergreen tree of the magnolia family

Shimoza: the area near the door where lower-ranking members of parties or meetings are supposed to sit (cf. *kamiza*)

Shinto: lit. "the way of the gods"; the Japanese indigenous religion

Shiriai: acquaintances

Shochūmimai: letters of summer greetings

Shōgi: Japanese chess

Shōji: sliding latticework doors, which are covered with translucent paper

Shōkō: burning incense for the soul of the deceased

Shodō: calligraphy

Shūdan ishiki: Japanese group consciousness

Shōgakuryokō: school excursions

Shujin: lit. "master"; a term used by Japanese wives to refer to their husbands (cf. *kanai*)

Shushigaku: the Japanese term for neo-Confucianism

Sodai gomi: lit. "big garbage"; a derogatory term for Japanese husbands who simply lay about the house and never do household chores

Sonkeigo: honorific language in which one expresses respect toward an addressee by raising the addressee's position through the use of certain expressions (cf. *kenjōgo*)

Sōretsu: the funeral procession

Sōshiki: Japanese funerals

Soto: exterior, outside; often used in Japan to refer to individuals who are outside the group to which one belongs (cf. *uchi*)

Sumiyaki: charcoal burners

Sunao: the state of being gentle and obedient

Takenoko: bamboo shoots

Tanabata: a festival taking place on the night of July 7 when the Star Weaver and Altar (her lover) are believed to cross the Milky Way and meet

Tanshinfunin: a job transfer made without one's family

Tanzaku: oblong sheets of paper hung on bamboo branches during the *Tanabata* festival

Tatami: a Japanese straw floor mat

Tatemae: official or public stance; in contrast to one's true feelings (cf. *honne*)

Teineigo: a polite level of speech

Tekireiki: the right age to marry; generally thought to be in the mid- to late-twenties for Japanese women

Terakoya: Buddhist temple schools of the Edo period

Tōitsu: integration and rapport with a skill one is learning

Tōkō kyohi: absenteeism or truancy; an increasingly serious problem in Japanese schools; also known as *futōkō*

Tokonoma: alcoves in Japanese houses

Tomobiki: a day that is avoided in the scheduling of funerals because it is thought to bring bad luck

Toshikoshi-soba: noodles eaten after midnight on New Year's

Eve, symbolizing a link or bridge between the old and
new years

Tsumi: a sin or crime

Tsurishiro: a document used in arranged marriage in which
information about the prospective couple and their
respective families is provided

Tsuya: a wake during which the bereaved family and relatives spend the night watching over the deceased in the
coffin

Tsuyu: the rainy season, usually lasting from June to July in
Japan

Uchi: interior, inside; often used in Japan to refer to individuals
who are part of the group to which one belongs (cf. *soto*)

Uguisu: bush warblers or nightingales

Ume: plums

Unagi: eels

Urenokori: a derogatory term to describe women who have
passed the right age to marry (*tekireiki*) and are still single;
originally used to refer to goods or food left unsold

Usu: a mortar; traditionally used in making Japanese rice
cakes

Wabi: simplicity as a Japanese ideal of beauty; *wabishii*: the
adjective form of *wabi*; *wabu*: the verb form of *wabi*; *wabi-
cha*: "the tea of *wabi*" (cf. *sabi*)

Wairo: bribery

Washitsu: a traditional Japanese-style room, usually with
tatami

Yōfuku: Western clothes

Yōshitsu: a Western-style room, often with carpeting

Yuinō: a marriage custom in which a man sends gifts and a
certain amount of money to his prospective bride and her
family

Yukan: the process in which the dead person's body is
washed with hot water in preparation for burial

Yukata: the most informal type of Japanese kimono, normally
worn in the summer

Zanshomimai: greeting cards sent in the summer

Zazen: silent sitting and meditating in Zen Buddhism
Zenekon: general building contractors
Zōni: rice-cake soup
Zōtō: the Japanese custom of gift giving